W9-BGH-988

Submarines
at War

**A History of Undersea Warfare
from the American Revolution to the Cold War**

Submarines at War

A History of Undersea Warfare
from the American Revolution to the Cold War

Michael Gunton

CARROLL & GRAF PUBLISHERS
New York

Carroll & Graf Publishers
An imprint of Avalon Publishing Group, Inc.
161 William Street
NY 10038-2607
www.carrollandgraf.com

First published in the UK by Constable,
an imprint of Constable & Robinson Ltd 2003

First Carroll & Graf edition 2003

ISBN: 978-07867-1455-1

Printed and bound in the EU

For Judith

Very many thanks to Commander Jeff Tall OBE, RN retd, and his staff at the Royal Navy Submarine Museum at Gosport for their invaluable help in the preparation of this book. In particular to Maggie Bigmead, Head Archivist, for her encouragement and advice.

Contents

List of Illustrations

All pictures are courtesy of RN Submarine Museum except those marked * which are courtesy of the U.S. Naval Institute Photo Archive.

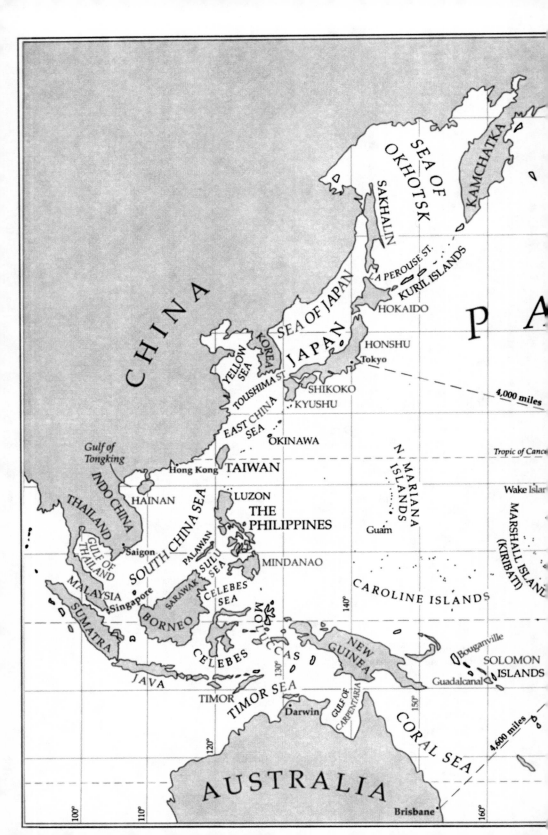

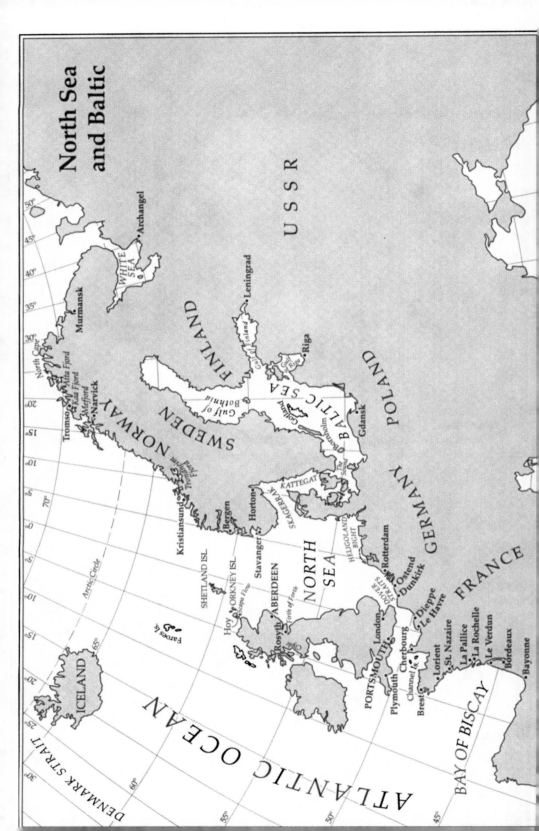

The Mediterranean

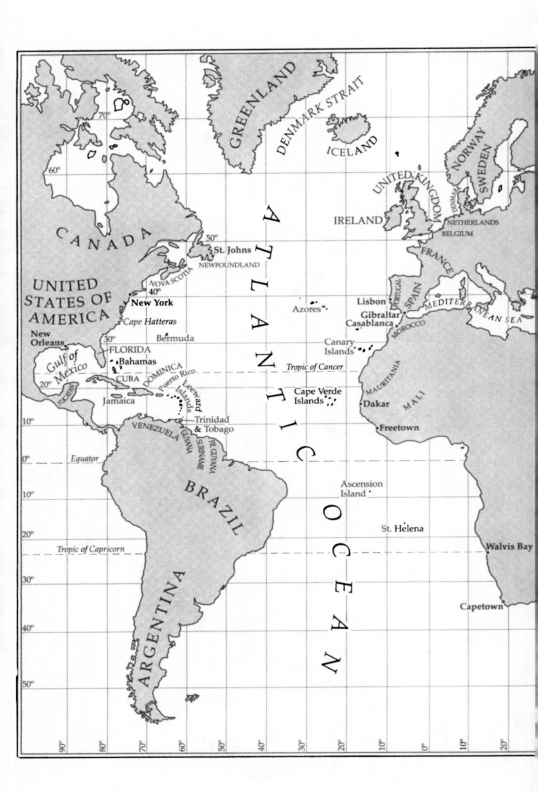

Introduction

*The submarine – its interior
and operation.*

S UBMARINERS of all nations are a very special breed, though they would not claim to be exceptionally brave, merely doing a job in very difficult circumstances. Most of them were volunteers in the two world wars. Only in the German U-boat service were men conscripted in any numbers, and this was forced on them by the tremendous manpower losses they sustained. Submarine commanding officers were largely in their late twenties or early thirties, although as the Second World War progressed, the increased demand and the losses sustained eventually brought down the average age to the early twenties, especially in the U-boat service.

All submariners operated in difficult and dangerous conditions which most people would find totally unacceptable. Imagine a London underground train comprising four carriages, about 200 feet long – and, in this case, about 26 feet wide, twice as wide as an actual carriage. All the seats, handrails and advertisements have been removed and the carriages joined together making an empty steel corridor – roughly similar in size to a Second World War submarine.

To take the London tube train analogy even further, in the rear carriage, which is now slightly tapered like the stern of a submarine, fit one large water trimming tank, which will take half the available space and be used to balance the vessel on the surface or submerged. Add an emergency steering unit, then make room for six or seven men, stokers, who are members of the engineering team.

Here is both living and sleeping accommodation, a table for eating, and lockers for their personal belongings and other equipment.

In the next carriage put a large 18 feet long, 4-stroke, 1250 h.p. at 450 r.p.m. diesel engine and an electric motor, the diesel provides power for both surface propulsion and recharging the batteries for the electric motor, which is used whilst submerged. Also squeeze in the lavatories or 'heads' and wash room for the whole crew.

In the third carriage put a small wireless office adjacent to a control room with its two periscopes (search and attack), sonar and radar equipment, motor and engine telegraphs, a navigation plot table and radio fixing equipment. Then add a small galley where food for up to 48 men can be produced, a Petty Officers' mess for three or four people and a wardroom for the four or five officers, both with their own small lavatory, and an engineers' mess.

In the front carriage, which is the fore-end of the submarine, fit in six torpedo tubes and twelve 1.5-ton torpedoes, each 22 feet long and 21 inches in diameter, some of which can be stored below the deck. Just behind them put a seamens' mess where 20–25 men can live, eat and sleep, and add a second trimming tank.

Around the whole of the submarine on the bulkheads (walls) fit miles of piping and tubes and dozens of instruments. Under the deck (or floor of the carriage) where the space available is roughly the same as that above the deck, put a small officer's cabin and two batteries, joined in parallel, both with 112 cells each of which produces 2.4 volts and weighs half a ton. The power from these batteries goes around the submarine in a ring-main joined by a series of junction boxes. The batteries, similar to old car batteries, have to be topped up from time to time with distilled water, so storage must be provided for about five tons of the liquid. Add a 250-ton oil fuel tank and an 18-ton lubricating oil tank.

A crew of between 36 and 50 men have to work, live, eat and sleep in the space that is left among all this hardware, and they could be at sea for as long as two months. Potatoes, bread which is specially wrapped to last some two weeks and is baked on board thereafter, other vegetables, some of them dehydrated, a vast amount of tinned food, fresh water and a few cigarettes must be taken on board and crammed into any space available – between instruments, machinery and equipment, between the stored torpedoes, anywhere there is a spare inch of space.

Sleeping is done on a shift basis. The crew is divided into three watches and while there are bunks for officers and petty officers, most of the crew have to adopt 'hot bunking' – where they share the same cot – although there are a few places to sling a hammock. Personal hygiene is not something which commands much attention; showers or baths are not possible and the opportunity to wash hands and face are rare. Fresh water is for drinking and is rationed. It follows that no clothing or bedding can be washed and an added difficulty is that the lavatories cannot be used when the boat is below 70 feet because of the complicated valve system that has to be used, which is when empty bottles and tins come in handy.

If the submarine is on the surface, where it spends as much time as possible, either charging batteries, patrolling at night or cruising during the day when there is no enemy around, it is subjected to the whims of sea and weather. With the deck so close to the waterline even a choppy sea will continually throw spray over the crew on watch. A rough sea can inundate the boat, throwing gallons of water down the conning tower and into the boat, soaking everything and making the hot atmosphere damp and humid; the hatches will have been left open to get air into the boat. Below, the crew and contents, including food, can be thrown around relentlessly with the pitching, tossing and rolling.

If the boat is submerged, life is smoother, but the atmosphere deteriorates as 36–50 men breathe and pollute it. If the boat is under water for a long period, because it is under attack or the enemy is patrolling the surface, the atmosphere, already dominated by the ever-present diesel fumes and the smell of damp and rotting food and sweat, becomes unbearable. This problem is solved using soda lime, or carbon dioxide absorbent, usually in four canisters through which air is drawn by an electric fan, while at the same time candles are burned to create oxygen. By using this system 5 to 6 per cent of the oxygen lost from the air is replaced.

Sleep is difficult as the continual change in air pressure affects the eardrums and this, combined with confined and narrow bunk space, encourages insomnia. Breathing becomes difficult and, of course, smoking is not allowed but would be impossible anyway because in the oxygen-starved atmosphere a match will not strike and a cigarette will not draw. Surprisingly, a crew can breathe with minimum oxygen for up to 15 hours without distress. The biggest danger is from chlorine gas caused by sea water mixing with the sulphuric acid in the batteries. The crew cannot go anywhere to relax, there is no room to go for a stroll, nowhere to go to relieve stress. Everyone is always in close contact with someone else.

This description applies generally to British and German submarines but not wholly to those used by the Americans who have always believed in having the biggest and the best. Sometimes it is true – it certainly was in the case of their submarines, so that another tube carriage has to be added to represent an American submarine bringing the total to five. This allows for more facilities and an increase in crew to around 90. Major differences come in the accommodation, compared to a British submarine or a U-boat. The Americans have the added comfort of a shower room, a cold-storage room and a cigarette deck, while the crew's quarters are divided between sleeping and eating. But then one has to consider the huge area American submarines had to cover – the Pacific Ocean, some 64 million square miles, is the largest ocean in the world, covers one third of the Earth's surface and is greater than all the planet's land surfaces put together.

On the order to 'Dive! Dive!' whether routine or emergency, the tanks are flooded while the two sets of hydroplanes, horizontal rudders fore and aft, are depressed as the submarine is driven forward. As it submerges quick calculations have to be made concerning the weight of the boat, auxiliary and compensation tanks inside the submarine, carrying around 30 tons of water, are used to balance it at the depth required. Surfacing involves the submarine going to periscope depth and blowing water out of the ballast tanks, using compressed air kept in around 20 bottles stored in the submarine. Pressure is kept at about 4,000 lb per square inch. As soon as any water has been blown out of the tanks the submarine has buoyancy; only a small amount of high-pressure air is used for as soon as the conning tower is above water the hatch is opened to allow in fresh air which can then be used to blow out the rest of the water from the ballast tanks. The hydroplanes, two horizontal fins on either side of the boat which steer the boat up or down, are also used. The diesel engines are now started to propel the submarine whilst the electric batteries, responsible for propulsion while submerged, are recharged; air compressors being used to replenish the compressed air used to blow the tanks.

Submarines carry escape equipment, the Davis Submerged Escape Apparatus invented by Sir Robert Davis. This DSEA comprises a mouthpiece connected by a flexible tube to a rubber bag which, in turn, is attached to a metal container charged with oxygen under pressure allowing the escaper to breathe under water. The oxygen in the bag must be at the same pressure as that of the water depth. On the way up oxygen from the breathing bag is automatically released as the pressure of the water decreases. The man escaping wears goggles and a nose clip which means that he can only breathe through his mouth. Two valves have to be operated so that he can breathe at the correct rate on his way to the surface; once there the mouthpiece is removed and the equipment acts as a lifebelt. The DSEA was used almost exclusively by the Royal Navy although German U-boats carried equipment that was similar in a number of ways.

There are two methods of escape, the first of which is the Twill Trunk. Submarines with this system fitted had two hatches in their pressure hulls each with a compartment which could be completely sealed, one at each end of the boat. Following an accident survivors had to go to the nearest escape hatch which was sealed off by water-tight doors and valves. A trunk was then lowered from the hatch to make a two foot diameter tunnel from the hatch to within a few feet of the deck. DSEA sets are put on to stop the men breathing in carbon dioxide gas and nitrogen under pressure while flooding as carbon dioxide concentration increases under pressure and becomes lethal. When air pressure is increased, the blood absorbs more nitrogen from the air than normal.

It takes about ten minutes to flood the compartment at 100 ft depth. When the pressure outside is the same as in the submarine the escaper enters the tunnel, opens the hatch and ascends to the surface. As he will have an excess of nitrogen which must be released slowly, an escaper must come to the surface in easy stages. The length of time he takes will depend on the time he has been breathing nitrogen under pressure and the depth from which he is ascending. Men escape in turn, one at a time.

The alternative method, the Escape Chamber, was incorporated into the design of the submarine, two escape chambers, with room sufficient for two men, being established at either end of the vessel. When in use the chambers are flooded and two men enter, lock the door, which has a glass inspection window, put on their DSEA breathing gear and flood the compartment. When the pressure in the chamber equals that of the water outside they open the escape hatch and proceed to the surface. Back on the submarine their escape is watched by the men left in the boat, the hatch is then closed by hand mechanism and the water drained out. Two more men can then use the equipment.

At the end of the Second World War methods of escape from a sunken submarine were re-examined using evidence based on the experiences of submarine survivors from several nations. The two methods of escape used in the Royal Navy were both shown to have disadvantages – there were dangers inherent in using the DSEA equipment, such as forgetting to remove the mouthpiece on surfacing and thus suffocating, there was not always enough escape equipment for those on board, and the DSEA equipment proved complicated to use by those suffering from the effects of carbon dioxide. As a result the 'free ascent' method was devised based on a Built-in Breathing System (BIPS). Escape compartments at either end of the boat are fitted with a ring of air valves, or breathing points through which the escaper can take a deep breath of pure oxygen. In an emergency escapers use the breathing valves while the compartment is being flooded. When flooding is complete the escape hatch is opened and the escapers go out one by one. They have no need to inhale as they rise to the surface because their lungs are full of oxygen, and keeping their mouths open during ascent allows air to escape as the air expands due to the lessening pressure. If a man making a free escape holds his breath he will burst his lungs due to the expanding air having no exit. Because escapers breathe in highly compressed air before leaving the submarine they do not have to rise in easy stages to avoid the 'bends'. 'Free ascent' has the advantage that no equipment is required, apart from a ring or life-jacket to give buoyancy on the surface, so that every survivor can use it, everyone having an equal chance.

A submarine, of whatever nationality, is home to its crew for anything up to two months. It can also be their tomb, as it was for 40,000 men of all combating nations during the Second World War.

CHAPTER ONE

The Development of the Submarine

History of development, equipment development, weapons, officers and men, depth charges.

THE first appearance of submarines in the arena of naval warfare was hardly a rip-roaring success. It took place in September 1776, during the American War of Independence, when the British Admiral Lord Howe, in his 74-gun ship of the line, *Eagle*, was busy supporting the armies opposed to George Washington as they gathered around New York ready to make their attack. In broad daylight his sentries suddenly spotted an egg-shaped object bobbing up and down in the water near the ship.

Before long the water around *Eagle* was the scene of frenetic activity with a number of patrol boats rowing in pursuit of the floating object. As they neared their target they suddenly saw another, smaller, object break away from the main one and begin to float towards them, carried by the tide. With no idea what it was they wisely began to row away as quickly as they could, since the small object suddenly exploded, sending up a plume of water. The very first submarine-launched 'torpedo' had gone off and made history. For the man in the floating egg it was a moment of supreme disappointment that his attempt to destroy the *Eagle* had failed.

With the Americans holding New York but almost surrounded by the British, a small group, led by a Yale College graduate called David Bushnell, had devised a method of attacking the British fleet with a submarine. Designed by Bushnell it had an egg-shaped hull strengthened by timber beams, the vessel's sole crew member being a man who turned a crank handle to provide propulsion, although he had first to trim the craft so that the top of the small conning tower was just above the waterline. He did this by adjusting the water level in the ballast tank and only then could he concentrate on propelling and steering the boat. It was a task that must have demanded considerable gymnastic ability. The handle could be operated by either hands or feet and moved a shaft which propelled two screws, one of which moved the vessel vertically, the other horizontally; it was steered by a tiller that fitted under the crewman's arms and worked a small rudder.

Having reached his target, the crewman, with hands and/or feet on the crank handle, and his eye on the level of water in the ballast tank, then had to edge up to the hull of the vessel he was attacking and attach a mine containing 150 lb (70 kg) of gunpowder. The mine had a protruding screw and the idea was that it would be lifted by a crank handle under the vessel and screwed into the wooden hull, remaining suspended until a clockwork firing device triggered it off and, theoretically, blew the target to pieces.

The periscope had yet to be invented so, to achieve what he planned, the crewman had to stick his head out of the conning tower which was, of course, almost awash. Only when he had attached the mine to his target could he duck down, close the hatch and submerge the boat by operating a foot-pedal to allow water to enter the ballast tank. If he let in too much water the boat sank like a stone to the bottom; if the water flow was insufficient then part of the vessel remained above sea level and could be easily spotted.

David Bushnell, being a scientist and therefore no fool, did not operate the submarine, whimsically called *Turtle*, himself but called for volunteers from the rebel army – three were forthcoming and from these Sergeant Ezra Lee was selected to be the world's first submariner. On the night of 6 September 1776, shut in the confines of *Turtle*, Lee was towed by two whaleboats towards the objective. A mile or two up river from the target the submarine was released from its towline so that it could drift towards the unsuspecting *Eagle* on the tide. Lee was able to keep his head out of the hatch without difficulty because the sea was calm and the night was dark and moonless. He navigated his vessel, if that is the right word, by picking up shore lights and watching his primitive compass, the needle of which had been painted with a phosphorescent substance so that it showed up in the dark.

It took two hours of hard work with the crank handle to manoeuvre *Turtle* into position. As he neared *Eagle*, Lee ducked down into the boat, shut and clamped the hatch and edged his craft under the warship. He then pumped out water until *Turtle*'s conning tower bumped quietly against *Eagle*'s bottom.

Now things began to go wrong. The first problem was that, unknown to Lee, *Eagle*'s hull was copper-sheathed against attack by teredo worms, so the screw on the mine would not penetrate. He therefore shifted his position and tried again. After several attempts he grew tired and breathless for there was no method by which fresh air could be supplied to the submerged *Turtle*, so Lee decided to give up and retreat. By the time he had extricated himself from under *Eagle* it was broad daylight but, because of the shortage of air, he could not remain submerged and had to semi-surface.

Turtle, although the first submarine or submersible to go into action, was only the latest in a long line of submersible designs which stretched back probably some 2,000 years. Alexander the Great, circa 340 BC, is reckoned to have used glass barrels to submerge and observe the wonders beneath the sea, although it was not the sixteenth century that designers really began to take the subject seriously – between 1575 and 1765 there were about 17 different submarine inventions.

A submarine of sorts was next in action during the 1850 war between Denmark and the German states when the superior Danish navy was blockading the northern German ports. A German corporal called Bauer designed a submarine which, using army funds, was constructed at Kiel. It had a metal hull and again was propelled by hand and armed with a mine which could be attached to the hull of the target ship. Named *Plongeur Marin*, it made only one sortie which, although it did not force the Danes to lift the blockade, certainly had them worried. It was subsequently lost at sea by acci-

11

dent and Bauer received no further encouragement from his own countrymen.

Like so many inventors before him Bauer had to leave his own country to get his ideas accepted, going first to Russia where he sold one of his designs, and then to England where he met British designer John Scott Russell. Later, during the Crimean War, Russell used one of Bauer's designs to construct a submersible vessel to assist in the attack on Sebastopol in 1855, although the project was a complete failure.

Cornelius van Drebbel is credited with being the first man to design a submarine in about 1630 which could be propelled through the water whilst being 'submerged'. He devised a vessel in which oars protruded through holes in the sides, made watertight by greased leather coverings. He is reputed to have navigated the River Thames on several occasions but, it is thought, the submarine was awash rather than fully submerged. During the following hundred or so years several further attempts were made, including the American Robert Fulton who demonstrated his submarine before a Royal Commission in England in 1809. Prime Minister William Pitt had considered buying the American's design but the Admiralty still held the view that the submarine was no threat to Britain's maritime superiority and vetoed the purchase.

Following *Plongeur Marin* the next example of a submarine in action came in 1864, again in America during the Civil War, when the hard-pressed Southern states were forced to adopt this method of naval warfare to try and break the blockade of Charleston by the powerful Union fleet. Called 'Davids', mainly because of their potential giant-killing capabilities, their submarines relied on motive power provided by a crew of eight working a crankshaft driving a propeller. They had a ballast tank to control their buoyancy and, an innovation, were equipped with hydroplanes (fins) to allow them to alter depth whilst being propelled. They were fitted with a spar torpedo – a long pole with a gunpowder bomb tied on the end of it which fired on contact with the target.

On the night of 5 October 1863 *David*, under the command of Lt William T. Gaskell, set out to attack the ironclad frigate, *New Ironsides*, which had been continually bombarding Charleston fort.

The submarine, despite being spotted by sentries as it approached, pressed home its attack and exploded its spar torpedo against the side of the warship tearing a large hole in its hull close by the engine room. The frigate, although badly damaged, did not sink, whereas *David*, by the very nature of its attack, had to get very close to its target. The explosion caused such a huge wave that the submarine was overwhelmed and sent to the bottom with the loss of all the crew except the captain.

Undeterred by these setbacks, design work was continued by Captain J.L. Hunley. A cigar-shaped 30 foot long submarine, nicknamed *Hunley*, was constructed and made ready for another attack on the Union fleet. Like its predecessor it had a crew of eight men, this time turning a crankshaft which drove a three-bladed propeller. Although it was designed to travel mainly on the surface with the captain navigating from an open hatchway, it could be fully submerged and controlled by hydroplanes fitted forward, but on a practice dive *Hunley* sank and all the crew died. Despite this, such was the patriotism of the Confederate forces that it was not difficult to find another volunteer crew to take the salvaged *Hunley* on another attempt to break the blockade. Setting off in the dark on 17 February 1864, under the command of Lt G.E. Dixon, it made for the outer harbour where the new wooden man-of-war *Housatanic* was anchored.

Again *Hunley* was quickly spotted by sentries, who had been warned to look out for anything suspicious floating nearby, but by the time the alarm was raised *Hunley* was so close to the warship that its guns could not be depressed low enough to be of any use.

The captain of *Housatanic* ordered the warship's cable to be cut and the ship got underway with all haste, but it was too late – the spar torpedo carried in the bow of *Hunley* rammed into the side of *Housatanic* just below the mainmast and blew a great hole in the ship's side. The Confederate warship quickly sank but so too did the gallant *Hunley* and its crew. Despite this second loss of the submarine and eight men, this episode did mark the first successful attack made by a submarine on a warship and as such deserves its place in history.

By the 1880s a whole host of designers were busy with their own plans for submarines and at one time there were as many as 40 schemes in hand. But the man who could rightly claim to be the father of the submarine was an Irish-American called John Philip Holland. Born in an Ireland devastated by famine, disease and unsympathetic English landlords, he saw a submerged war weapon as a good way of hitting back at the British by attacking their mighty fleet, so he emigrated to America where he encountered anti-British organisations which funded his early efforts and eventually a proto-type was launched. Although it immediately sank it was refloated, adjustments were made, and it was then a success. A second proto-type, known as *Fenian Ram* was launched two years later and worked well, but Holland's Irish-American moneymen decided to take control of the submarine themselves and the project fell apart. Holland, however, managed eventually to sell his design to the US Navy and subsequently the USS *Holland* was launched.

The British, though they thought submarines an underhand method of warfare, were persuaded to take the development seriously and acquired the rights to build five Holland boats, surprisingly, it seems, without any objection from Holland. *Holland II*, considered by some to be the most advanced submarine design achieved by 1900, was 31 feet long, displaced around 19 tons and had one of the earliest internal combustion engines, the Brayton, which developed 15 h.p. for surface propulsion. Holland also introduced the principal of diving rather than just sinking beneath the surface by using horizontal rudders fitted into the stern of the vessel. The Holland submarine thus became the prototype for all subsequent vessels.

In 1896 the French Marine Minister organised a competition for the design of a submarine and as a result 29 of them arrived on his desk. The winner was a boat called *Narval*, designed by Monsieur Laubeuf, which was duly built in 1899 and had dual propulsion; a steam engine gave it a surface speed of 11 knots and could also recharge the boat's electric batteries which were responsible for its submerged speed. Its behaviour both on the surface and submerged was excellent but, most importantly, the hull was constructed in two parts – an inner pressure hull surrounded by an outer hull, the space in between the two being occupied by the water ballast tanks which could be filled or emptied to make the submarine dive and resurface. It was a design that was soon to become standard, its one drawback being that like so many other submarines that used steam for propulsion, it took a long time to dive, around 12 minutes, and conditions were exceptionally hot for the crew when submerged.

A contemporary development of *Narval, Gustave Zede* finally proved the viability of underwater warfare, when, during trials it showed that it could torpedo battleships both in harbour and out at sea, also demonstrating its mobility by making the 410-mile journey from London to Marseilles without any trouble. There, using the battleship *Magenta* as a target, and with no periscopes, which meant it had to break surface from time to time so that the captain could have a good look around, it successfully launched its attack. Although it was easily spotted from *Magenta* it was generally agreed that it was visible for such a short space of time the battleship's guns would have been unable to fire a shot at it.

Then, in 1901, the French Mediterranean fleet was leaving Ajaccio when, without warning, the battleship *Charles Martel* was 'torpedoed' by *Gustave Zede*. The French fleet had no idea that a submarine was even in the vicinity because *Gustave Zede* had earlier crept secretly out of the harbour to launch the attack.

This incident vastly increased French enthusiasm for submarines. They now saw them as a weapon of war which could give them superiority over the traditional maritime enemy, the British – always a desirable dream in the French mind – and went ahead with their development. The final triumph as far as the French were concerned, and a terrible omen for the future, came in 1906 when, during manoeuvres, a flotilla of submarines successfully 'torpedoed' 21 ships which were ostensibly defending Toulon, Marseilles and Bizerta.

As the twentieth century dawned the development of the submarine was being carried out with enthusiasm by all the major naval powers. The French, with plans to rebuild their fleet, included 38 submarines but, in view of what had happened with the *Gustave Zede*, they spent a considerable amount of time considering defence against submarines. Nevertheless, the British became concerned with their development plans, while the same concern was expressed about US Navy plans even though these were mainly concerned with providing a strong coastal defence to protect New York, Long Island Sound, and the Delaware and Chesapeake Bays as well as San Francisco.

In Germany the development of the submarine had been held back by Admiral von Tirpitz's belief that it was not a practical weapon of war, but in 1905 the Korting heavy-oil engine was developed and the first Unterzeeboot, the U-boat, was built. From 1907 onwards the Germans embarked on an energetic programme of building large 'overseas' submarines similar to those being constructed by the British.

The British attitude changed with the appointment of Sir John Fisher as First Sea Lord in 1904. He saw that the submarine could be a valuable addition to the fleet although the emphasis was still on using it as a defensive weapon. Subsequent technical development meant that the submarine could be used for more extensive operations and with its endurance increased it became clear it would also be a useful offensive weapon, an attitude adopted mainly by the British and German navies.

In the first 15 years of the century the number of submarines grew from under 20 to over 400 in 16 of the world's navies and they began to bring about a fundamental change in sea strategy.

During the years between 1918 and 1939 all the major nations continued to develop their submarines, the general aim being to develop boats which could operate for long periods far from their bases. A number of technical innovations were adopted which increased manoeuvrability and operational safety, structural strength was increased to allow submarines to go to greater depths and hydraulic systems were improved for rapid and remote control of valves, air vents and rudders; more effective escape systems were adopted. Torpedoes were also developed to carry a greater weight of warhead, faster, more accurately and for longer runs. After a variety of experiments the choice narrowed down to either a single-hull submarine with external tanks or double-hull vessels, with fuel kept inside the pressure hulls of the former and between the hulls of the latter.

Diesel engines, based on the original German designs, had become largely six-cylinder, four-stroke, solid injection engines which gave submarines a maximum surface speed of around 15 knots. As explained earlier, the diesels provided the surface propulsion, while electric motors powered by three 270-volt batteries joined in parallel provided the underwater motivation.

When the batteries were run down, and the time this took depended largely on the speeds adopted when submerged, they had to be recharged, which had to be done on the surface using the diesels. The process took some two to three hours if the batteries were really low, and while this was being done the submarine was, of course, in constant danger of being spotted by enemy patrol boats or aircraft. By the time the Second World War started, submarines could dive deeper than ever before and because of the stronger pressure hulls, could carry out the diving process more rapidly as well as being better controlled underwater.

In the early 1900s a British naval officer, Captain Bacon, helped by an Irish optician, devised a system of mirrors, set in a tube, which could give a clear view of what was going on above the surface when submerged. The snag, and it was a minor inconvenience at the time, was that this early periscope could give an upright view ahead, an upside-down view astern and one on its side on either beam because of the arrangement of the mirrors. It did not have an adjusting mechanism so it could not be adjusted up or down – it was either all the way up or all the way down, but it was better than nothing. Although the French were also devising and fitting a periscope at the same time it was the British system that the Americans eventually adopted.

Second World War submarines were usually equipped with two periscopes which could be extended as much as 30 feet above the submarine's hull. The lower-power, or attack periscope, had a monocular and unifocal lense which gave normal vision and was used in the final stages of an attack; it had a very small top so that it left very little wash on the surface of the sea. The high-power periscope was binocular and bi-focal and included range-finding and sky-search facilities. Its diameter was in the region of nine inches, tapering at the top to five inches, and gave a substantial wash which could easily be spotted by an alert lookout. On a clear day it could give clear vision up to 10 miles. Periscopes were raised and lowered by wire pulleys operated by oil pressure rams and where they passed through the submarine's hull there were special glands designed to resist the external pressure of the sea.

During the First World War Allied ships had great difficulty in combating the U-boat menace until the development of hydrophones, an underwater microphone which could hear the noise of a submarine's machinery or propellers, although its value was considerably limited by the fact that all surface ships in the vicinity had to stop engines, to cut out the noise they were making, so as to allow the hydrophone operator to try to differentiate more easily between the various sounds on his equipment. Using several hydrophones on different ships, the position of a submarine could be fixed with some accuracy by cross bearings.

During the years between the world wars the League of Nations strove to get international limitation on the number of submarines that could be built – as with larger warships – but it failed in this and its attempt to get an international agreement on banning the use of submarines in indiscriminate attacks on commercial shipping.

It soon became clear that any method that would enable surface ships to detect the presence of submarines would revolutionise anti-submarine warfare. The British extended their efforts in this direction and although the hydrophone had its limitations these were surmounted in the early 1920s by the development of ASDIC – Anti-Submarine Detection Investigation Committee, established in 1917. ASDIC was an acoustic system which was active, listening for any sound a submarine might make whether its motors were running or not, by sending out supersonic sound waves which, when they hit a solid object, caused an echo to be reflected back to receivers. Using ASDIC, a submarine as far away as two miles could be picked up and pinpointed since the sound waves were directional. Unlike the old hydrophones it could still be used whilst the operating ship was cruising at a moderate speed and could give the range of the submarine as well as its direction.

The introduction of ASDIC was the first major defensive step against submarines. The second came during the Second World War with the development of radar, particularly when it was used in aircraft. Radar is similar, in some ways, to ASDIC in that it is a method for detecting and locating objects using reflected short or very short radio waves. Using radar an object can be pinpointed very accurately and precisely. When eventually fitted in aircraft radar allowed the Allies to make considerable headway in the fight against U-boats as it was ideal for picking up a boat on the surface, particularly at night; the Germans developed their own version later in the war.

The submarine needed a weapon which could be carried and fired without blowing itself up in the process. Captain Guiseppe Luppis of the Austrian Navy (Austria was then part of the Austro-Hungarian Empire, which had a coastline on the Adriatic) had come up with an idea for a floating torpedo propelled by steam or clockwork and directed from a submarine by a guide line. The idea was turned down by his own government so he took it to Robert Whitehead, an English inventive genius, to turn his basic idea into something more practical.

It took Whitehead two years to come up with a solution and he first produced the Whitehead torpedo in 1866. It was some 22 feet long, 14 inches in diameter, tapering to a point at bow and stern, carrying 18 lb of dynamite and weighing around 300 lb. Once started it could run submerged in a straight line for a short distance without guidance, its depth-keeping ability being improved two years later with the invention of a balance chamber mechanism in which a pendulum, connected to the horizontal rudders, automatically corrected fore and aft tilt. It carried its own turbines, oil tank, depth engine, gyro steering engine, immersion mechanism, starting lever, depth indicator, combustion tank, ignition, fuel tanks and a warhead of 500 lb of TNT. Steam which supplied the motive power was generated by forcing a spray of water through a torch of burning alcohol; steering was by the gyroscopic mechanism; a delicate hydrostatic device, reacting to water pressure, governed depth control; the explosion was triggered through contact or magnetic influence. Although the Austrians were still not interested, the British Admiralty, showing uncharacteristic foresight, gave Whitehead £15,000 (a vast amount of money at that time) for the secrets of his torpedo and the right to manufacture it.

The torpedo, the submarine's major weapon, was increased in size from 18 inches to 21 inches in 1923 and to around 22 feet long. It was fired by a short burst of compressed air and when it left the tube it functioned under its own mechanism. Generally early torpedoes achieved speeds upto 30 knots and could run for more than 8,000 yards.

The torpedo as used in the First and Second World Wars was launched from its tube by a short burst of compressed air; starting gear on the rear of the torpedo was then mechanically triggered by operating valves, which threw the starting switch, spun the gyro mechanism and drove the steering mechanism. It was automatically steered at the required speed, depth and course, vertically by a depth gauge and horizontally by the gyro mechanism, and was propelled by a small battery-driven motor. An advantage of such a torpedo was that did not emit exhaust smoke, was silent and did not leave a trail of air bubbles to give away its position.

Great care had to be taken when loading a torpedo into the tube, and when firing, because the weight distribution within the submarine changed dramatically and had to be counter-balanced, otherwise the bow would come up, the boat would surface and give its position away. When a torpedo was loaded and the rear loading door shut, the space left was quickly filled with water from a special internal loading tank under the tube, allowing the bow door to be opened without a sudden inward rush of water making the vessel bow heavy. After the torpedo had been fired, the sudden loss of weight was compensated for by an extra supply of water from the internal loading tank to provide the balancing weight. The bow door was then closed and water pumped back into the tank from which it came so that the rear doors could be opened for reloading.

The number of torpedo tubes on each submarine varied but typical examples were: the British S-Class, six tubes all forward and a stock of 12 torpedoes; the American S-Class, four forward tubes and a stock of 12 torpedoes; the X1-Class U-boat, eight tubes, six forward and two aft with a stock of 22 torpedoes. In some cases, such as the British T-class submarine, they carried two external tubes but these proved impractical as they could only be used while surfaced. Torpedoes were devastating when functioning correctly, frustrating and dangerous when they were not. In the early days of the Second World War, in both the Atlantic and the Pacific, there were major problems as will become plain in later chapters.

The first gun was carried aboard a submarine in 1909, and there have been arguments about its viability ever since. The guns carried by submarines in the Second World War were usually no bigger than 4-inch calibre and some of the larger submarines, certainly the majority of U-boats, were also equipped with smaller-calibre anti-aircraft guns.

The depth charge designed by the British during the First World War was the main offensive weapon against the submarine and while it did not alter much in character later on the method of despatch certainly did. It consisted of a large cylinder filled with TNT exploded by hydrostatic detonator and was usually rolled off the stern of the ship two at a time. Until its invention the only method of blowing up a submerged vessel had been by catching it with a towed explosive sweep, but the advantage of the depth charge was that it did not have to hit to do damage with the shock waves it produced.

In the Second World War delivery methods were developed which enabled a number of depth charges to be fired at once in pre-determined patterns. A more powerful explosive called Torpex – a mixture of RDX, TNT and aluminium which reduced the size of the depth charge considerably – was used. The casing was also streamlined to make it sink faster and to improve accuracy.

British submarine commanders during the Second World War were around 27 years old and, before the war, went through an arduous training programme. The maximum age for a British submarine commander was 35 years and this rule was strictly applied even during wartime. On being commissioned as an officer they spent two and half years in a submarine as a lieutenant before being promoted to First Lieutenant, second in command. After another one and a half to two years they were sent on a three-month Commanding Officers' course and then had two years general service on a warship to learn how the fleet works, before being given command on their tour in a submarine.

Ratings in Britains' submarines were largely volunteers, 95 per cent of whom had chosen the submarine service. They could only join after being fully trained in the specialisms of torpedoes, ASDIC or seamanship, did five years' service in a submarine and could then volunteer for more, or go to a surface ship; ten years' service in submarines was the maximum.

The crew of a British submarine included five officers – the captain, first lieutenant, navigator, armament officer and engineering officer – with 55 ratings, half of them seamen and half stoker mechanics. The crew was headed by a coxswain who controlled the men, established routines and looked after provisioning. He was also responsible for the escape equipment and was usually supported by four specialist petty officers, each with their own departmental responsibilities – torpedoes and ASDIC, electrics and main batteries, radar and wireless, and communications.

US submarines, because of the large distances they had to cover, were larger than British and German. As a consequence they had an average crew of eight officers and 54 men, but as the war continued these figures grew to eight officers and 95 men.

US submarine commanders spent most of their training at university where they studied for around four years. At the start of the war their average age was 40 but this fell dramatically as the US Navy opted for younger men, like the Germans cashing in on the exuberance of youth. As in the Royal Navy every officer and man, all volunteers, was a specialist in his job. A new officer or crew member had to pass stringent written and oral examinations on all the equipment in the submarine so that every man had a good idea of every other man's job and responsibilities.

German U-boat commanders, before the conflict, had an equally long and difficult training period, aimed at developing character and practical skills and involved six month's basic training, 114 weeks on a sailing ship, 14 months on a cruiser, a year in the classroom and another year on a warship receiving practice in command.

German commanders were aged between 26 and 30 years, although as the war progressed they went for younger men. U-boat crews averaged 20–24 years at the beginning of the war but by 1945 this had dropped to 17–18 years. They came largely from industrial and technical jobs, were from the working and lower middle class and had to meet strict physical qualifications. Until 1939 most German submariners, officers and men, were volunteers but this policy was dropped early in the war.

Japanese Navy submarines were officered and manned by an elite of volunteers who had to pass strict tests of fitness and temperament. They had one aim and that was to attack and sink American capital ships. Officers, all graduates of naval academies, had to spent two or three years on a surface warship before qualifying as a submarine commander. At the outbreak of war the Japanese submarine service was convinced that it was the best in the world – as the war progressed it proved to be the worst. Japanese crews, again volunteers, of which there was no shortage, were trained on the job on a submarine attached to the Submarine School.

Readers might wonder why, when some British submarines in the book have names, others have less romantic numbers. After the First World War the Royal Navy had a tradition of naming their submarines rather than using soulless numbers. When the Second World War started, however, any new submarines were identified only by their numbers. It was not something that submariners particularly liked but that was the way it was – until Prime Minister Winston Churchill became involved. In the midst of the war, with many other important things to think about, he wrote to the First Sea Lord: 'Let me see the list of submarines that will come into service by 31 December 1943 in their classes and also those at present in the service with no names. I have no doubt whatever that names should be given and I will myself make some suggestions that may stimulate others.'

A month later he wrote again to the First Sea Lord: 'I am still grieved to see our submarines described as "P-21" etc in our daily returns. I thought you told me you would give them names. It is in accordance with the traditions of the service and with the feelings of officers and men who risk their lives in these vessels. Not to give them a name is derogatory to their devotion and sacrifice.'

Later that month a happier Winston wrote: 'These names for submarines are certainly better than the numbers. I have no doubt a little more thought, prompted by a dictionary, would make other improvements possible. Now do please get on with it and let them all be given names in the next fortnight.' By the time the Prime Minister arrived in Algeria on 3 February 1943 the submarines of the Mediterranean fleet all had their names in evidence.

CHAPTER TWO

The First World War

Three cruisers sunk, the tragedy of the Lusitania,
*Britain's naval base at Scapa Flow penetrated,
U-boats off USA, Britain helps Russia.*

A T the outbreak of the First World War no one understood how
effective submarines were going to be or if they were going to
be of any value at all, however it did not take long for them to
prove their worth and show just how dangerous these underwater
vessels could be.

German U-boats began in August 1914 by searching for the British
Grand Fleet in the North Sea, which it was patrolling between Britain
and Norway. The first contact came when U-19 sighted one of the
battle squadrons and fired a torpedo at the battleship *Monarch*.
Unfortunately for the crew of the U-boat the torpedo missed its
target but gave away the submarine's position, British escorts
immediately attacked and U-19 was rammed and sunk by the cruiser
Birmingham, thus becoming the first German U-boat casualty of
the war.

U-18 was then part of a U-boat attack on the British fleet which,
the Germans believed, was anchored at Scapa Flow. By the time the
attacking U-boat flotilla arrived on the scene, however, the fleet had
put to sea. U-18, which had overcome eight miles of turbulent tidal
streams in the Pentland Firth, did not know this, and forced its way
through the wide and deep entrance to Hoxa Sound. It was right in
the middle when it was sighted and attacked by a patrolling destroyer
which rammed it. Although it was able to limp away eastwards, it

finally had to give up the fight for survival and scuttle itself near the Pentland Skerries. The success of U-18 in penetrating the British naval base led to a feeling of outrage, shock and a vast improvement in its defences.

Although this event really brought the potentiality of the submarine to the world's notice history had already been made a few days earlier when Korvettenkapitan Otto Hersing in command of U-21 put his name in the record books by sinking the light cruiser *Pathfinder* off St Abb's Head. It was the first successful action by a submarine since the Confederate navy's *Hunley* had sunk the Federal man-of-war *Housatanic* more than 50 years before.

The admittedly old armoured cruisers *Cressy, Hoque* and *Aboukir* were steaming along the Dutch coast at a speed of 10 knots under the command of the senior officer, Captain John Drummond. A strong gale had been blowing and had driven the destroyer escort into harbour, but the sea had now moderated to a heavy swell. Earlier U-9 had been on the surface recharging its batteries but when the masts of three vessels were sighted on the horizon to the south the submarine submerged. It waited, lurking beneath the surface as the three ships sailed slowly towards it. Their speed was dangerously slow, which was nothing to do with the state of the weather but, as it was claimed later, was the decision of the senior officer who wanted to conserve fuel. It made life much easier for U-9, which had plenty of time in which to manoeuvre into position for the attack. The submarine was armed with six torpedoes, having four torpedo tubes, two in the bow and two in the stern, and the bow tubes could be reloaded if necessary. Its main task was to prevent British landings on the Belgian coast during the Battle of the Marne.

When *Aboukir,* commanded by Captain Drummond, was within 500 yards U-9 fired one torpedo – it was not yet the days of the deadly salvo – and hit the cruiser a mortal blow on the starboard side. Drummond thought his ship had struck a mine and ordered the other two cruisers to close up to take survivors onboard and, possibly, help save his ship.

The lessons of submarine warfare were, of course, still being learned at this stage and so it was not surprising that the captains of

Cressy and *Hoque* drew close to the stricken *Aboukir*, hove to and lowered their boats to pick up survivors – it very quickly became accepted that a warship did not stop to pick up anything if it was thought that a submarine was lurking in the area. But these were early days.

U-9, followed the practice of the day, and after firing a single 18-inch torpedo had dived deep to reload. When it returned to periscope depth its captain saw the *Aboukir* sinking and the two other cruisers stationary nearby. This time the U-boat fired two torpedoes at *Hoque*, which was so close it was impossible to miss. Both torpedoes hit the cruiser and the only danger now was that the U-boat, which had continued steaming ahead, might collide with its victim – the German vessel had to go sharply astern to avoid disaster.

Cressy, her boats lowered to pick up *Aboukir's* crew, sighted the U-boat's periscope just as it turned to fire its stern torpedoes. It was too late for the British ship. As *Cressy* got under way and went full steam ahead to try and ram the U-boat she ran straight into its two torpedoes and, with a mighty explosion, stopped dead. U-9 turned again and fired its last torpedo from the bow tubes, hit the target, and sent *Cressy* to the bottom.

Sixty-two officers and 1,397 men of the 2,000 aboard the three cruisers lost their lives on that day – it had taken under an hour for the U-boat to send three ships to destruction and kill so many men. U-9 withdrew from the scene of carnage, recharged its batteries and returned to Germany in triumph.

It took some time for the British to realise that the disaster had been caused by a single submarine and for some time they were under the impression that the attack had been carried out by a whole flotilla of U-boats. The incident was explained away as an insignificant blow, while a powerful fleet remained and there was little need for concern. But the British Admiralty was now left in no doubt as to the danger of the German U-boat.

The lessons of the submarine menace were as quickly being taught to the Germans, and Britain's famous submariner, Lt Cdr Max Horton was their first tutor. Horton was in command of E-9, one of the class of submarine that bore the brunt of the undersea war in the First World War. Dawn was breaking on 12 September 1914 as

E-9 slipped slowly past the German island of Heligoland at periscope depth. Horton was peering through the eyepiece when he suddenly spotted the white bow wave of a warship, clearly of some size. Manoeuvring the E-9 into an attacking position, he waited. The German light cruiser *Hela,* on exercise and confident that she was safe in German waters, sailed on. She was some 600 yards away from the submerged British attacker when her voyage suddenly ended. Two torpedoes from E-9's bow tubes rent the German ship asunder, and when Horton took his final look at the scene an hour later all he saw was floating wreckage and German trawlers looking for survivors.

Horton and E-9 were in action again within three weeks, this time off the Ems estuary. On 6 October the German destroyer S-116, again on patrol in what its captain thought were safe waters, was the victim of another determined attack by Horton and sent to the bottom. The sinking of *Hela* and S-116 had a dramatic effect on the German High Command and all ships exercising were immediately withdrawn to the Baltic Sea, which, they thought, was as safe as any sea could be for the German fleet.

In the space of only two months since the outbreak of war the British and German navies had learned to their cost that the submarine was a weapon of war that could mean disaster – U-9 underlined this later in October when, off Peterhead, it torpedoed and sank its fourth British cruiser, *Hawk,* with the loss of 500 lives.

The submarines that fought in the First World War were as different from the sophisticated weapons of the Second World War as a Model T Ford is from today's family saloons. On the British side, once it had been decided that they were proper weapons of war, no expense was spared and the outbreak of the conflict saw the Royal Navy armed with 74 submarines with another 14 being built or projected. The Germans, on the other hand, had 33 U-boats commissioned with another 28 under construction. The difference, however, was not so overwhelmingly in favour of the Royal Navy as it appears. The vast majority of British boats were coastal types and only 18 of their submarines were of ocean-going or 'overseas' D- and E-class types while all the commissioned German boats were capable of overseas operations.

British D-class 500-ton submarines were constructed from 1906 and were fitted with German diesel engines. Their batteries had enough capacity for them to remain submerged throughout the daylights hours but they could not, of course, be used when submerged because they needed air to function, and when the submarine was under water this would be used up very quickly and the crew would have been asphyxiated.

These submarines had a range of some 2,500 miles and could do just over 14 knots on the surface and a sharp sprint at 10 knots when submerged. Normally submerged passage was much slower, only 4 or 5 knots. They were the first submarines with twin screws and created another precedent by having ballast tanks fitted outside the hull. They carried two 18-inch bow torpedo tubes with one tube in the stern. Some, the later D-class boats, became the first British submarines to carry deck guns – a single two-pounder. They were also the first boats to be fitted with wireless; aerials were rigged to a mast, which had to be lowered and carefully stowed along the vessel before it submerged.

In D-class submarines the crew could actually stand up whilst in the boat, and also for the first time the officers and crew were provided with accommodation. Despite all these modern 'conveniences', life was incredibly cramped with the men virtually living among the machinery and torpedoes.

E-class submarines which, with the Ds, fought through the entire war, had further developments with slightly more power and endurance. With a displacement of 700 tons, and four 18-inch torpedo tubes, two forward and two aft, they could make over 15 knots on the surface and had a range of 3,000 miles.

Submarines, both British and German, could travel submerged for about 60 miles provided they kept at economical speeds. After that the batteries ran flat and they had to return to the surface to recharge using the diesels to act as generators. This took between two and three hours if the full supply was to be restored. When submerged the interior air pressure was maintained at the same level as the outside atmosphere. The deeper the boat dived the greater the external water pressure – 16 tons per square foot at 500 feet, for example – so this severely limited the depths to which a submarine could dive.

The Germans did not order their first U-boat until 1905 and this, U-12, was much in advance of its British contemporaries having a double hull and twin screws with heavy-oil/electric drive and an extremely reliable engine. The later class, known as the Mittel-U type, was better still than U-12, the most notable new feature being the deck gun, an 88 millimetre, sometimes 105 millimetre, which enabled them to sink a large number of ships with gunfire rather than using expensive torpedoes.

Submarine activity during the first months of the First World War was not confined to the British and German navies. In the Mediterranean in February and March 1915, the Austrian Adriatic ports were being continually blockaded by the French fleet patrolling the Straits of Otranto. The blockade was lifted by a small submarine of the Austrian Navy. The French cruiser *Waldeck Rousseau* was attacked and missed by the Austrians but shortly afterwards the new dreadnought *Jean Bart* was badly damaged by submarine attack and the blockading battleships were forced to retreat to Bizerta. Cruisers and smaller vessels were left behind to continue the confinement of the Austrian fleet but this reduced force was further weakened when another Austrian submarine offensive resulted in the sinking of the cruiser *Gambetta*.

The submarine was certainly proving to be a useful weapon in the war at sea. Pre-war theories that its advent would bring an end to the old strategy of close blockade by surface ship were quickly proved correct. Likewise British submarines patrolling off the Ems estuary were close to establishing a blockade there, deterring the German fleet from leaving its Baltic training grounds via the Kiel Canal.

Both British and French submarines were involved in the Dardanelles, entering the Sea of Marmara in December 1914, a prelude to the Gallipoli campaign. The first victory in this sector of the war came from the French submarine B-11 which, after bravely diving under a minefield torpedoed and sank the Turkish armoured vessel *Messoudieh* in the Straits of Gallipoli.

The first British boat to attempt to break into the Sea of Marmara, E-15, ran aground halfway up the Straits and was lost; the Australian boat AE-2 did get through but was sunk by a torpedo boat (it was part of the massive Australian military effort at Gallipoli). The third submarine to try the dangerous passage was the British E-14, which got through and did considerable damage to Turkish shipping. Under Lt Cdr White it was sent to try and sink the German battlecruiser *Goeben* which, after being trapped for some months in Constantinople, had attempted to break out but had run aground off Nagra Point. E-14 failed to find the *Goeben* but torpedoed and sank another ship. It then tried to force its way through the Narrows but came under heavy bombardment from shore batteries, during which its captain was killed by shrapnel.

E-11 followed in next with what was the most successful of the patrols carried out by British submarines in the Sea of Marmara. It lasted 29 days during which time the Turkish battleship *Barbarousse Haireddine,* was sunk, together with a gunboat and 30 other ships.

During the nine-month campaign nine British and four French submarines carried out 15 patrols in the Sea of Marmara. Four were lost on the inward journey and one was sunk on the way out. The French submarine *Joule* hit a mine, the *Mariotte* was caught in anti-submarine nets and the *Turquoise* ran aground. The British E-7 was also caught in submarine nets, while E-15 was another which ran aground in the very shallow waters; E-20 was sunk by a German U-boat, UB-14. On the other side of the balance sheet the submarines sank a battleship, a destroyer, 5 gunboats, 11 transports, 44 steamers and 148 sailing vessels.

German U-boats did not ignore pleas for help from the Turkish Navy and in April 1915 U-21, commanded by Korvettenkapitan Otto Hersing, sailed from Kiel to Gallipoli. Although sighted by the British, the U-boat managed to evade attacks and subsequently sank the battleships *Triumph* and *Majestic*. Both warships were pre-Dreadnought (heavily-armed battleship) but this did not diminish the Germans' achievements which did something to redress the balance and detract from the success of British and French submarines.

During the first nine months of the war the U-boats in the Atlantic had little effect on the trade routes which were so vital to Britain – fewer than 50 British steamers were sunk and these were quickly replaced. In April 1915, however, U-20, commanded by Leutnant Walther Schweiger, left Wilhelmshaven on a voyage which was to have major repercussions on the conduct of the war and besmirch the name of the German submarine service for many years. Four days into its voyage U-20 was on station south of Ireland. The patrol started well when two British steamers were sunk by gunfire and a third with a torpedo fired without warning.

The lack of warning when firing a torpedo had some significance because, according to international law at the time, submarines were obliged to surface and ascertain the identity of a potential target before sinking it. They also had to make adequate provision for the safety of its crew and passengers before sending it to the bottom. It was a difficult law for submarine captains to follow for not only was it impossible for a small submarine to take survivors on board, but the Germans faced the problem that the British had started arming its merchantmen and thus to surface and ask questions put a U-boat commander at some disadvantage.

Originally the defensive measures advised for merchantmen attacked by U-boats was to turn towards the attacker forcing it to dive and then run directly over it using superior speed to escape. This tactical ploy was only partly successful and so other methods, such as arming merchantmen, were adopted by the British. Another ploy was the equipping of 'Q' ships, merchant vessels secretly manned by Royal Navy crews and with a concealed heavy gun. When an unsuspecting U-boat surfaced to challenge the 'Q' ship, the gun's camouflage would be thrown down and the gun would open fire. 'Q' ships were soon recording a number of successes – a U-boat on the surface, investigating before an impending attack and making arrangements for the welfare of potential survivors, was a very handy target for well-trained gunners.

U-boat commanders, with self-preservation at the forefront of their minds, thus became increasingly inclined to ignore the law, tending to shoot or torpedo first and ask questions afterwards. They understandably put forward the proposition that an armed merchantmen was the equivalent of an ordinary warship. The first British merchantman to be sunk by a U-boat was the SS *Glitra* in October 1914, and in this instance the submarine had put a boarding party on the vessel, opened the sea cocks to sink the ship and hurt no one. The new British tactic put an end to this chivalrous activity and when U-20 torpedoed the steamer without warning, it was therefore carrying out what was fast becoming standard practice.

On 7 May 1915, U-20 was at the end of its patrol off southern Ireland with only two torpedoes left and the thoughts of its captain and crew turning towards home and family. Their reveries were abruptly halted when, out of the afternoon mist, loomed a large ship heading straight for them. The U-boat captain's reaction was spontaneous – without waiting to check the details of the approaching vessel he fired his remaining torpedoes straight at the ship. Both of them smacked into their target, which sank in 20 minutes. A highly successful attack, thought Walter Schweiger, while the crew rejoiced at their success.

The snag was that the unescorted, unarmed vessel that was now lying on the ocean floor was the British liner *Lusitania* carrying nearly 3,000 people across the Atlantic to New York. Some 128 neutral Americans were among the 2,000 who lost their lives. The attack was quite illegal and drew heated protests from the Americans and a shocked and horrified world. But it is difficult to decide exactly what the U-boat commander should have done, suddenly faced with a large vessel heading straight for him in hostile waters when he was not fully acclimatised to battle conditions.

In August 1915 over 40 British ships totalling 135,000 tons were sent to the bottom by U-boats, although the unrestricted attack campaign came to a temporary halt at the end of that month, following the torpedoing of the British liner *Arabic*. This time only 40 lives were lost but these included three Americans. A second wave of protests from the United States had its effect and U-boat commanders were ordered not to sink passenger vessels of any nationality, without giving warning and saving the passengers and crew. It was a respite that was to last only four months for the German High Command had second thoughts and became convinced that an unrestricted attack by U-boats would bring Britain to its knees within a year. The removal of restrictions was confirmed in March 1916 when UB-29 sank the unarmed French steamer

Sussex, killing or injuring many of its 380 passengers, again including several Americans.

July and August 1916 saw the record cruise by the German U-boat U-35, during which 54 ships totalling 91,000 tons were sunk in the Mediterranean, nearly all of them by gunfire; British, French and Italian ships were among the victims. UB-35 was commanded by Commander Lothar von Arnauld de la Periere, the German U-boat ace, whose story will be dealt with in greater detail later.

It was in the same year that the Germans found a new use for submarines. The *Deutschland,* the first of six U-boats being built as merchant submarines, was sent to the still neutral United States to bring back a cargo of nickel, tin and rubber. It was a successful trip and on its second voyage it was escorted by another new breed of U-boat, UB-111, which had a much longer range and greater offensive power than any hitherto. As it happened it was not needed as an escort vessel for the British were not, as expected, lying in wait for the *Deutschland.* Instead UB-111 exhibited its capabilities by sinking five ships off the American coast.

The uncompromising spirit in which the war at sea was being fought was clearly indicated in the autumn of 1916. Submarine activity was very heavy off the North Cape and on 2 September the munition-ladened steamship *Olive Branch* was attacked by U-28 under the command of Korvettenkapitan Schmidt, the crew taking to the lifeboats after a warning that their ship was about to be sunk. When they were clear of their vessel, U-28, at a range of only 250 yards, opened fire, the second shot being a direct hit on the *Olive Branch's* ammunition hold. So violent was the resulting explosion that U-28 itself was wrecked. The U-boat's crew were forced to abandon ship and, without lifeboats, had to try and persuade the crew of the *Olive Branch* to take them aboard their already over-ladened lifeboat. Their request was refused and the U-boat crew perished.

It was not only around the British Isles, in the Atlantic and the Mediterranean that British submarines were active. In the Baltic in 1914–18 the Russian fleet was inferior to the German in both numbers and quality and its submariners were insufficiently trained, so it was decided to send three Royal Navy submarines to help them.

Lt Cdr Max Horton in E-9, Lt Cdr Noel Lawrence in E-1 and Lt Cdr Martin Naismith in E-11 – all three officers were eventually to become admirals – were selected for the task.

On 18 October 1914, E-1 and E-9 penetrated the shallow waters between Norway and the Danish Island of Sjaelland and avoided the German patrols; E-11, however, was sighted and forced back. This submarine was bedevilled by mechanical troubles, not unknown in British submarines of that time, and although it made a deter-mined effort to follow its colleagues into the Baltic, attacks by the Germans, and shallow waters which made evasive action difficult, eventually forced the submarine to give up and return to base. E-11's failure on this mission was amply compensated by its later heroic action in the Dardanelles.

Meanwhile E-1 and E-9 successfully broke through into the Baltic but failed to find the patrolling German High Seas fleet. Both submarines had unsuccessful skirmishes with the German Baltic fleet, and some near escapes, and they finally reached Russia where they were put under the operational command of the Admiral of the Russian Baltic fleet.

For two weeks the two submarines patrolled without success, spotting the enemy only when it was impossible to set up an attack. The famine ended, however, in January 1915, on the final patrol before winter really set in and the Gulf of Finland froze over, when Horton sighted a solitary destroyer and fired a single torpedo. A tremendous explosion signalled success and when E-9 surfaced after only four minutes the German destroyer had disappeared.

When spring came, naval operations in the Baltic resumed and soon Horton was in action again, sinking a German transport in the midst of a well-protected convoy and E-9 was being hunted by destroyers and cruisers. In June, Horton sank a destroyer and a collier, again in a well-protected convoy.

The following month Horton joined in one of the rare battles between the German and Russian Baltic fleets by attacking the armoured cruiser *Prince Adalbert,* the German flagship. The cruiser was hit twice and badly damaged and only just managed to limp back to base with her bows submerged. Ironically the *Prince Adalbert* was quickly repaired and sent back into the fray, only to be torpedoed and sunk by E-8 which, only a short time before, had joined E-9 in the Baltic. It was, in fact, one of four boats sent out to reinforce the British support effort; E-13 was another of the four but it was sunk somewhere on the way.

E-1, after some time in port with a defective engine, now rejoined the battle, sinking the battlecruiser *Moltke* in the Gulf of Riga. Meanwhile E-19 scored another success by sinking the light cruiser *Undine*. The small British submarine force was really proving its worth in 'German home waters'.

Patrols continued with occasional successes, but with the loss of two submarines. The end came in 1917 with the Russian Revolution and the signing of the Treaty of Brest-Litovsk, when the Germans insisted that all British submarines in the Baltic should be surrendered; they were, in fact, scuttled and their crews evacuated overland.

The third unrestricted German submarine campaign, launched in February 1917 with a front-line force of over 100 U-boats, was a deliberate gamble aimed at bringing the United Kingdom to its knees before the USA could enter the war. In its early stages it looked like succeeding, Allied shipping losses averaging 630,000 tons a month with a peak of 866,000 tons in April 1917. But in that month the Allies adopted the convoy system which produced both a fall in Allied losses and higher U-boat losses.

Until early in 1917 thousands of merchantmen had sailed independently presenting U-boats with easy targets, but between May and July a convoy system, grouping ships together, sometimes over 200, and providing them with a strong naval escort, was adopted. In these three months only 300 ships had joined the convoy system but already losses were beginning to fall. There were three reasons for this: ships were better protected where before they had little or no protection; U-boats found it more difficult to find the convoys; and once a U-boat fired a shot or torpedo and its presence was detected the escorts immediately attacked. The effect was immediate and Allied merchant shipping losses fell to around 250,000 a month by the end of 1917. The total effect of ocean convoys was to reduce the losses in UK overseas trade from nearly 5 per cent in April 1917 to around half a per cent at the end of the war.

Some 370 U-boats were built by the Germans in the First World War; of which 178 were lost, and nearly 5,000 men; they sank 5,708 ships totalling over 11 million tons. The ravages British shipping sustained in the years 1914–18, inflicted by German U-boats, remained seared on the British mind long after the end of the conflict.

When U-boats appeared off America's east coast in May 1918 it was a major shock to both the American people and the military, being the first time for over 100 years that a foreign power had invaded their eastern seaboard. For the U-boats the campaign was as easy as shelling peas. They sank over 165,000 tons of shipping in a very short space of time, causing chaos in the process. Ships moved closer into the shore to avoid the marauding enemy thus increasing the chances of collision, particularly as no lights were allowed during the hours of darkness. To make life even more difficult for the Americans naval craft were sunk or damaged by the guns of freighters which fired at anything dubious. All this chaos was created by five U-boats; six were sent but one was recalled at the last moment.

U-151 was the first to arrive. It was some time before the Navy Department admitted the presence of enemy submarines off the coast, and it is said that the delay was responsible for the loss of 14,000 tons of shipping (six vessels), 13 deaths as well as imperilling the lives of over 400 people. U-151 was commanded by Koevetten-kapitan von Nostitz and on arrival in the area he attempted to torpedo the British steamer *Huntress* about 1,000 miles East of Cape Hatteras. The *Huntress* notified shore stations of the attack. The American steamship *Nyanza* was the next to be attacked but managed to escape after send out an 'SOS'. It was not going U-151's way because it then attacked the American ship *Johancy* but missed again. Although the *Johancy* sent out radio signals they made little impression on those listening.

There were several more encounters before, at long last, the British tanker *Cheyenne,* after a short battle with U-151, reached Delaware with the astounding news that there was a U-boat in the area. At last the Fourth and Fifth Naval Districts, the two nearest the scene, took action against the intruder. In the meantime U-151 disappeared.

Unbeknown to the Americans it had temporarily turned itself into a minelayer, sowing them off Virginia, before continuing to sink ships – several of them, albeit small ones. U-151 was eventually joined by U-156, U-140, U-117, U-155 and U-152, the latter being quickly recalled. Between 15 May and 9 November 1918 they sank 45 American ships, eight British, 15 Norwegian, 14 Canadian, three Portuguese, and one each from Japan, Italy, Sweden, Belgium, Cuba and France. As well as these casualties from direct actions it is estimated that 11 American ships were lost through accidents caused by the U-boat presence; these 11 vessels had a total tonnage of 30,655, bringing the total tonnage attributable to U-boat activity to 197,761 tons. Some 435 lives were lost, but to keep things in perspective, in this same period 1,142 ships carried over two million American soldiers safely to France. Thus the U-boats' American campaign was ultimately a failure, only serving to give further impetus to America's will to win.

During the years between the wars the British strove, with the League of Nations, to get international limitation on the number of submarines that could be built – as there was with larger ships – but they failed. They also failed to get an international agreement on banning the use of submarines in indiscriminate attacks on commercial shipping.

CHAPTER THREE

World War Two

Britain/Germany

A CTION was not long in coming when the Second World War started – on the very first day of the war, U-30, commanded by Fritz-Julius Lemp sank the liner *Athenia*. The action by the U-boat's commander was probably instinctive – war had broken out only hours earlier and then he suddenly found a dark shape looming out of the mist. He fired without thinking, which could have been equally disastrous for Germany for, unbeknown to him, the German liner *Bremen* was also in the vicinity and it could well have been his target.

The *Athenia*, like the *Lusitania* in 1915, was carrying American passengers and the Allied propaganda machine made the most of the U-boat's action. But sinking on sight was in no way the accepted policy of the German U-boat command at that time, although one suspects that the U-boat's captain was not too severely reprimanded.

In the first weeks of the war nine U-boats played havoc in the Western Approaches where shipping lanes to and from Britain converged, making it essential that Britain did something about it, and they chose to send two aircraft carriers, *Royal Oak* and *Courageous*, whose aircraft could give some protection. Among the nine U-boats was U-29 commanded by Otto Schuhart, who had already sunk a 10,000-ton tanker, *Regent Tiger*, when the war was but five days old. It looked as though fortune was on his side when he attacked another 8,000-ton tanker, *British Influence*, but while he was doing so, he had the shock of seeing the carrier *Ark Royal* in his sights. Reacting quickly he fired a salvo but was confounded when he saw two torpedoes explode prematurely.

A few days later, on his was back to base having completed his patrol, he sighted a Swordfish bi-plane and deduced therefore that there must be a carrier in the vicinity. Moments later he saw smoke on the horizon and it was not long before the carrier *Courageous* came into view. Schuhart altered course towards the carrier even though he saw two destroyers and aircraft protecting her. His problem then was to catch up with the enemy ship. He could not surface because of the aircraft and his submerged speed was only 8 knots, while the carrier was capable of 26 knots. After ninety minutes of tenacious pursuit the British carrier suddenly altered course towards him, having turned into the wind so that aircraft could land on her deck. Schuhart immediately attacked, firing three torpedoes at a range of 3,000 yards and then dived deep. He and his crew heard two certain hits. The carrier simply rolled over and sank, taking with her half her 1,260 crew. The two destroyers then commenced a vigorous attack which lasted over four hours. When it finally went quiet he slipped away to home and safety; every member of the crew of U-29 was awarded the Iron Cross 2nd Class.

Perhaps the best-known U-boat commander of the Second World War was Kapitanleutnant Gunther Prien of U-47, largely because he achieved a spectacular coup by taking his boat through the defences of the British naval base at Scapa Flow, where U-18 had been unlucky in 1914, but this time part of the British fleet was there.

The night of 13 October 1939 was the selected time of attack and, such was the secrecy surrounding it, that the crew of U-47 had no idea they were to undertake such a dangerous mission until the U-boat was lying on the sea bed within sight of the Orkney Islands. The first hurdle to overcome were the treacherous currents that swirl around the islands of Kirk Sound; then Prien had to skilfully manoeuvre his boat between sunken ships that blocked the Sound itself. Although U-47 temporarily fouled one of the cables from a blockship it got through the Sound just after midnight. Taking his first look through the periscope Prien saw what he thought were two battleships which were in fact the battleship *Royal Oak*, the seaplane carrier *Pegasus*, and several destroyers. At 4,000 yards he first fired four bow torpedoes at the *Royal Oak*, one of which struck the battleship but did little damage, two missed and the fourth misfired. He then turned away expecting a hail of depth-charges to fall around him but there was no reaction from the British. The officers aboard *Royal Oak* sent to discover the cause of the explosion had come to the conclusion it was something internal.

Surprised by the lack of reaction Prien withdrew some distance to reload his torpedo tubes, returning an hour later, on the surface, to fire three more at the battleship which towered over the diminutive submarine. This time the blow was fatal. Two torpedoes struck the *Royal Oak* amidships and 13 minutes later she rolled over and sank; 24 officers and 809 men died.

Prien now received the reaction he had previously expected, as patrol boats raced around throwing depth charges in every direction. Still on the surface and with engines at full powers, he raced away from the scene clinging as close as he dare to the dark coastline. With total chaos behind him he navigated U-47 between the blockships once again, out through the Sound and vanished into the ocean depths.

The Iron Cross 1st Class was awarded to Prien by Grand Admiral Raeder immediately on the boat's return to Kiel. Prien and his crew became national heroes overnight for, not only had they attacked the Royal Navy in its lair, they had avenged the German Navy's greatest moment of defeat in 1918 when, after the surrender, the fleet had been taken to Scapa Flow and scuttled.

When the British and German fleets opposed each other at the beginning of the Second World War, the British had 69 submarines at their disposal, 6 of which were minelayers and 33 of which had been built before 1935.

The German U-boat arm was almost caught by surprise when war was declared, having only 57 boats at their disposal, 27 of which were large enough for operations in the North Sea. True, they had plans to build over 200 and many were under construction, but when the war started they were ill-prepared.

Before war was declared, between 19–29 August, 17 ocean-going U-boats sailed from their various bases to take up station in the North Sea, while on 21 August seven minelayers set out to lay mines off the British and French Channel ports. Four days later six coastal boats set sail for the central area of the North Sea, followed by nine more of their smaller boats. By the time war broke out they were all on station waiting for action.

Very quickly the Germans determined that the major target for their U-boats was to be merchant shipping, although their original plan was not a sink-on-sight policy. Under instructions from Adolf Hitler they had to obey the law of the sea, finding out a ship's cargo and destination before opening fire. This was in no way an altruistic policy laid down by the German dictator for he had wrongly surmised that once Poland was overrun, and it was too late for the Allies to do anything about it, they would sue for peace. He thus did not want anyone upset at this early stage of the conflict by indiscriminate sinkings. It was a policy that was not to last for very long, for the order restricting U-boats in their attacks on merchant shipping was removed in October 1939 when the German High Command gave the U-boats permission to attack all ships identified as hostile, without warning. By the end of the year the U-boats were in full cry after merchant shipping and had sunk 114 ships with a total tonnage of 421,000 tons; it was not yet the day of the well-escorted, highly organised convoys. However, life for German U-boats during the early days of the war did not go entirely in their favour. The closure of the Dover Straits meant that to reach the Atlantic they had to go by the northern route, sometimes travelling on the surface, so that they were often sighted and attacked by aircraft of Britain's Coastal Command.

There were two more damaging attacks on Royal Navy capital ships during this period. The *Ark Royal*, which became Britain's most famous aircraft carrier (partly because of the number of time the Germans claimed to have sunk her) was narrowly missed by U-39, commanded by Gerhard Glattes. The torpedoes passed close astern and, although the U-boat was attacked by the destroyer *Faulkner*, sunk and its crew of 44 captured, it was a near miss that worried the British. By the end of the year nine U-boats had been sunk – U-27, U-35, U-39, U-42 and U-45 by British escort ships, U-36 by the submarine *Salmon* and U-12, U-16 and U-40 by mines.

The U-boat war against Allied merchant shipping gathered momentum during the early months of 1940. By the end of January, 40 ships totalling 110,000 tons had been sent to the bottom; another 45 ships totalling 170,000 tons were added the following month.

The main target for U-boats at this time was supposed to be the British battleship *Renown* returning from West Africa but she managed to evade attack and unfortunately merchant shipping paid the price. U-53 sank four ships before being attacked and sunk by the destroyer *Gurkha*, while the minesweeper *Gleaner* sank U-33 in the Firth of Clyde. On 18 February, U-boats attacked a Norwegian convoy and although the convoy itself escaped, the destroyer *Daring*, one of its escorts, was sunk.

In March 1940 there was an unaccountable decline in the number of U-boat attacks and sinkings with only 23 merchant ships totalling 69,000 tons being lost. This however had nothing to do with the efficiency of escorts or anti-submarine patrols – the Germans were regrouping their boats ready for the invasion of Norway.

While the U-boat arm was having its successes in the Western Approaches and the North Sea the British submarine service was not inactive, neither was it that lucky, for German anti-submarine activity in the Heligoland Bight had brought the destruction of three submarines, *Seahorse*, *Undine* and *Starfish*. Their colleagues were busy, not sinking any enemy merchant ships but stopping them, examining their cargo and, if necessary, escorting them into port. Some German ships were sunk however for on 10 January the *Bahia Blanca*, caught by ice when trying to evade British submarine patrols in the Straits of Denmark, holed herself and sank.

By the time the Second World War broke out Max Horton, whose earlier career has been described in the previous chapter, had been knighted, promoted to Vice Admiral and was immediately put in command of the British submarine service. When he became clear in his mind that the Germans would invade Norway he sent every available submarine, about 19 of them, to Norwegian waters to be ready to attack the invasion fleet. He was strongly criticised for this because it was thought to be a dangerous policy, as submarines could only spend a limited time at sea and could not wait for long on the off-chance that the Germans would invade.

The submarine *Truant*, patrolling off Christiansand, caught the German cruiser *Karlsruhe* as she left harbour and torpedoed her. Other submarines in the area now had permission to attack German merchant shipping off the coast of Norway without having to observe any of the formalities.

In May 1940 Horton was convinced that the Germans would invade Holland and Belgium so he again disposed a considerable force of submarines off the coast of the two countries; again there was criticism; again he was right. The Germans invaded both countries on 10 May but this time, with the memories of the disasters during the Norwegian invasion, their ships kept well away. By July the Germans had captured French, Dutch and Belgian ports on the west coast of Europe and were able to move their U-boats into bases much more ideally placed for attacks in the north and south Atlantic. In consequence the British reorganised their convoy routes round the north of Scotland through the Pentland Firth.

Horton's powers of prognostication did not end in 1940. In the Mediterranean in 1942, the Italians attacked Gibraltar with mini-submarines (see Chapter 13) and although they were unsuccessful on this occasion, back in Britain the question was being asked: 'Do we have mini-subs?' No, we did not but Horton had already thought of it and had ordered their design. On 9 November 1942 he gave up the command of the submarine service and was promoted to Commander-in-Chief, Western Approaches. His job was done and the British submarine service was in a very healthy state.

This is a good point at which to divert from the narrative to discuss the major problem of torpedo malfunctioning, which hit all the navies in both the Atlantic and Pacific Wars. For a long time, the Germans in particular, but also the British and later the Americans, were hampered by a series of torpedo failures – they either fired prematurely, varied their depth, went too low because of inaccurate depth gauges or, worst of all, swung back towards those that had fired them.

German U-boats suffered during the Norwegian campaign and were made temporarily useless. Britain's aircraft carrier *Ark Royal*, for example, was a sitting target for U-39 but its torpedoes exploded prematurely giving away the U-boat's presence and allowing the carrier to take evasive action.

During the Japanese attack on the Philippines when US submarines were operating in a defensive mode and made attacks on several ships, these were thwarted by malfunctioning torpedoes. Indeed, torpedoes were the weakest link in the U-boat arm. They had the advantage that they were powered by electric batteries and so did not leave a trail as they sped towards their targets. But they had the same problems as the Americans were to suffer later, detonating after only a short run, or running deep or going wild. New magnetic pistols were exploding the torpedo prematurely, then contact pistols failed, whereupon it was found that they were running below the depth set. At one time the Germans estimated that some 30,000 tons of shipping would have been sunk if the torpedoes fired at them had worked. Both Prien in U-47 and Shultze in U-48 suffered. British ships did not even know that they had been targets because the torpedoes were so bad.

The US submarine service suffered unforgivable faults in their torpedoes. Frederick Warder in *Sea Wolf* fired four torpedoes at one Japanese ship and all missed, the sort of thing to cause a dangerous lack of confidence among submarine commanders and their crews. Lt Cdr Scott in *Tunny* fired four stern torpedoes and had the satisfaction of hearing four hits. Later, Japanese reports picked up by listening stations showed that there had been four premature explosions. *Tunny* also made an impeccable attack on Japanese carriers, firing almost perfect salvos from the forward torpedoes at one and the stern tubes at another. One carrier was damaged by one torpedo and all the other torpedoes exploded prematurely.

Tinosa tracked and attacked two giant Japanese oil tankers from a position from which it was impossible to miss. One tanker was slightly damaged, the other was hit but nothing happened: the torpedo was a dud.

Such faults were highly frustrating to the submarine commanders and their crews and could give away the presence of a submarine to the enemy anti-submarine patrols. But one of the worst examples occurred when US Navy submarine hero, Richard O'Kane in *Tang* was hit and sunk when a torpedo fired by him at a Japanese target circled back and struck his submarine (see story on pages 178–9). *Tullibee* was also lost in the same way.

That there was something wrong became apparent as soon as submarines went into action, but for a long time the authorities in all countries failed to act even though their experts were adamant. As a result it took almost two years before such faults in all the submarine services were finally corrected.

From July 1940 Britain was under threat of invasion by the victorious Germany army, and although British submarines were deployed things did not go well for them. On 6 July *Shark*, commanded by Cdr P.N. Buckley, reported that he could not dive and was returning to base. It was not heard of again. In fact, as later reports showed, it was forced to surface in daylight after being attacked by aircraft, its guns having run out of ammunition so that it could not defend itself and so was scuttled by the crew. This was one of the first occasions attacking aircraft had been able to use depth-charges – an advantage not yet available to British anti-submarine aircraft patrols.

The Dutch submarine 0–13 and the British *Salmon*, *Narwhal*, *Thames* and *Spearfish*, as well as *Shark*, were all lost during this drastic period. Not only were German aircraft equipped with a new deadly weapon but the Germans had also perfected their wireless interception techniques which caught many British submarines in these early days.

U-boats attacks on Allied shipping, although not yet as spectacular as they were going to be, still brought considerable success. It was the period when the individual U-boat aces Prien, Kretschmer, Endrass and others were having what they themselves described as a 'Happy Time', for their attacks were aimed mainly at ships sailing independently, and there were still a large number of them about. In one four-month period, June to October 1940, 144 unescorted and 73 escorted vessels were sunk by U-boats with only 6 of the latter being destroyed. During 1940 a total of 2,186,000 tons of Allied shipping was sent to the bottom.

In the following months, indeed until early 1943, British submarines were mainly deployed to attack German warships, with merchant ships only a secondary consideration. To do this they had to cover an exceptionally long coastline, from northern Norway and the Baltic right down the coast of Western Europe and the Mediterranean in order to search for enemy warships leaving or returning to their bases. In this activity the submarines had both their successes and failures – in February 1942 the *Sturgeon* sank a German oil tanker off Obrestadt but *Snapper* was sunk without trace, probably the victim of a mine. At this time the patrol line of British submarines was drastically thinned when several were withdrawn to Atlantic convoy escort duty.

On 28 October 1940, the British merchant service navy suffered another major disaster when the liner *Empress of Britain*, on passage home from the Middle East, was bombed and set on fire by enemy aircraft off Ireland. She was taken into tow and was to have been escorted home by two destroyers but U-32 put a torpedo into her which ended her career, U-32's career, in turn, being ended shortly afterwards when it was attacked and sunk by the escorting destroyers.

It was about this time that German U-boat policy made a significant turn which had a dramatic effect on the course of the war, to the detriment of the Allies. The most famous name in the German U-boat arm was that of Karl Doenitz who was, in fact, considered the father of the service. He was one of the leading U-boat aces of the First World War and narrowly escaped death when his boat was sunk in the Mediterranean. The experience taught him many things and set him to thinking about the wolf pack tactics that he was to use to such good purpose in the second major conflict. In 1935 he, as Captain Doenitz, was appointed to command the new German U-boat arm. He immediately laid plans to expand the service, develop the wolf pack, and increase cooperation between his boats and reconnaissance aircraft. The German naval staff wanted to build large ocean-going U-boats with an armament of heavy guns, but in the end they were persuaded by Doenitz to build submarines in the 500-ton range for attacking convoys.

The ultimate aim of Doenitz's wolf pack tactics was a night surface attack on a convoy with a large number of U-boats. Although

Doenitz made it clear that he wanted at least 300 at one time he never got them, as the Allies were sinking them almost as fast as they could be provided. His aim was to spread all available U-boats across the expected routes of convoys. When a convoy was sighted the observing boat could call up a number of its colleagues, most of whom came surfaced at high speed, so that a concerted attack could be made. Until the beginning of the 1941 he did not have enough U-boats to use this strategy for he could only use a third of his U-boats strength in the field at any one time – one third was always on passage either to or from the battle area while the other third was in port for rest or refit.

But by March 1941 he had infiltrated enough boats into the Atlantic to execute his plan, which depended first on the position of a convoy being determined by U-boat command based at Lorient. Once this was known the information was passed to the pack leader at sea who, when one of the boats actually sighted the convoy, could organise the mass attack. During daylight hours the pack would withdraw clear of the convoy but when darkness fell the U-boats would attack en masse, on the surface – tactics which took the British by surprise.

There were however limitations. First, the Germans depended on the shadowing U-boat being able to keep in constant touch with the convoy; if it was attacked and sunk the others would have no director to guide them. Secondly, it required considerable use of radio air waves and thus made detection easier for the British. But these weaknesses were not realised at first, by which time the U-boats had already made inroads into Allied shipping.

But before the wolf packs started to bite, in the same month of March 1941 it was the turn of the U-boat service to suffer major losses. In an attack on convoy OB-293 on the 7th and 8th, two U-boats, U-70 and U-47, were sunk by the corvettes *Camellia* and *Arbutus* and the destroyer *Wolverine*. On the 17th two more, U-99 and U-100, were sent to the bottom in an attack on convoy HX-112. The tragedy as far as the Germans were concerned was that with those boats went Gunther Prien, Otto Kretschmer and Schepke – three of the leading U-boat aces, Kretschmer was, in fact, captured with his crew before his boat sank and spent the rest of the war as a prisoner.

The reason for these sinkings was that in the first months of 1941, the Allied convoy system had begun to build up and escorts had become more efficient in tracking down and attacking U-boats. The Germans' answer to this was to move their boats further to the west beyond the range of air escorts. The result of this move was an agreement between the Allies and the Americans that the latter would provide air escorts for convoys some 600 miles off the Canadian coast. With air escorts from Britain only capable of covering convoys 700 miles out into the Atlantic, this still left a gap of 3,000 miles where no air escorts could go. This disadvantage was immediately used by the U-boat wolf packs who made a mass attack on convoy SC-26, sinking six ships. Surface escorts were quickly called up and accounted for U-76 and the attack ceased, but only a few days later four ships were sunk in another convoy.

Forty-three ships were sunk in April, but only 10 of these were in a convoy at the time. Despite these successes the U-boat command realised that the number of sinkings was not rising in proportion to its efforts and decided to swing its area of attack nearer to its home ports, to the waters round Ireland and Iceland. But this time the British had anticipated such a move and had increased air and surface anti-submarine patrols, and in August made 18 attacks against U-boats. U-452 was sunk by a Catalina, U-570 surrendered to Hudson aircraft (see page 181) and other U-boats were sent into panic crash-dives when they were caught on the surface.

In September 1941 the U-boats regained the initiative. Convoy SC-42, of 65 ships, was heading for Britain and had just passed the southern tip of Greenland. Unbeknown to the senior officer of the convoy, or the British Admiralty, 17 U-boats were waiting for it and 17 merchantmen including a number of tankers were destroyed. The U-boat pack lost U-501 (see page 183) and U-207. U-boats were also very active in the southern Atlantic at this time and 36 ships were sunk during the three summer months.

In September there was also an important change in the conduct of the Battle of the Atlantic as far as the Allies were concerned. After a meeting between Britain's Prime Minister, Winston Churchill, and American President Roosevelt, it was agreed that American warships would not only seek to destroy any German surface raiders attacking the routes between the United States and Iceland but that the US Navy would escort convoys comprising non-American ships. Starting on 16 September 1941 American escorts were provided for certain Atlantic trade routes eastwards as far as mid-ocean.

Before the actual escorting work had begun, however, on 4 September, the American destroyer *Greer*, on her way to Iceland, was attacked by U-652 and replied with depth-charges. Then, on 17 October, the destroyer *Kearney* was torpedoed and on 31 October the first American loss took place when the *Reuben James*, escorting a British convoy, was sunk.

The last big convoy battle of 1941 took place on 12–21 December when convoy HG-76 was attacked off the coast of Spain. The battle started well for the Allies with U-127 sunk on the first day, before developing into a fight between the U-boats and the convoy's escorts, finally being won by the latter; only two merchantmen were sunk, whereas U-131 was sunk on the third day, U-434 was depth-charged to the surface and abandoned as it sank on the fourth day, U-574 was rammed as it was diving and was sunk the next day, and U-567 was sent to the bottom on the sixth day.

The British destroyer *Stanley*, which had helped in the destruction of the first two U-boats, was herself sunk, the sloop *Stork* was damaged when ramming U-574 and the auxiliary aircraft carrier *Audacity* was also sunk. Although the attacking U-boats were reinforced by three more during the battle it was a triumph for the escorts as a total of five U-boats had been destroyed.

During 1941 the Allies lost 432 ships, totalling nearly 2,200,000 tons, to U-boat attack while the Allies, through various means, disposed of 35 U-boats and, in the Atlantic, 7 Italian submarines.

On 22 June 1941 Russia was attacked by Germany and immediately Britain's Prime Minister, Winston Churchill, promised as much support as possible. As far as submarines were concerned this led to the immediate despatch of two boats – *Tigris* commanded by Cdr H.T. Bone and *Trident* under Cdr G.M. Sladey – to northern Russia, which were in action almost immediately attacking German supply ships along the Norwegian coast.

Life was not easy for the British submariners. Although they were given a base by the Russians at Polyarnoe at the entrance to the

Kola inlet, it took them over a month to make it habitable. Cooperation was not a word which had much prominence in the Russian language. They had little, if any, experience in submarine warfare and laid down a set of rules and regulations which the British had difficulty in understanding, never mind obeying. For example, it was demanded that submarines arrive at a specific spot outside the Kola inlet and at a special time. The rule completely ignored the fact that there were a number of navigational difficulties, there were no recognition signals and, of course, there was the weather. For half the year there was almost continual daylight and for the other half almost continuous darkness. For much of the time it was exceptionally windy, and when it wasn't windy it was foggy.

Life on a submarine is difficult at the best of times but usually there is the opportunity of a break and a breather ashore. In Russia British submariners did not even get this. The landscape was bleak with rarely a tree in sight and for the best part of the year it was covered in snow. Food too, was a problem with reindeer meat the dish of the day – every day – with potatoes. Vodka was the stable drink and if you didn't like vodka, and British sailors didn't, then tough luck. Being at sea was no fun either. In the winter when a submarine surfaced, the upper deck and all the equipment immediately froze solid. Total darkness, foul weather, long patrols in tempestuous seas called for extreme courage and devotion to duty.

It also fell to British submariners to teach the Russians the finer arts of submarining, including how to attack with a spread salvo of torpedoes, which was a revelation to them. Although Russian seamanship gained some respect from the British they were surprised when Russian destroyer skippers refused to sail in bad weather, although in fairness to the Russians it has to be said that such skippers did seem to be phased out shortly afterwards.

Tigris and *Trident* were eventuality replaced by *Saline* and *Seawolf* and this 'shift system' continued until the Germans were finally driven from Norway.

The Allies gained an important advantage in May 1941 with the sinking of U-110 and the capture of an Enigma M3 coding machine and other secret papers (see page 79) which gave the position of every U-boat at sea and where Doentiz's patrol lines were being directed. This gave them the opportunity to route convoys around them.

In early 1942, the Battle of the Atlantic moved to American waters for the first time, since the Americans had officially joined the war and U-boat commanders had what they had earlier described as a 'Happy Time'. By mid-January seven of their 750-ton U-boats had arrived off Newfoundland ready for an attack on merchant shipping, but they found the convoys well guarded and the weather bitterly cold. Like any good tourist they moved south to the sun and found that not only had the weather improved but so had the chances of attack. The American coast was lit up as in peacetime, navigational buoys were still illuminated, albeit dimly, and many ships went about their business with lights ablaze and seemingly no thought of war.

Success was immediate as U-123 sank six ships, totalling some 32,000 tons, off Cape Hatteras, North Carolina, in as many days; a good example to other U-boats whose numbers had now increased to 12. Within a few weeks 500,000 tons of shipping had been sent to the bottom – 58 ships, half of them valuable oil tankers. A further 500,000 tons were sunk in April and only one U-boat was destroyed.

Around this time the first of the new U-boats, the U-tanker, came into service and its arrival on the scene extended the period that U-boats could stay in the Western Atlantic, Caribbean and Gulf of Mexico. The German Navy realised that U-boats would have to operate in waters far from their bases and therefore would be at sea for long periods. Purpose-designed U-tankers, and larger minelayers known as 'milch cows', were put into service to refuel and supply the smaller U-boats at sea. They were widely used to supply the 'aces' and thus increase their chances to sink more ships.

It was 1918 all over again and in the first seven months of 1942 a total of 681 ships and a massive, 3,500,000 tons were sent to the bottom, yet there were never more than 12 U-boats in the area.

By the end of this period, however, the Germans had suffered the loss of seven U-boats: U-85 was sunk by the USS *Raper* on its way to the battle area; U-352 was lost to the American coastguard cutter *Icarus*; U-157 was sunk by another US cutter, the *Thetis* off Cuba;

U-153 was sunk by the US destroyer *Landsdown* in the Caribbean; U-158 was destroyed by aircraft in the Bermuda area; and U-701 and U-576 by aircraft, off the American east coast.

In the second half of 1942, the Battle of the Atlantic continued unabated with constant U-boat attacks on convoys. A pack of 18 U-boats attacked convoy SC-94 in August sinking 11 ships for the loss of 2 U-boats. The following month 29 ships were sunk. In October one convoy lost 8 ships in exchange for 3 U-boats while another 3 U-boats were lost in November when the Allies lost 15 ships. In December, the odds were slightly in favour of the Allies when a pack of 22 U-boats attacked a convoy, and although they sank 2 ships, they also lost 2 of their number.

The successful passage of the last convoy was due largely to much improved aircraft escorts. The planes were able to pick up U-boats by radar and radio direction equipment when on the surface at night and attack them with depth charges with which they were now equipped. By mid-1942 RAF Coastal Command had 500 aircraft, and convoy escort ship numbers were up to 400.

In the last five months of the year U-boats were able to sink an average of 100 ships a month totalling 500,000 tons for the loss of about 2 U-boats every month. Although U-boat losses appear high they were considerably less than the number of new boats joining the German fleet, so the Germans, who were convinced they could win the war by winning the Battle of the Atlantic, were not overly concerned.

The year 1943 dawned with Admiral Karl Doenitz finding himself in the happy position of having over 200 U-boats at his disposal and he started off by attacking a convoy which, because of bad weather, had no air cover, and was therefore vulnerable; 7 ships were lost.

By February Doenitz actually had over 100 U-boats at sea in the Atlantic, Caribbean and south of the Azores, with an almost constant stream of U-boats passing through the Bay of Biscay and the North Atlantic, going to and from the patrol areas. Allied shipping casualties rose again dramatically and during the month 63 merchantmen were destroyed, but so were 13 U-boats.

In March shipping losses grew to 108 ships, totalling 627,000 tons. It was during this month that the largest convoy action of the war took place when 40 U-boats attacked two convoys. On 16 March 8 U-boats were shadowing convoy SC-229 comprising 40 ships. Ahead of it was the much slower convoy SC-122 and gradually the two closed up together to form a mass of ships covering a broad area of the ocean. Other U-boats were called up and a five-day mass attack on the convoys began. It was a complete disaster for the Allies with 21 ships, totalling over 140,000 tons, being sunk; the U-boat wolf pack lost only one boat, U-384, through air attack.

Fortunately for the Allies this run of successes for the U-boats was not to last long, for the Allies were able to bring to bear much more efficient anti-submarine methods. Firstly, the air gap in the mid-Atlantic escort of convoys was closed by the introduction of long-range aircraft which meant that convoys could have air cover for the entire Atlantic passage. Next, the Allies adopted a policy of larger convoys, which meant that more escorts could be concentrated around the ships; and coincidentally, new radar sets, which German receivers could not pick up, were introduced.

In April the number of ships being sunk began to fall while the number of U-boats sunk began to rise. For example, in May U-boats succeeded in sinking only 2 ships while losing 18 of their number. Suddenly the picture was changing for not only was the pendulum swinging in the Allies' favour in the Atlantic, but their aircraft were having considerable success in the Bay of Biscay attacking outgoing and incoming U-boats on their way to and from the wolf packs. For the first time for many months Doenitz found he was losing more U-boats than his building yards were supplying.

By 22 May the Germans made up their minds that they must accept defeat and withdraw the surviving U-boats from the battle scene. Doenitz declared that the withdrawal was only temporary 'to avoid unnecessary loss of life in a period when our weapons are shown to be at a disadvantage'.

Doenitz's response to this defeat was to fit his U-boats with more efficient warning receivers, more and more powerful anti-aircraft guns, and with the new acoustic torpedo. He also obtained approval for a new building programme which would produce bigger boats capable of greater speed under water.

The survivors of the May defeat, 16 boats in all, were formed into a new group and sent to cover an area some 600 miles west of the Azores. Doenitz also looked for other areas, such as off the Brazilian west coast and West Africa, where convoy defences would not be either as concentrated or as alert. He began sending his U-boats out through the Bay of Biscay in groups so that, if subjected to air attack, they could return more concentrated firepower at their attackers. The new tactic initially accomplished very little. Seven U-boats based in the western Atlantic in June sank only two or three vessels while losing U-521 to the USS PC 565 off Cape Hatteras. Meanwhile in West African waters they fared little better and managed only to damage one ship; the results in Brazilian waters were also disappointing.

During the last days of July 1943 the U-boat arm suffered yet another morale-sapping blow when eleven U-boats, including two U-tankers, left western France to cross the Bay of Biscay, the U-tankers being given a special escort, U-504. The three of them were on the surface together when they were spotted by aircraft, more aircraft were called up and the attack on the boats began. One tanker, U-461, was sunk by a strange coincidence by aircraft from 461 Squadron, and the other, U-462, was badly damaged by a 600-lb bomb, the first time such a weapon was used on a submarine. U-462 did considerable damage to the aircraft, one of which had to limp away from the scene, before it too finally sank. The escorting U-504 promptly dived to safety. That, however, was not the end of the fight. Eight U-boats from the original flotilla were still left in the Bay and on 1 August U-454 was attacked by a Sunderland and sent to the bottom, but not until it had shot down the aircraft. Another aircraft spotted U-383 and sank it, while the following morning a US Liberator aircraft accounted for U-706. By late evening the same day U-106, which had been subjected to constant attack, also finally sank. This was another shattering defeat for Doenitz who immediately recalled the other boats and cancelled all further group sailing.

And still the U-boats were constantly attacked and sunk: U-647 was the victim of a mine; another U-tanker, U-489, was sunk by aircraft; and surface escorts to convoy OS-51 disposed of U-135. Aircraft from the USS *Card* sank a U-tanker off the Azores, damaged U-66 and then went on to sink U-664 and U-525 two days later.

Shipping losses to the Allies were by now becoming insignificant with, in early August, only two ships being lost in exchange for two U-boats destroyed. At the end of the month the USS *Card*'s aircraft were again in action, sinking U-874.

During the three months June to August 1943 in all waters, excluding the Mediterranean, U-boats sank only 58 Allied merchant ships but lost a massive 74 of their number. The final defeat of the wolf packs came in the last quarter of 1943. Twenty U-boats had formed a patrol line in mid-Atlantic, refuelling in mid-ocean from the tanker U-760, and were waiting to catch slow Allied convoys on the outward-bound passage.

Before they could start their attack U-341 was sunk by a Liberator aircraft. The 19 remaining boats then fell upon two convoys that were in the same wide area, in a five-day battle that was to result in the sinking of 6 merchantmen totalling 36,000 tons, and 3 escorts, in exchange for the loss of 3 U-boats sunk and 3 more severely damaged. This was the first occasion that the U-boats had used their new acoustic torpedoes. Unfortunately for them the British had a similar weapon and had devised measures to counter it: towing a noise-making machine astern of the ship so that it attracted the acoustic torpedo.

The German U-boat command now reformed its boats to await the next west-bound convoy, but they were again spotted by aircraft and the convoy was diverted to another route. Subsequent convoys were then attacked through the remainder of the year by varying numbers of U-boats, but on each occasion the German boats came off worst. Eventually they dropped the idea of waiting for convoys and the wolf packs were dispersed.

It was in March 1944 that Admiral Doenitz finally admitted that his U-boats had been defeated. He called in all his boats from the central Atlantic and cancelled all further operations against convoys. Never again were Allied convoys seriously threatened.

The Battle of the Atlantic had been a bloody contest. Some 3,500 Allied merchant ships were sunk in the North Atlantic and British home waters and between 75,000 and 85,000 Allied seamen died. Some 648 and 784 U-boats lost during the war were sunk in the Atlantic and around two-thirds of the 28,000-plus U-boat men who died lost their lives in the Atlantic.

In the final section of this chapter it is worth mentioning 'the vicious and the virtuous' – those submarine commanders who were responsible for atrocities and those who did their best to redress the balance.

Propaganda was widely used during the Second World War and it was successful British Government 'spinning' or propaganda, that gave U-boat commanders, in general, a very bad name. Submariners, of whichever nation, are brave men with exceptionally high morale, great skills and strong patriotism – just as true for the men serving in German U-boats as it was for those in any other navy. Lurid novels and emotional, highly inaccurate war films in both Britain and America have continued to paint a picture of heartless villains attacking women and children, unarmed ships and helpless survivors. But the courage and devotion of U-boat captains and crews during the Second World War compared favourably with those shown by Allied submariners. There are, in fact, only two fully documented instances of actions by U-boat commanders which cannot be excused, one in each of the two world wars.

On 27 June 1918 the British hospital ship *Landovery Castle*, fully illuminated and clearly marked, was torpedoed by U-86 commanded by Oberleutnant sur See Helmut Patzig. The survivors took to the ship's boats which were subsequently sunk by gunfire. There was no excuse for this action and in 1921 two of the U-boat's officers were tried and found guilty by the German Supreme Court which clearly stated that 'the firing on the boats of the *Landovery Castle* was an offence against the law of nations'. Patzig had disappeared and could not be brought to trial.

On 13 March 1944, as dusk was falling, Kapitan Leutnant Heinz Eck, in command of U-852 and on passage from Kiel to the Indian Ocean, torpedoed the British-built Greek tramp steamer *Peleus*. The 8,000-ton freighter carried a crew of 35 British, Greeks, Chinese, Egyptians, Chileans, Russians and Poles.

They took to the boats and Eck ordered that one of the survivors, Third Officer Stavros Sogias, be brought aboard the U-boat for interrogation. When this was complete and details of convoy routes and escorts obtained from the frightened officer, Sogias was ordered back to the lifeboat. Eck and his crew then proceeded to obliterate all evidence of his attack. The U-boat turned and rammed the lifeboats, machine-gunned the survivors and destroyed life rafts with grenades. When the vile task was completed the U-boat left the scene and continued its journey southwards, not knowing that despite all efforts five survivors, all desperately wounded, were left behind as unforgiving witnesses.

Thirty eight days later, after one survivor had died, the four remaining were picked up by a Portuguese freighter. On 2 May U-852 was forced to beach in Somaliland on the east coast of Africa after an air attack, at which point Eck made his second fatal mistake in that he failed to destroy the U-boat's log book. When the crew of 59 was taken prisoner the log was closely examined and showed clearly that the submarine had torpedoed a vessel in approximately the same area that the *Peleus* had been destroyed, and at approximately the same time. The evidence, on the face of it, was damning.

The captured Eck and his crew were taken to Britain and thence to Germany where, on 7 October 1945, they were put on trial by the British-sponsored war crimes court in Hamburg. The trial lasted four days, and all the accused pleaded guilty to 'violating the laws and usages of war and being concerned with the killing of members of the crew of the *Peleus*'. Eck claimed that he destroyed the *Peleus* rafts because he thought they might be carrying signalling equipment and he might have been spotted by aircraft. He and two of his officers were sentenced to death and shot on 30 November 1945; another was given life imprisonment and a fifth sent to prison for 15 years.

Cruelty, however, was not confined simply to U-boat commanders, though there was, for example, no vociferous propaganda or outcry when the Russian submarine S-13, commanded by Captain 3rd Class Marinesko, sank without warning the fully illuminated *Wilhelm Gustloff* in the Baltic on 30 January 1945; the *Gustloff* was carrying 5,000 refugees and wounded servicemen.

Neither has much been said or written about the Japanese submarine commanders who killed the survivors of sunken ships almost as a matter of course to remove any evidence of their presence, or one who torpedoed and sank a fully-illuminated hospital ship in the Pacific.

There are also the infamous incidents carried out by the Japanese I-8, under the command of the notorious Cdr Tatsunoke Ariizumi, who sank the Dutch merchantman *Tjisilak* in the Indian Ocean and then proceeded to take the 98 survivors on to the deck of the submarine and murder them with swords and spanners. There is little doubt about the truth of this story because evidence was given by two survivors who were left for dead in a lifeboat and were subsequently rescued. The same man was also responsible for the murder of 60 members of the crew of the *Jean Nicolet*, an American merchantman, after torpedoing her. Ariizumi eventually shot himself as he entered Tokyo harbour just before the war ended.

Of course it was not only the Axis partners that were accused of alleged 'atrocities'. Lt Cdr Anthony Miers VC of the British submarine *Torbay* was said to have machine-gunned survivors of a troopship sunk off Crete in July 1941. Captain Dudley Morton of the US submarine *Wahoo* allegedly killed survivors of a Japanese troop transport. Both men took the view that the survivors were troops who, if they were rescued or reached the shore, would soon be back in action shooting their countrymen. Another American submarine was accused of failing to rescue survivors of a sunken merchantman, but considering the dangers inherent in stopping the vessel to carry out a rescue, it is not surprising.

There was another incident involving the British when accusations of a 'barbaric action' were made. In August 1944, U-385 under the command of Hans-Guido Valentiner was sent to harass the Allied invasion fleet. It was spotted by a Sunderland aircraft, attacked and severely damaged. The submarine crash-dived and remained submerged until it was discovered that diesel fumes were entering the submarine. The U-boat came to the surface and was immediately fired upon by the sloop *Venus* of the crack 2nd Escort Group, even while the submarine crew was abandoning ship. The German captain immediately accused the sloop of firing on survivors, but the captain of the sloop explained that it had all happened so quickly he could not give the order to cease fire fast enough. Both sides accepted the explanation. Only one German crew member lost his life.

Such accounts should be balanced by examples of courtesy and humanity, even in the presence of great danger. One of the most famous of these was the rescue of the crew of the Portuguese freighter *Cabalho* by Captain Salvatore Todaru, the Italian submarine commander who sank her – his story is told on page 141.

There were similar actions by the commanders of German U-boats. When Kapitan Leutnant Herbert Schultz of U-48 stopped the British steamer *Royal Sceptre* with a shot across the bows, according to the practice at the time – it was 5 September 1939 – the British captain decided to make a run for it. Schulz fired another shot as black smoke from the steamer's funnel billowed out indicating an increase in speed. Schultz then fired a third shot which hit the ship and stopped her. The crew immediately took to the boats but while they were doing so the ship's radio operator was frantically signalling their positon and predicament so that it would not be long for before British ships or aircraft came racing to the scene.

Schulz could have aimed to hit with the U-boat's deck gun straight away and destroyed the *Royal Sceptre*, but instead he waited until the survivors had pulled clear of the stricken vessel. When they were a reasonable distance away he fired a torpedo and the British ship blew up and sank. No sooner had this exercise been completed than Schultz sighted smoke on the horizon. It was another British ship, the freighter *Browning*. U-48, still on the surface, and with Schultz on the bridge, approached the newcomer within hailing distance and told the captain that British survivors were floating nearby and instructed him to go and pick them up, which he did.

Schultz again showed humanity on 11 September 1939, after he had destroyed the British freighter *Firby*, which had also tried to make a run for it. This time, when survivors were in their lifeboats, Schultz drew close and he and his crew tended to the wounded, put them on the right course for home, and then radioed their position to the British Admiralty in London.

Kapitanleutnant Heinrich Liebe, another U-boat commander, had no choice but to blow up a British oil tanker even though it had stopped as instructed. For even as the captain was being rowed toward the U-boat with the ship's papers, the radio operator was again signalling frantically. One torpedo turned the tanker into a ball of fire with flames covering the water around it so that the crew, who had already taken to the boats, were in terrible danger of being engulfed by the flames. Without hesitation Liebe took the U-boat into the conflagration and towed the lifeboats to safety. With the survivors on deck the U-boat then searched for and found an American ship, and put them on board.

After September 1942 any U-boat commander who stopped to help survivors would have contravened direct instructions from the Commander-in-Chief, Doenitz – an order given for a very good reason. On 12 September 1942, U-156 under Kapitanleutnant Wilhelm Hartenstein torpedoed and sank the troopship *Laconia* which was carrying 268 British servicemen and their families and 1,800 Italian prisoners of war. Doenitz ordered all U-boats in the area to go and help pick up survivors.

While Hartenstein had his U-boat full of survivors and was towing lifeboats to meet French ships from Dakar, he was attacked and bombed by American Liberator aircraft. Hartenstein transferred all the survivors on board to the already over-crowded lifeboats and submerged to safety. Meanwhile U-506 had been helping U-156 but before it could unload the 142 women and children it had on board to other vessels, it was attacked by a flying boat. However, it was able to quickly submerge and was 200 feet below when the bombs fell.

On 19 September Doenitz ordered that U-boats should in future only take Italians on board and transfer any other survivors from sunken or sinking targets to lifeboats before leaving the scene. The distortion of the truth which Allied propaganda was capable of at this time was such that Doenitz was described as ordering that all survivors should be killed by U-boat commanders.

CHAPTER FOUR

The Final Sacrifice

The British – David Wanklyn, Edward Bickford,
John Linton, Edward Tomkinson.
The Americans – Sam Dealey, 'Mush' Morton,
Howard Gilmore, John Cromwell.
The Germans – Gunther Prien, Joachim Schepke,
Englebert Endrass, Fritz-Julius Lemp.
The Enigma story

TWENTY-EIGHT-YEAR-OLD Lt Cdr David Wanklyn, the bearded, piratical-looking commander who took over the submarine *Upholder* in August 1940, was the first submariner to win Britain's highest award for bravery, the Victoria Cross. He was undoubtedly one of the finest of British submarine commanders, much admired for his sterling competence but also much criticised for firing a salvo at the impossible range of 6,400 yards. Described as 'modest, able, determined and courageous', he was the top scoring ace of the war with a tally of 15 transports totalling 119,000 tons, 2 submarines, 2 destroyers, an armed trawler and damage to a cruiser.

He chose the submarine service in 1933 despite his 6 feet 2 inch stature and his enthusiasm for the difficult life was not diminished when he married in 1938. On his first wartime patrol off the coast of Tripoli in the early days of 1941, he sank an 8,000-ton supply ship, probably sank another and carried out a determined attack on a destroyer. Wanklyn and *Upholder* would soon become a legend in the Mediterranean. But such was the fickle nature of the undersea war that *Upholder* followed early success with four patrols during which it had no luck at all, despite a number of torpedo attacks.

On the fifth patrol the Wanklyn luck changed for the better. Off the Tunisian coast he sighted a convoy and in an immediate attack sank the 5,500-ton *Antoinetta Laura*. The following day Wanklyn was ordered to the Kerkenan Bank to finish off a supply ship which had run aground. On arrival he found that not only was it impossible to approach the stricken vessel submerged, but that there was a grave danger that *Upholder* would be grounded in the shallow water, however he managed to manoeuvre the 200-feet-long, 630-ton *Upholder* alongside, board the supply ship and set it on fire.

A few days later a convoy of five ships was sighted and attacked even though it had a four-strong destroyer escort. The German ship *Leverjusen* of 7,500 tons and the 3,000-ton *Arcturus* were both sunk while evading persistent attacks from escorting destroyers.

Upholder was soon again in action off the coast of Sicily. On this, the submarine's seventh patrol, two merchant ships had fallen victim to its torpedoes and it had sustained minor damage during attacks by patrol boats. Now there was another convoy in its sights, but unfortunately Wanklyn had only two torpedoes left. It was on this attack that Wanklyn won the Victoria Cross.

The convoy that Wanklyn had sighted was a submarine commander's dream – four of Italy's best ocean liners, the *Conte Rosso*, *Marco Polo*, *Victoria* and *Esperia* carrying thousands of troop reinforcements for the Afrika Korps. An escort of four destroyers provided a close screen while two cruisers and three destroyers covered the outer areas of the convoy. A magnificent target – and only two torpedoes!

There was nothing for it but a point-blank attack and to hell with the escorts. *Upholder* crept close to the four liners and let go her two torpedoes, immediately diving to 150 feet to avoid the expected vicious counter-attack. As the torpedoes struck home, rending the *Conte Rosso* asunder and sending 2,279 soldiers and her crew to the bottom, the counter-attack arrived as a destroyer raced overhead letting off patterns of depth charges that tossed and turned *Upholder* around the Mediterranean depths.

More depth charges, more twisting and turning, shattering glass, gushing leaks and flickering lights. The atmosphere in the submarine became damp and disgusting with its contents – instruments, food and vegetables, foul-smelling damp clothes, mouldy shoes – being thrown around haphazardly. The noise was ear-shattering, the continuous vibrations nerve-wracking. Any member of the crew with a tendency towards panic was immediately calmed by the imperturbability of the captain, who gave his orders in the same matter-of-fact tone that he used during normal exercises. He wasn't panicking so why should anyone else?

For two hours the frantic escorts threw depth charge upon depth charge into boiling waters. As the cruisers and destroyers raced above Wanklyn skilfully manoeuvred his boat, twisting and turning to avoid the worst of the attack. Eventually it was all over, and the *Upholder* slipped quietly away from the scene.

During subsequent patrols Wanklyn added a 2,500-ton vessel, a 6,000-ton supply ship, a trawler, the 5,000-ton *Trio*, a 4,000-ton tanker, two 19,500-ton liners, *Neptunia* and *Oceania,* a 4,500-ton trawler, the Italian submarines *Amiraglio Saint-Bon* and *Tricheco* and the destroyer *Libeccio* to his score, as well as badly damaging the Italian cruiser *Garibaldi*. (A full account of the sinking of the two submarines will be found on page 187.)

On 2 April 1942 *Upholder* sailed on its last patrol, the 25th, before returning to the United Kingdom for a refit and a well-earned rest for its crew. Their task was to land agents on the African coast which was completed with the usual efficiency, before being ordered to join a patrol line with two other submarines. Wanklyn and *Upholder* were never heard of again.

The submarine *Salmon* under the command of Lt Cdr Edward Bickford, described as one of the brightest young officers, though also a comparative old timer, was early into action, in the Skaggerak on 4 December 1939. While on patrol submerged, Bickford spotted what he thought was a box floating on the surface but careful examination showed that it was in fact the conning tower of a U-boat. More in hope than certainty he fired a long-range salvo and was rewarded minutes later by the sight of U-36 disintegrating in a massive explosion. Bickford surfaced but found only debris and no survivors. Later, however, fishing boats found that miraculously there had been four survivors whom they were able to rescue.

A week later Bickford sighted the large German liner *Bremen* which crossed his bows at a range of 2,000 yards. *Salmon* surfaced and ordered the liner to stop, this being in the days when some decencies were still observed in the war at sea. But the *Bremen*'s captain decided to ignore the instruction and make a run for it. Bickford was preparing to open fire when the arrival of an escorting aircraft forced him to take avoiding action and the opportunity was missed. He had, in any event, decided at the last moment that as the German ship did not carry any offensive armament she should not be sunk. His decision not to sink the passenger vessel was later confirmed as correct by the Admiralty.

The following day Bickford was rewarded with the sight of three light cruisers, *Nuremberg*, *Leipzig* and *Koln*, escorted by five destroyers. At first the German squadron was too far away for an attack to be contemplated but as luck would have it, the cruisers altered course and turned in Bickford's direction. The salvo from *Salmon* was deadly, hitting *Nuremberg* and *Leipzig* at least once. Although both ships were damaged neither was sunk.

The wartime career of Bickford and *Salmon* was, unfortunately, short-lived. On 14 July 1940 the submarine, which had been on normal patrol in the North Sea, was due to arrive at Rosyth, but never did, having probably been the victim of another deadly mine.

Cdr John Linton VC was 30 years old when he had taken command of his first submarine *Snapper* in 1936, and was awarded the Distinguished Service Cross in May 1941 while commanding *Pandora*, taking part in actions against the French off Oran and supplying the beleaguered island of Malta. He then took over the submarine *Turbulent* in January 1942 and was immediately despatched to the eastern Mediterranean. Within two months he had sunk four enemy vessels, albeit small ones but during the following months they claimed one cruiser, one destroyer, one U-boat and 28 supply ships, which were headed for North Africa and Rommel's army. When one sees figures like these it is easy to understand why it is generally agreed that the submarine service played a vital role in the defeat of Rommel and the Afrika Korps. For this he was awarded the Distinguished Service Order in September 1942.

Variety is the spice of life and Linton also spent time bombarding the enemy coast. He was able to claim a goods train, a road convoy and an electric train; there were a number of operations landing or picking up agents as well. By February 1943 *Turbulent*'s crew were badly in need of a rest when they sailed on a last patrol before returning home, this time off the Corsican and Sardinian coast. Its last reported position was near to a known enemy minefield, but nothing further was heard so it was assumed that they were destroyed by a mine, just like *Upholder* on its last patrol. On 25 May 1943 Cdr Linton was posthumously awarded the Victoria Cross for his brave exploits.

Lt Cdr Edward 'Tommo' Tomkinson and *Urge* started their careers in the Mediterranean by sinking the Italian cruiser *Bande Nere* and several supply ships. Tomkinson was a cheerful personality who hated war and despised its rewards, yet was extremely efficient in the art of submarine warfare. He was a man of forthright opinions and would take a strong stand against authority if he was sure that he was right.

On patrol in December 1941, he made a daring attack on the pride of the Italian Navy, the battleship *Vittoria Veneto*, which he hit with three torpedoes but failed to sink. He was bitterly disappointed but his emotions could not be compared with those of the Italians over the damage to their beloved and, it must be said, beautiful battleship.

The submarine's career then followed what had become the established pattern of submarine warfare in the Mediterranean with constant attacks on enemy convoys punctuated by special duties such as landing and picking up agents on the enemy coast. It was an unpredictable period with success followed by failure, followed by success.

Once Tomkinson heard the sound of distant depth charges and deduced that a convoy was in the area. The Italians at that time had the disquieting habit of hurling depth charges into the sea around a convoy on the off chance that marauding submarines planning an attack would be hit, or at the least put off. Before long Tomkinson did indeed see an Italian convoy, but it was too far away to attack. He made up for this disappointment shortly afterwards with an attack on another convoy during which the 5,000-ton *Zeffo* was sent to the bottom and a similar ship, the *Perseus* was severely damaged.

Switching now to special duties *Urge* landed commandos on the enemy coast and then, for variety, on 1 April 1942, sank the six-inch gun Italian cruiser *Giovanni* off the Sicilian coast.

After 18 successful patrols *Urge*, together with the rest of the flotilla, was ordered from Malta, now under constant attack from German and Italian bombers, and were temporarily withdrawn to Alexandria from what were becoming heavily mined waters. But *Urge* was never heard from again. Somewhere in the deep blue water around Malta, it is believed to have struck a mine and a gallant captain and 50 men died. Tomkinson had sunk 52,600 tons of shipping, one cruiser and damaged another, and put a battleship out of action for a long period.

No one is likely to dispute that the hero of the American submarine service was the modest but daring Lt Cdr Sam Dealey, captain of the almost legendary submarine *Harder*. June 1943 saw the start of the Dealey-*Harder* partnership that was to inspire a nation and yet, like so many submarine stories, end so sadly.

When Dealey was sent to cover the sea lanes from Tokyo Bay westward, he took the instructions very seriously, and even ventured to within 6 miles of the Japanese coast looking for enemy vessels trying to avoid detection by skulking along the shoreline. It was not long before he found what he was looking for – a couple of Japanese merchantmen.

Dealey attacked on the surface and although one of his torpedoes detonated prematurely, the other struck home. The *Harder* had recorded its first success but it was nearly paid for dearly. The torpedo that exploded had attracted the attention of enemy escorts which reacted with great speed and were soon launching their first depth-charge pattern when *Harder* had scarcely submerged. With control lost, it plunged to the sea bottom 300 feet below. No serious damage was done but it rammed its nose into the deep mud there and at first, despite all efforts, flatly refused to move. Desperate situations demand desperate remedies and Dealey had to order full power with tanks fully blown – even though there was a danger that *Harder* would break free and shoot to the surface too fast. It took a further 45 minutes before the submarine had pulled itself free.

The following day *Harder* was again in action, badly damaging the 7,000-ton *Sagara Naru* and once again had to endure a determined attack by Japanese escorts. Two days later another Japanese freighter was damaged, and then another two. Escorts fought back desperately but were avoided by the crafty Dealey.

Three blank days followed and Dealey, with only two torpedoes left, was beginning, like the rest of the crew, to count the time before they could return to base for a rest. Then on 29 June 1943, he suddenly sighted another enemy vessel apparently sailing eastwards. As he drew closer he realised that the ship had in fact stopped and was aground and down in the water. A surprised Dealey realised it was the Japanese freighter *Sagara Naru,* the ship he had torpedoed on the second day of his patrol. He was just about to finish her off when another four Japanese vessels hove into view, which put him in a dilemma – he had only two torpedoes left, yet he had four targets. Deciding that he had to be selective he chose the largest transport in the group and fired both torpedoes. The first one hit its target blowing the transport to pieces, the second torpedo missed the transport but hit a tanker lying just behind it. How lucky could a submariner get? Two out of two did not seem a bad score, so Dealey set course for home highly satisfied with his first patrol.

Harder carried out two more successful patrols before returning to the United States for a refit. Then it was back into action in April 1944, just when the Commander of the US Navy decided it was time Japanese warships were added to the list of targets for American submarines, as well as merchantmen.

Harder patrolled off the Caroline Islands looking for likely targets but had no luck during the early days. Such was the lack of action that when he was caught on the surface by an enemy aircraft, Dealey decided not to submerge but in the hope that the Japanese plane would report his location to a nearby warship. The ploy worked for only 90 minutes later Dealey saw a Japanese destroyer racing towards him, so he decided he would wait until dark before he made his presence felt. When it was time to go into action Dealey saw through his periscope that the destroyer was still patrolling the area and was heading his way. He fired his first salvo at a range of 2,000 yards. It did not need a second – the destroyer was mortally hit and in a cloud of smoke began to go down. In four minutes the *Ikasuchi* was on the bottom.

On his fifth patrol Sam Dealey was instructed to rescue a party of agents from the coast of North Borneo and then search the area for a Japanese fleet that was believed to be in the region. *Harder* was manoeuvring carefully through the dangerous channels near the pick-up area when he sighted a convoy of tankers, escorted by three destroyers, bound for the Borneo port of Tarakan. Dealey surfaced to give chase but was soon sighted by a destroyer as the night was clear and brightly lit by the June moon, so he turned away, ostensibly to escape the enemy. But that was not Dealey's way. As *Harder* raced off at 19 knots, the aft torpedo tubes were made ready. At a range of some 8,000 yards, when he was expecting the destroyer to open fire, he ordered the submarine to dive and swing sharply to port knowing that the destroyer would probably race ahead and present a full side view to the stern of *Harder*.

As so often happened with Dealey's plans, the scheme worked and as the destroyer *Minatauki* sped past the spot where the submarine had last been seen, two torpedoes smashed into its side sending it to the bottom in five minutes. On going back to search for the convoy he was soon being attacked by another destroyer which was racing to pick up survivors from the *Minatauki*. Diving deep *Harder* avoided the attack and continued with its original task of heading towards the waiting party of agents.

By now *Harder* seemed to have a magnetic attraction for Japanese warships and deep in the Sibutu Passage, Dealey sighted a 2,100-ton destroyer heading his way. Although he thought that his periscope might have been spotted he held his ground and waited until his attacker was only 650 yards away before firing a salvo which stopped the *Hayanami* in its tracks, struck in the bows by the first torpedo and in the stern by the second. Meanwhile another destroyer had arrived on the scene and proceeded to blast *Harder* with depth charges but Dealey dived deeper and escaped.

In Japanese destroyer attacks such as these often over 100 of these deadly weapons, set at various depths, would be hurled at the submerged vessel. In the claustrophobic atmosphere, the bulkheads damp and dripping, the interior in darkness or dimly lit by temporary lighting, the crew would wait silently in the midst of chaos, broken glass and water. As the attack continued the hull would shudder and tremble with the force of the explosions and the great pressure of the sea around it. Often this went on for hours, the air becoming foul and breathing difficult. The crew knew that at any moment an accurately aimed depth charge could deliver the fatal death blow bringing the sea crashing through the boat and ending life. It was this sort of experience that submarine crews all over the world faced whenever they were attacked by enemy ships.

Dealey pressed on with his operation and was eventually able to reach the rendezvous and pick up the agents, before carrying out his second assignment of searching for the Japanese fleet. He did not have to search for long and, as so often happened, trouble came to him, in this case, in the shape of two destroyers on anti-submarine patrol. The Japanese warships had no idea that an American submarine was in their area so they came quietly towards the waiting *Harder* without, one would suppose, a care in the world. When they were 1,000 yards away they were greeted by a salvo of four torpedoes. The destroyer *Tanikaze* ran straight into them and blew up. Dealey then turned *Harder* around and gave the second destroyer, unidentified, a second salvo. There was a mighty explosion, her stern rose high in the water and then plunged to the depths.

Shortly after this Dealey completed his mission by locating the Japanese battle squadron and reporting its position. With five Japanese destroyers to his credit Dealey then returned to base at Fremantle in Western Australia.

Dealey should now have been given some leave, but instead he went to sea again in *Harder*, leading a small pack of submarines. On 24 August 1944, *Harder* and its sister boat, *Hake* were operating off the Philippines. In the middle of an attack on two small warships, one let off a pattern of depth charges which *Hake*, some distance away, clearly heard. Sam Dealey and the crew of *Harder* were never heard of again.

Lt Cdr 'Mush' Morton and *Wahoo* was another pairing of famous names in the United States submarine service. Morton took over *Wahoo* at the end of 1942 and on 24 January 1943 sighted his first enemy destroyer and attacked, but after firing a salvo which missed he became heavily involved with avoiding other enemy escorts. Then, raising his periscope after an abortive attack he saw the destroyer coming straight at him, so he fired two torpedoes, watched the first one miss, but saw the second blow off the destroyer's bows.

Wahoo then began a series of patrols which netted a total of 20 ships and 60,000 tons, around the Carolines, in the Yellow Sea and the Sea of Japan, in fact, anywhere the enemy was lurking. Its exploits during Operation Barney are described later on page 126, but finally on 13 October a Japanese anti-submarine aircraft reported surprising a submarine on the surface and dropping depth charges on it as it submerged. Such was the end of *Wahoo*.

Commander Howard W. Gilmore was one of the most famous of US submarine commanders but, sadly, with one of the shortest careers. His submarine *Growler* was launched only five weeks before the attack on Pearl Harbor and was immediately ordered to the submarine base on Hawaii. Despite the treacherous attack, and the fact that war had broken out, the crew of *Growler* was looking forward to the sunshine and delights of the Pacific Island, but their luck was out.

US Naval Intelligence discovered that the Japanese intended to force what was left of the US fleet into battle and destroy it. Part of the Japanese plan was to strike at American bases on the Aleutian Islands off Alaska, so a number of submarines, including *Growler* were sent to counter this. Afterwards *Growler* was once again ordered to Hawaii only to be diverted to Formosa where she did what she did best: sink Japanese ships.

With a score card of one destroyer and four merchantmen sunk and another destroyer badly damaged, Gilmore was more than satisfied with his boat and his crew. They were a closely knit, successful team.

At the end of 1942 *Growler* was based in Australia and was sent on its fourth patrol to the Gilbert Islands, which started well. Gilmore intercepted a Japanese convoy and sank a transport, and then, two days later, another. In another part of the Pacific the battle for Guadalcanal was in full spate and large amounts of shipping were moving north of the Solomon Islands.

Growler's luck did not hold. It attacked seven more convoys but the malfunctioning torpedoes problem caused all the attacks to fail so that not one hit was recorded. For a time things went quiet, then the Japanese launched a huge operation to evacuate Guadalcanal, a development not known to Gilmore or to US Navy Intelligence.

On 30 January 1943, Gilmore found another convoy and managed to at least damage a merchantman, but Japanese escorts were alert and immediately launched a counter-attack which Gilmore managed to evade. That night *Growler*'s radar picked up a contact some 18 miles away and Gilmore was quickly after it, deciding to make a surface attack, slowly closing on the target which was identified as a 3,000-ton Japanese gunboat. Gilmore waited until the range closed and then fired two torpedoes. He was relieved to see them running straight and true, but the smile of satisfaction on his face was quickly wiped off when he saw them suddenly reverse course and come back at him. He ordered 'full speed' and 'left full rudder'. *Growler* lurched sideways and only just avoided the speeding missiles before Gilmore ordered a 'crash dive' and managed once again to escape.

He found another convoy and determined upon a surface attack, getting into position to await the arrival of a 10,000-ton merchantman. When only 5,000 yards away an escort spotted *Growler* and opened fire with every gun it had. The submarine was severely damaged as shells exploded all around it and Gilmore was forced to dive, just in time to avoid a destroyer bent on ramming him. *Growler* was then subjected to a massive depth-charge assault and around 04.00 hrs an explosion temporarily destabilised the submarine. It quickly regained its equilibrium, but a main ballast tank had been ruptured. Two hours later the submarine surfaced and managed to carry out sufficient repairs to make it possible for it to continue its patrol.

In the Steffen Strait Gilmore sighted another possible target, a 2,500-ton Japanese patrol boat. Unseen by the enemy Gilmore managed to close the range but the wake of the submarine on the flat surface of the sea caused the gunboat to roll slightly and an alert officer on deck noticed this. As the patrol boat turned sharply across the path of the *Growler* the submarine's radar operator spotted the danger and warned Gilmore, who ordered all watertight doors shut but no sooner had he given the order than the submarine hit the patrol boat full on and came to a shuddering stop.

Machine-gun fire sprayed *Growler*'s bridge killing two men and wounding two others. Gilmore himself was also badly injured, his shoulder smashed by bullets. Holding the periscope standard for support, he ordered 'clear the bridge' and the injured men were taken down. The men waiting below moved to help him down but he had been hit again and ordered them to stay below and shut the hatch. Unable to move and with enemy machine guns still spraying the bridge Gilmore ordered the crew to dive the submarine, *Growler*'s executive officer, Cdr Schade, obeying with great reluctance.

Its fore end was crumpled, its bow twisted and there was serious flooding but Schade skilfully took the damaged *Growler* 2,000 miles back to Brisbane without its brave commander.

Gilmore was awarded the Congressional Medal of Honour, the first to be given to a submariner. *Growler* went on to sink two Japanese destroyers before, on 8 November 1943, it joined its former commander on the ocean floor after being depth-charged off Luzon.

Another submarine commander awarded the Congressional Medal of Honour was Lt Cdr John Cromwell, senior officer assigned to coordinate attacks by a group of submarines on Japanese forces off Truk, in the Caroline Islands.

On 16 November 1943 he sailed in *Sculpin*, commanded by Cdr Frederick Connaway. Two days later they received a signal informing them that a Japanese convoy was due to leave Truk for the Marshall Islands. Connaway was ordered to intercept the convoy, but *Sculpin* was quickly spotted by Japanese escorts and forced to dive deeper.

After a time Connaway decided to surface only to find a Japanese destroyer waiting for him. He dived again and waited for several hours before deciding to go up again and find out what was happening. As the submarine surfaced the depth gauge jammed so the crew had no idea of their actual depth, but they soon found out when they burst to the surface close by the destroyer, which immediately attacked. A full salvo of depth charges severely damaged *Sculpin*, destroying the pressure hull and disabling the steering gear and hydroplanes.

Connaway realised that the only way to handle the situation was to defend the ship with their gun and ordered the gun's crew on deck. But the destroyer closed quickly before they had time to do anything and fired a salvo which hit the conning tower, killing Connaway and two officers, and destroying the diesel engine air inductor. The senior officer Lt G.E. Brown gave the order to scuttle the submarine and abandon ship.

Cromwell, who was well acquainted with both Japanese methods of torture and the value of his knowledge of the submarine service and its organisation, decided to stay with his ship. When the rest of the crew had abandoned ship as ordered, Cromwell, one junior officer and a volunteer crew of ten took *Sculpin* on its final dive. As far as the US submarine service was concerned it had simply disappeared, as had so many submarines on patrol. It was not until after the war when some of the survivors, one badly injured, were rescued from a prisoner-of-war camp that the full story of Cromwell's sacrifice became known.

Perhaps the best known U-boat commander of the Second World War was Kapitanleutnant Gunther Prien of U-47, largely because he achieved the impossible and spectacular by taking his boat through the defences of the British naval base at Scapa Flow and sinking the battleship *Royal Oak* (see page 40).

Prien found himself in the spotlight for a different reason some weeks later when U-47 first attacked three large transports and the battleship *Warspite* without success, the fault being not with Prien and U-47 but with unreliable German torpedoes. On a number of occasions U-boats made attacks on important British warships, including major battleships, only for the torpedoes to either run wild or fail to explode on impact.

In June 1940 Prien attacked several convoys and sank 6 ships before running out of torpedoes and then, in October, he led 4 U-boats in an attack on another convoy and sank 14 ships, ultimately becoming the first U-boat commander to sink 200,000 tons of enemy shipping and receiving the highest possible decoration of the Oak leaves to the Knight's Cross.

March 1941 saw Prien in action again, sighting and reporting convoy OB-293. Other U-boats joined in the attack and sank two ships, but unfortunately for them the convoy's destroyer escort was also extremely active and gave the German U-boat service its worst blow of the war. An old boat, UA, was so badly damaged it only just managed to escape while U-70 was sunk after its captain and crew surrendered following the attack which blew them to the surface. Prien and U-47 and another U-boat hero, Kretschmer in U-99, were driven off.

Prien continued to shadow the convoy but on 7 March he was spotted by the British destroyer *Wolverine* commanded by Lt Cdr J.M. Rowland. U-47 crash-dived as *Wolverine's* depth charges thrashed the water. The U-boat's propeller was badly damaged and the noise it created was a constant indication to the *Wolverine* of its position. Another depth-charge attack was sufficient to put a final end to Prien and U-47, after the U-boat commander had sunk 28 merchant ships.

Joachim Schepke had joined the submarine service because he did not like the spit-and-polish and routine of big ships, which did not give an officer the opportunity to use his initiative. As commander of U-100, his was one of the many U-boats which created havoc among Allied shipping in 1940–41. He sank 37 ships with a total tonnage of 145,000 and was looked upon as a U-boat commander with a great future.

Convoy HX-112 comprising 50 ships, which left Halifax in March 1941 and was watched over by the 5th Escort H Group, was attacked by a wolf pack with great success and several ships were sunk. The U-boat ace Kretschmer (page 48) made a devastating attack during which he sank six ships including four tankers, putting the escorting warships in a frenzy.

Schepke in U-100 had been picked up by ASDIC and was damaged in the subsequent depth-charge attack which forced him to the surface. When he did so he was shocked to find that his diesels would not start because their fuel lines had been severed. A destroyer was closing fast to attack when Schepke disastrously ordered the electric motors to take the submarine astern instead of ahead. It quickly became clear that the destroyer was going to ram U-100 so Schepke ordered 'abandon ship' but it was too late to do anything. The destroyer crashed into the submarine hitting it abreast of the conning tower and killing Schepke instantly. The U-boat sank with its crew and dead commander.

Engelbert Endrass had been Prien's First Watch Officer in U-47 and, in fact, was responsible for firing the salvo which sank the British battleship *Royal Oak* in Scapa Flow in 1939. He was eventually promoted to command U-46, sinking 26 Allied ships and 142,000 tons. He was then given command of a training school for a time before joining U-567 in October 1941 – one of six U-boats which made contact with Allied convoy Homebound Gibraltar 76 before moving into an attacking position.

In an attempt to defend his convoy the senior officer ordered a number of escorts to draw away and stage a fake battle, which would draw off the U-boats. But instead, the fake battle fooled several merchant ship commanders in the convoy who fired off a number of star shells which illuminated the scene and the convoy. As a result Endrass was able to torpedo a 3,300-ton tanker before convoy escorts, racing to the scene, sighted U-567 on the surface and turned to attack. Endrass immediately dived and took avoiding action but was not fast enough to avoid the depth-charge attack launched by them.

Twenty-six-year-old Fritz-Julius Lemp and the crew of U-30 were one of 21 U-boats that had been secretly patrolling off the British

Isles and the Straits of Gibraltar for almost a month before war was declared, one of the reasons he happened to be where he was when the *Athenia* crossed his path and was sunk (see page 39). Lemp reported afterwards that he thought the *Athenia* was a troopship while the German hierarchy strongly denied that a U-boat had sunk the passenger liner, frightened of the reaction that might come from the United States. After this incident Lemp was very careful about what he did. Having sunk a 4,500-ton freighter, he gave the survivors whisky and cigarettes and saw them safely into their lifeboats.

Although a successful U-boat captain who sank a large number of ships in a comparatively short space of time – 17 ships totalling 68,600 tons in 10 months – he could not be described as a lucky captain. For instance, when he stopped a freighter with his deck gun, the crew abandoned ship so he decided to put a boarding party on the ship and sink it with explosives. As he was in the middle of doing this destroyers and aircraft were seen approaching so he quickly dived. Unfortunately he forgot to cut loose the ship's dinghy which bobbed above the submarine like a marker buoy, and he was subjected to a sustained attack by aircraft from which he only escaped with difficulty.

Lemp was transferred to U-110 and sent on patrol off southern Iceland where he sighted a 50-ship incoming convoy. Calling up the rest of the wolf pack he crept into the convoy himself and sank a tanker. Approached by two destroyers he dived quickly and got away.

There is a moment in every war, every battle, every military engagement and, indeed, in everyday life, when an event, a decision, or an action turns the flood of fortune in one direction or another. It may not be obvious at the time but on reflection, when the battle is won or lost, that moment takes on its true significance. The capture of the German Enigma M-3 coding machine in May 1941 from U-110 was one such. It was kept secret at the time and in fact the submarine was recorded as sunk in the first edition of the official history of the war at sea by Captain S.W. Roskill. It was only some time later that the full story became known.

U-110 sailed for the North Atlantic to patrol the convoy routes. On 8 May Lemp sighted a convoy but because the night was bright and clear he delayed his attack, and radioed details of his find to base. The message was intercepted by U-201, commanded by Adalbert Schnee, who immediately changed course to join Lemp. The two commanders drew up their plan of attack which was to be made in daylight, submerged. The two U-boats manoeuvred into position and it was just one minute before noon on 9 May when the U-110 fired its first salvo. Two ships in the convoy were hit during this initial attack but, unfortunately for Lemp, his periscope had been sighted by the convoy escort HMS *Aubretia*. After about 30 minutes of depth-charging the submarine was suddenly blown to the surface.

Events happened fast. The captain of *Bulldog*, Cdr Addison Joe Baker-Cresswell, seeing the panic-stricken crew abandoning U-110, wheeled round on a ramming course. Lemp clambered to the bridge, saw the danger and immediately shouted an order to abandon ship, fast. The crew needed no second order. Down below those whose duty it was to destroy vital equipment and throw documents overboard either decided to put their personal preservation first, or simply forgot, and left the boat. With no crew manning the submarine's gun, Baker-Cresswell realised the possibilities. He did not need to ram, he told himself, but could capture the U-boat intact with any vital equipment or documents on board. So he altered course, brought his boat to a stop, opened fire, mainly to encourage more panic, and lowered one of the ship's boats.

While Baker-Cresswell was planning his future moves Lemp was seen swimming away from his boat with some of his officers, never to be seen again. Some German authorities believe that when he saw the U-boat was not sinking, he decided to swim back and was shot, but there is no confirmation of this.

Bulldog's boat moved alongside and a boarding party clambered on the deck. Fearful of being trapped if the U-boat should sink under them, they grabbed everything they could lay their hands on. The Enigma machine was still plugged in, as if it was being used when the attack occurred. Everything that could be moved was loaded into *Bulldog*'s whaler and ferried back to the destroyer whilst *Aubretia* picked up the U-boat's survivors.

None of the boarding party knew anything about submarines, so they could do little to ensure U-110's buoyancy. Nevertheless it was taken in tow and an attempt made to take it to Iceland, but the following day the U-boat sank.

The Enigma machine and code books were sent to the Government Code and Cypher School at Bletchley Park in Hertfordshire but nothing was revealed about what had been captured aboard U-110. It is thought that the documents included a list of secret refuelling points to service the *Bismark*, other raiders and long-distance U-boats and that, as a result, this network was wiped out.

The captured Enigma machine had eight different rotors which could be used when the code tables were changed. It also enabled the breaking of the U-boat cyphers which gave the position of every U-boat at sea and where Doenitz was directing his patrol lines, as a result of which a large number of convoys were rerouted around them. Some estimates suggested that this saved at least 300 ships from being sunk. Bletchley Park was also able to read details of German GE-7 electric torpedoes and confirm what U-boat survivors had said, that new U-boats could dive to a depth of 600 feet.

CHAPTER FIVE

The Undaunted
- The Allies

The British – Bryant, Cayley, Hutchinson,
Haggard, Miers VC, Roberts VC, Gould VC, Mars.
The Americans – Fluckey, Street, Ramage, Warder,
Klakring. The Pole – Karnicki.

L T CDR BEN BRYANT, the 34-year-old commander of *Sealion* did
not make an impressive start to his patrolling career. While on
anti-invasion patrol off Norway in 1940 he was forced to temporarily withdraw from his patrol to recharge his batteries. His luck
was out for while he was doing so the entire German invasion fleet
passed through his patrol area; and then he was attacked off the
Danish coast and his main motors put out of action. *Sealion* only
just made it home by hugging the Danish coast to avoid detection,
and then limping across the North Sea at dead of night.

Bryant and his crew could be forgiven for feeling despondent, but
not for long. Success came at last, off Oslo Fjord on 11 April 1940,
when *Sealion* attacked and sank a small transport. Then on her
eighth patrol bad luck struck again, followed by near disaster.
Travelling at periscope depth Bryant sighted a U-boat surfacing
astern only 300 yards away – a prime target for *Sealion*'s stern tubes
which were already fully loaded. It took time for Bryant to get his
boat correctly lined up, time that enabled the unsuspecting U-boat
to increase the distance between the two vessels and present a narrow
end-on target. Bryant fired both stern tubes but the torpedoes missed

and by the time *Sealion* surfaced to fight it out with guns the U-boat had submerged to safety.

Later that same night a mine bounced and scraped its agonisingly slow way down the side of *Sealion*. Tension rose almost to breaking point at the intermittent grinding sound – any second one of the deadly horns could touch the hull and blow it and its crew to pieces, but eventually the mine simply floated away.

On 6 August 1940 *Sealion* had yet another near escape. Having sunk the leading transport of a German convoy, it was nearly run over by a closely following ship which smashed *Sealion*'s main periscope, although there was little other damage.

The German ship *Leonhart* of 2,600 tons was the next victim in that eventful patrol, sunk on 11 August. Then Bryant intercepted the Norwegian vessel *Fylke*, evacuated the crew, and set the ship on fire by bombarding it with the submarine's gun.

Shortly after this Bryant was promoted to Commander and given a new ship, the improved 5-class *Safari*, a boat in which he had more luck, more action and the opportunities which eventually put him on a par with the nation's leading submariners. He sank a 5,000-ton armed merchant cruiser, a 3,000-ton water carrier and a 3,000-ton supply ship, before being sent to the Mediterranean where, at that time, submarine action was falling off. Unfortunately for Bryant most of Italy's large merchant fleet had by now been destroyed, and success depended on finding small targets which, despite their size, were given strong air and sea protection.

Bryant became very adept at 'winkling out' these small targets and then avoiding the heavy counter-attacks which always followed. By 1943 he had discovered that minesweepers, anti-submarine yachts and trawlers were particularly vulnerable to surface gun attack and wreaked havoc in the Tyrhennian Sea, ending the war a Captain.

In contrast to Ben Bryant, Lt Cayley opened *Utmost*'s score sheet with a successful attack on three transports which made up an unescorted convoy, sinking them all. After successfully carrying out an agent-landing operation Cayley and *Utmost* were off on patrol again. After sinking the troopship *Capo Vita* and severely damaging the Italian cruiser *Duca d'Abruzzi*, Cayley came across

E-19 – First World War submarine

U-71 – U-boat under attack

Oberleuntnant Fritz-Julius Lemp,
commander of the *U-30* and
responsible for sinking the liner
Athenia at the beginning of
the Second World War

Grand Admiral Karl Doenitz,
father of the U-boat service

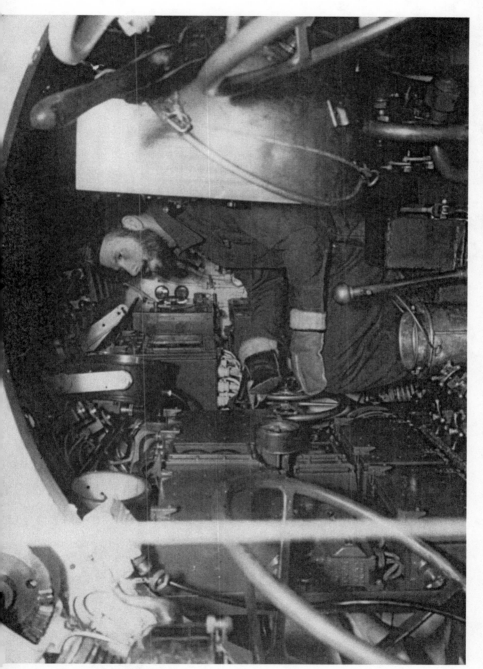

X-craft interior: cramped control room in an X-craft

Cdr John Linton VC, DSO, DSC, RN

Lt A.C.G. Mars RN

Cdr Anthony Miers VC, DSO, RN

Singapore X-craft VC's

Lt L.E. Fraser VC

Leading Seaman J.J. Magennis VC

Life on board: a submariner goes for a stroll

A chariot on the warpath

Lt P.S.W. Roberts VC   Petty Officer Tom Gould VC

Heroes of *Thrasher*

Lt Cdr A.C.C. Miers VC DSO,
commander of the British
submarine *Torbay*

Responsible for the attack on *Tirpitz*

Lt B.B.C Place VC DSO

Lt D. Cameron VC

a convoy of five ships off Kerkennan Bank and sank the German vessel *Heraklea* which carried troops and supplies destined for the Afrika Korps.

Although his reputation was already well established Cayley enhanced it during this period with an exploit which demanded both the highest courage and skill. A 55-mile-wide Italian minefield across the Sicilian Narrows had been proving a constant danger to British submarines, causing them to take a wide diversion and waste a lot of time when going to and from patrol areas off the northern coast of Sicily. It was therefore decided to try and find out if the minefield could be crossed by a submarine travelling at a depth of 150 feet – Cayley was given the task of forcing a way through. He set off with those back at base hoping for the best but expecting the worst. For 12, 18, then 24 hours nothing was heard from *Utmost* which was going through a huge area strewn with mines with no idea of the pattern in which they may have been laid or even how many of them there might be. It was like walking through a field of landmines while blindfolded. The tension mounted inexorably and they had almost given up hope, when suddenly there was a signal: 'Next please!' it said.

Sadly too many of these submarine stories have an unhappy ending and the story of *Utmost* is no exception – the submarine and its crew disappeared whilst on patrol off Sicily only a few weeks after Cayley had left for a new submarine, P-311, a new vessel designed especially to carry two-man human torpedoes. But, after successfully completing the launch of such a torpedo off northern Sardinia P-311 disappeared and was never heard of again. Although after the war historians endeavoured to discover what had happened to her by searching German and Italian records, they found nothing to tell them how the brave captain and his submarine met their end.

The submarine *Truant* was ready for action when the war started and saw the war out after some splendid action, having the good fortune to be commanded by two of Britain's leading submariners. An established and experienced officer, Lt Cdr Hutchinson was in command at the outbreak of hostilities and was immediately in action patrolling the waters of the North Sea. Then on 23 March

1940 *Truant* chased the German merchant vessel *Edmund Hugo Stines* right into, at that time, neutral Norwegian territorial waters. The Germans were made nervous by such tenacity and quickly scuttled their ship.

Two weeks later Hutchinson sighted the German cruiser *Karlsruhe* as she sailed from Kristiansund after landing troops on the Norwegian coast and attacked her, but was initially thwarted by the cruiser's evasive zigzagging tactics. Hutchinson pressed on, however, until he was in position to fire a salvo of ten torpedoes, ideally spaced. The tracks of the torpedoes were quickly spotted by lookouts and the cruiser took more evasive action, but one caught her in the stern, putting both engines and the ship's steering gear out of action, damage that was sufficient to sink the cruiser.

Her departure from the scene was the prelude to an intensive counter-attack as escorting destroyers raced back along the tracks of the torpedoes. The submarine was wracked by massive explosions striking the hull like heavy industrial hammers. The hull shuddered and shrieked in protest but, despite many leaks and damage to some machinery, *Truant* managed to hang on at a depth of 300 feet. After a time Hutchinson brought the boat up to periscope depth but found another anti-submarine group quietly waiting on the surface. Returning to the depths, and after waiting patiently for 19 hours, Hutchinson came up again to find that all the enemy ships had disappeared. He was able to surface and let in precious fresh air for the crew, before *Truant* returned safely to base.

It was shortly after this incident that Hutchinson, victim of an Admiralty policy which put an age limit of 35 years on submarine commanders, was forced to give way to Lt Cdr Hugh Haggard who had joined the submarine service in 1933 and who was to remain with *Truant* throughout the rest of her career.

Haggard's first success was the sinking of the 8,000-ton *Preussen* off northern Norway in May 1940. The following month *Truant*, in company with several other submarines, was posted to the Mediterranean to reinforce the flotillas already there. Haggard joined in the Mediterranean battle with gusto, encouraged by an incident that took place whilst he was on his way there.

In the Bay of Biscay he and *Truant* intercepted a Bordeaux-bound ship, the Norwegian motor vessel *Tropic Sea*, one of the vessels attacked and captured by the German raider *Orion* which had put a prize crew on board. In addition to them there were the Norwegian captain, and his wife and the captain and survivors of the British ship *Haxby* which had earlier been another victim of the *Orion*. The German prize crew was short of courage when faced by a warship which could fight back so they scuttled their ship, but not before the prisoners were rescued and taken aboard *Truant*. On the voyage to home and safety it was recognised that this was probably the first time that a woman had ever made a trip on a submarine.

It was not long before Haggard and *Truant* were imitating the growing habit of other submarine commanders and following enemy ships right into their harbours in order to sink them. One such act of daring carried out by Haggard and his crew included entry into the harbour of Buerat El Sun and firing two torpedoes at a tanker moored there. The torpedoes, unfortunately, went under the tanker which was unladen, but blew the quayside to pieces. In order to escape Haggard had to surface and endure the attacks of small patrol boats before he could get clear. Shortly afterwards he attacked and sank the Italian destroyer *Alcione*.

At the end of 1941 *Truant* and *Trusty* were ordered to the Far East, the first reinforcements to be sent there since the outbreak of war. The move was forced upon submarine command by the fact that the Japanese were sending large expeditions against Sarawak and Borneo, forcing the United States fleet to withdraw to meet them.

Truant arrived two weeks before the fall of Singapore and when this tragic event happened was put under the command of the Royal Netherlands Navy at Batavia (now Jakarta). Its first task was to look for a Japanese convoy reportedly off Bali. Haggard found the waters there full of ships, including destroyers and anti-submarine vessels and fired a salvo of torpedoes at a Japanese cruiser, two of which hit the target but failed to explode. *Truant* managed to escape and make its way, as ordered, to the British base at Ceylon (now Sri Lanka) but the submarine repair ship was no longer there which meant *Truant* had to return to Britain for its long overdue refit. At least it was still in one piece.

Lt Cdr Anthony Miers VC, already described on page 59, was another to be ranked among the finest submarine commanders of the war. He was also an officer about whom his contemporaries had very positive and differing views. To some he was 'a turbulent friend and implacable foe', 'cocksure, self-willed to the point of arrogance', 'boorish and bullying'. To others he was 'resolute, bold, determined, decisive with great honesty of purpose, whether on duty or off'. An example of these diverse opinions was shown when his submarine *Torbay* was despatched on an emergency mission leaving half its crew ashore. Those abandoned were assigned to another submarine but when the two vessels met later in Alexandria they were offered the opportunity of rejoining *Torbay* – they all declined with thanks.

Miers sailed as a Lieutenant Commander in charge of *Torbay* in 1941, joining the British flotilla that was creating havoc among enemy shipping in the Mediterranean, soon being awarded the DSO for his attacks on supply ships and promoted to the rank of Commander.

The *Torbay*, along with 21 other Mediterranean submarines, was diverted to the Atlantic in 1941 when the German battleships *Scharnhorst* and *Gneisenau*, and the cruiser *Hipper* were on the rampage threatening Allied shipping. It was a short-lived interval for by the time the submarines had got to the scene the two German battleships had fled back into port. Back on its former beat, *Torbay* torpedoed an enemy ship which, although badly damaged, did not sink. Miers waited submerged until nightfall, surfaced, went alongside the now anchored vessel, put a boarding party to set charges and blew her up.

Torbay nearly came to grief during one patrol when she was caught on the surface by a destroyer while charging her batteries. She began her crash dive with customary speed and efficiency until Miers, who as captain was the last man down the hatch, found he could not close it properly. He gave up because of the proximity of the oncoming destroyer and so the submarine's future depended entirely on the strength of the lower hatch. The destroyer passed over the submarine releasing a pattern of depth charges as it did so. *Torbay* shuddered but continued to go deeper and deeper until it reached safety. When the submarine finally surfaced the crew was greeted by a deluge of water which poured in once the lower hatch was opened. To Miers's constant embarrassment it was discovered that the main hatch would not close because of a pillow, which the captain himself had been using for a nap while the batteries were being re-charged, and which was jammed between the top of the hatch and its cover. It was some time before Miers could live that down.

Patrolling the Aegean Sea, Miers sank the Italian submarine *Jantina* as a prelude to sinking a schooner and three caiques, all flying the Nazi flag and carrying troops, petrol and captured British ammunition. Off Corfu in March 1942 Miers torpedoed but failed to sink a destroyer, despite which he decided to follow a convoy right into harbour. It was extremely dangerous but, as he told a colleague, he was not coming all that way for nothing.

Negotiating the narrow channel entrance he slipped quietly in and found not only the newly-arrived convoy but six or more destroyers. As it was almost nightfall, and much too late to attack efficiently, he stopped engines and waited. Matters came to an interesting head when it was pointed out to Miers that the batteries urgently needed recharging, an exercise that could only be done on the surface. Being a clear moonlit night he decided to go ahead right in the middle of the harbour, surrounded by enemy ships. The three-hour operation complete *Torbay* dived again until dawn and when it was daylight, surfaced to find a dismal scene – all but two ships in the convoy had departed and there was only one destroyer left. Miers attacked all three vessels but was only able to sink the merchant ships. The destroyer made a series of intensive depth-charge attacks but despite being shaken like a pea on a drum *Torbay* remained undamaged. After 17 hours in the enemy harbour Miers then navigated the submarine out the way it had come in and sailed 40 miles back to base.

This action gained Miers the Victoria Cross and other officers and 24 ratings also received awards. He then established a precedent.

When he went to Buckingham Palace to receive his medal he insisted that all the recipients, both officers and men, should receive their awards at the same time – the first occasion on which both officers and men attended the same investiture ceremony

Two more Victoria Crosses were awarded to submariners working in conventional submarines, both for the same incident.

Lt Peter Roberts, First Lieutenant and therefore second in command of the submarine *Thrasher*, joined the submarine on 1 January 1941 and after trials and tests of new equipment, sailed to Malta, Alexandria and the Aegean. Roberts, incidentally, had earlier served with David Wanklyn VC so he had received the very best training.

Off Crete on 16 February 1942 *Thrasher* attacked and sank an escorted merchant ship as she was entering Suda Bay. It was immediately counter-attacked by anti-submarine vessels and two aircraft. As *Thrasher* dived to avoid the attack the crew heard two bangs, the sound of metal hitting metal, but as the boat continued the dive they were distracted by the 33 depth charges dropped around them.

Eventually it was safe for *Thrasher* to surface. When the boat's crew came through the hatch on to the bridge they found a bomb trapped on the deck. The deck casing which covers a submarine's hull above water when surfaced is perforated so that the submarine can submerge. Without perforations air between the deck and the hull would be trapped, making the boat too buoyant.

The captain, Lt H.S. Mackenzie, and Roberts selected Petty Officer Thomas Gould from the many volunteers to assist in disposing of the highly dangerous device. The night was pitch black when the two men went on deck and after a few moments to allow their eyes to become accustomed to the dark, Roberts went aft to examine the bomb. He discovered that there was not one bomb but two and coolly informed his colleagues that the problem was made even worse as the second one was trapped between the deck and the outer hull of the boat. The fact that the bombs might explode at any moment destroying *Thrasher* and its crew was bad enough, but what made matters even worse was that if, for any reason, the submarine had to take avoiding action and crash dive, Roberts and Gould would probably be trapped between the deck and the hull and be drowned.

The two bombs were rolling about as the submarine pitched and tossed in the choppy sea, and the first thing to do was to secure them with ropes and sacking. They then began edging the first one towards the stern of the submarine. Gently pushing and pulling, interspersing their exertions with fervent prayers, Roberts and Gould finally got it into position. At a signal from Roberts, Mackenzie sent the submarine full ahead and jerked the bomb into the water and to safety.

The second bomb presented a more difficult task, having smashed its way through the deck so that it was trapped between it and the hull, tangled up in a maze of pipes. To reach it the two men had to clamber through the hole it had made and shuffle along the narrow space to where it was sitting. Working in the confined space on their stomachs between the deck and the hull of a tossing and rolling submarine, they pushed and shoved the lethal object more than 20 feet towards a break in the grating that would allow them to lift the bomb on to the deck and heave it over the side. While they were engaged in this dangerous activity strange noises kept coming from within the bomb, a constant and urgent encouragement, as if one was needed, to do the job as quickly as possible.

It took them almost half an hour to get the bomb to the opening where another member of the crew helped them lift it on to the deck. After more minutes of tension and effort they had rolled it to the stern of the boat and, in the same manner as the first, deposited it in the sea. Their immediate reward was a large double scotch – their second, a Victoria Cross each.

Twenty-eight-year-old Lt Alistair Mars, had joined the British submarine service at 21 and had already been the First Lieutenant (second in command) of *Perseus* when he took over *Unbroken*, another of the highly successful U-class of submarines, when it was completed in November 1941. It was the first submarine to arrive in the Mediterranean island of Malta when the harbour reopened after a three-month shutdown caused by enemy action.

Mars had been outspoken about the severe early losses of submarines which he put down to 'inexperience and unimaginative training'. His first duty was to land the well-known agent Captain Peter Churchill (well known after the war that is) on the coast of the Riviera. Later *Unbroken* was patrolling off Genoa when Mars sighted a 4,000-ton freighter but because of the target's distance and speed, he was forced to fire his salvo of torpedoes at a range of 8,000 yards. Despite that it was an accurate shot and *Unbroken* scored its first success.

Shortly after this, in May 1942, Mars showed the true Nelson touch (Nelson, it will be remembered, put his telescope to his blind eye when he did not want to see a particular signal recalling him from action). Sent to patrol a particular area off Malta as part of the Island's much-needed defence, he decided to move to another one because he was convinced he could get there as his original position was too well patrolled by the enemy. There must have been a moment of panic aboard *Unbroken* three days later when Mars received a signal informing him that enemy cruisers were heading his way – his way, of course, being where the base commander thought he was.

Mars reasoned to himself that the enemy squadron must have been sighted by aircraft and would know that their position had been reported, so they would alter course. He also convinced himself that if the squadron did alter course it was likely to head for the area in which he was now waiting. It was an incredible gamble that could not only have ruined his naval career if it had gone wrong, but could have had a disastrous effect on the war in the Mediterranean at that time.

After an agonising wait of almost 24 hours *Unbroken*'s ASDIC picked up the sound of fast-moving propellers. When he peered through his periscope Mars had all his doubts removed for there, in exactly the right position for attack, were four cruisers. The fact that they were escorted by eight destroyers and two anti-submarine aircraft was only a matter of passing interest to Mars, or at least until *Unbroken*'s presence became known.

Ignoring the fact that three of the escorting destroyers passed right over him Mars pressed home the attack, firing four torpedoes at the oncoming cruisers. Then, in the common vernacular of the time, he got the hell out of it. Two of the torpedoes struck home. The heavy Italian cruiser *Belzano* was hit amidships while the light cruiser *Atendolo* had her bow blown off. Neither ship sank but they took no further part in the war.

In the following hour or so over 100 depth charges were dropped around *Unbroken* as it twisted and turned to avoid them. When the enthusiasm of the escorts finally began to wane *Unbroken*, at a depth of 120 feet, silently slipped away.

The next attack was almost *Unbroken*'s last. In October 1942, instructed to intercept a heavily escorted convoy, Mars carried out his orders to the letter even though the escorts were unusually alert and efficient. The submarine sank an Italian oil tanker but in doing so gave away its position so clearly that an attacking aircraft was able to drop a marker over it so that the destroyers were easily able to locate it. *Unbroken* was shattered and shaken, battered and buffeted so badly by their depth charges that its hydroplanes and one motor were put out of action. It was the nearest the submarine came to destruction but happily both the captain and his crew came through the war intact.

When the US submarine *Barb* was taken over by Lt Cdr Eugene 'Lucky' Fluckey early in 1944, results were immediate and between 31 May and 13 June *Barb*, together with *Herring*, sank five Japanese cargo ships totalling 16,000 tons. Although there was some elation over these successes this was soon shattered when *Herring*, which had served with *Barb* for many months in the Mediterranean and the Atlantic, was sunk.

Herring, commanded by Lt Cdr D. Zabriski Jr, had left Pearl Harbor on 16 May with *Barb* to patrol off the Kurile Islands between northern Japan and Kamchatka. On 31 May they made contact with a Japanese convoy and sank the escort vessel *Ishigaki*. Maintaining the attack *Barb* sent the freighters *Koto Maru* and *Madra Maru* to the bottom, while *Herring* disposed of the *Hokuyu Maru*. The following day, off Matsuwa Island, *Herring* was in action sinking the *Hiburi Maru* and the *Iwaki Maru*. Unfortunately, while pressing home this attack it was sighted by shore batteries which immediately opened fire, hitting *Herring* a fatal blow in the conning tower.

Barb continued its patrol and on 31 August encountered and attacked an eight-ship convoy of small vessels. The 5,600-ton *Okuni Maru* was quickly sunk and Fluckey and his crew were then subjected to a 58-depth-charge attack by escorts. It would have been easier for Fluckey and *Barb* to slink away to safety but instead, when the counter-attack was over, he came up to periscope depth and sank the 20,000 ton *Uno*.

It was then time for a rest, but the situation in the Pacific demanded that it not be for long. On 20 December 1944, *Barb* left Guam in a three-strong wolf pack to search for prey again around the Kuriles. Fluckey set the tone of the proceedings by sinking about 18,000 tons of shipping – *Shinyo Maru*, the tanker *Santo Maru* and the large *Anyo Maru* – by which time he had already done enough to get his name into the record books; but his big moment was yet to come.

On 23 January 1945 he arrived off Namkwan Harbour and much to his surprise found a submarine captain's dream – 30 Japanese vessels, all at anchor, neatly laid out in three columns of ten. Fluckey had no problem with aiming, he could hardly miss. Moving carefully into position he let go a salvo of 10 torpedoes and recorded 10 hits. Through his periscope he saw three vessels on fire and sinking, many others were also burning but he had no time to hang about counting his victims.

Cdr Fluckey was commended for 'his courage, initiative, resourcefulness and inspiring leadership combined with brilliant judgement and skill'. He was described as an inspiration to all submarine personnel, and was awarded the Congressional Medal of Honour.

There is an epilogue. Still in command of *Barb*, in June 1945 Fluckey was patrolling off one of the main islands of Japan, Hokkaido, when he saw a substantial warehouse which could, he thought, easily contain valuable material. So he woke up the population of the port, Shari, with an impressive 'fireworks' display which destroyed the warehouse. He then attacked the island of Kaihyo and added more property, a railway train, shore defences, railway lines and a town to his impressive list of ships sunk. With Japan defeated, Fluckey and *Barb* sailed home to peace.

Cdr George L. Street took command of the new US submarine *Tirante* as the war in the Pacific was coming to an end, the pendulum having swung very definitely in favour of the Americans. The Japanese were still trying to get vital supplies from China and Manchuria so the sea lanes in the Yellow Sea were relatively busy. George Street knew he was late on the scene and felt very strongly that he had to make up for lost time – which he did on his very first patrol. Leaving Pearl Harbor on 3 March 1945, *Tirante* returned on 25 April having attacked 12 enemy ships and sunk half of them.

Knowing that the number of enemy targets was shrinking fast Street decided to go looking for areas where an inquisitive submarine would be least expected – the dangerously shallow coastal waters. Here he sank two large freighters, a tanker and a transport loaded with troops; despite frantic depth-charge attacks which bounced *Tirante* on the rocky ocean bottom, he also managed to sink a 1,500-ton patrol vessel before escaping.

This attack was highly successful and fully vindicated Street's theory so he decided not to leave the area. After all, no one would expect him to hang around after what had happened and he was convinced that the enemy was making use of a concealed harbour on the northern side of Quelpart. So he headed for his target area despite the fact that, as the water was shallow, he would have to go in on the surface, through mined waters, and avoid shoals and reefs. There was also a shore-based radar system, a number of patrol vessels and very good air support. The odds were really not in his favour. Street crept into the harbour where he found a 10,000-ton tanker into which he placed two torpedoes. The force of the explosion almost flattened *Tirante's* crew on deck and, helped by the light of the tanker fire, two Japanese frigates went straight into the attack.

Street quickly brought *Tirante* round towards the leading frigate and fired two torpedoes, then he swung around and fired his last torpedo at the other frigate. Immediately ordering full speed, he headed out of the harbour just as the first salvo blew the first frigate to pieces; then the second shot hit the other frigate which also sank.

Tirante headed at speed along the coast into deeper water. But Street was not yet finished, sinking a 100-ton lugger with gunfire and then picking up the two-man crew of a Japanese aircraft which had been shot down. He too was awarded the Congressional Medal of Honour.

Audacious and sagacious were words often used to describe Lt Cdr Lawson P. Ramage, commander of the US submarine *Trout*. After taking part in the battle for Guadalcanal in 1942 he proved the first adjective by entering an enemy harbour and torpedoing a large tanker moored at Mri in Northern Borneo, having had a lean time trying to find targets. When Ramage took a long-distance look at the harbour and saw the vessel at anchor he decided to move in for a closer inspection. She was too far inside the harbour for a direct attack, at a depth of less than ten fathoms where there was strong tidal current, but, he thought, a night surface attack might solve the problem.

After waiting for darkness to fall, Ramage surfaced, charged the batteries and, using the electric motors, silently moved into the harbour. When the range was down to 1,700 yards he fired three bow torpedoes, two of which hit the target. He then turned *Trout* round and fired a stern shot which failed to detonate. The explosions obviously lit up the scene like a floodlit arena so Ramage decided not to hang around.

He was then given command of the submarine *Parche* and was off Formosa when he, together with *Hammerhead* and *Steelhead* sighted the tell-tale smoke of a convoy which, it turned out, was well protected by an umbrella of aircraft. The three submarines attacked immediately.

Ramage lived up to his reputation and went into the convoy like a ferret in a rabbit warren. He penetrated the strong escort screen and attacked on the surface firing 19 torpedoes in 46 minutes. Hemmed in on all sides by enemy ships and escorts trying to counter-attack he moved skilfully into position, firing bow and stern shots, damaging a freighter and sinking a second. Raked by machine-gun fire, and illuminated by flares, he reloaded and fired stern shots at a damaged tanker that was now firing at him. All lookouts, and anyone not vital to the action, were sent below, but Ramage stayed at his post and continued firing with bow and stern tubes, having to move sharply to avoid a freighter trying to ram him and to dodge concentrated gunfire.

Although completely boxed in, he fired 'down-the-throat' (see page 120) at another would-be rammer and stopped it dead, before sinking another with a stern shot. As dawn broke and with the enemy guns becoming too accurate, he cleared the area having sent four ships to the bottom and damaged several others.

When Ramage was congratulated on his feat he replied: 'I got mad!' He also got the Congressional Medal of Honour.

In the first few months following the destruction of a large part of the American fleet at Pearl Harbor, and until the carrier battles of the Coral Sea and Midway in May and June 1942, the war at sea in the Pacific was fought almost entirely by submarines, only 28 of which were immediately available in the area.

Like the Germans, the Americans were plagued with early torpedo troubles either through faulty depth keeping or defecting actuating pistols. As has been said, it took almost two years before it could be considered that they were consistently reliable.

Lt Cdr Frederick Warder in *Sea Wolf* had more problems than most with his torpedoes. On 14 December 1942 he found himself a prime target, a 12,000-ton seaplane tender, fired at it from a position from which it was impossible to miss . . . and missed. Shortly after this he had no less than four Japanese cruisers in his sights. He fired at the flagship of the squadron and thought he had secured a hit. When darkness fell he came up to periscope depth for another look and to his surprise the same cruiser appeared still to be there. Warder could only surmise that the cruiser he had fired at had been sunk and that the Japanese Admiral had transferred his flag to another ship, but he could not be sure, so he fired again but then had to crash-dive to avoid anti-submarine attack and when he next looked through his periscope all the cruisers had vanished. Warder could not be certain how successful his attacks had been. The crew of *Sea*

Wolf had certainly heard the explosions caused by their torpedoes but this could have been because they had exploded prematurely, as had happened before. It was a fact at that time that no submarine commander could have full confidence in the efficiency of his torpedoes.

When the torpedo problems were solved *Sea Wolf* made a number of attacks on Japanese shipping sinking a total of 18 with a tonnage of 71,000 tons.

Warder was replaced as the submarine's commander by Lt Cdr R.L. Goss who continued the submarine's run of success. Then Lt Cdr A.L. Bontier took the submarine on its 15th and final patrol. Sent to carry supplies and personnel to the Philippines *Sea Wolf* became involved in a search for a Japanese submarine that had sunk an American destroyer but with *Sea Wolf* submerged it seems that it was mistaken for the Japanese attacker and destroyed.

Another submarine high in the record books, with 21 ships and 100,000 tons sunk was *Flasher* commanded by Lt Cdr W. Grider, who took the boat on its fifth patrol in November 1944 in the South China Sea. There Grider found himself and his boat in the midst of a small Japanese convoy, all tankers.

He began the attack by firing four torpedoes, two set shallow to catch a destroyer and two set slightly deeper to hit the tanker on the far side of the warship. The shot was perfect. The first two sent the destroyer *Kishinaki* to the bottom by the stern, while the second two stopped the tanker even though it had turned away at the last moment. When Grider looked through his periscope he saw the destroyer going down, the tanker burning well and, to his surprise, another destroyer standing by motionless, so he attacked again and ended the career of the destroyer *Iwananami*, before finishing off the tanker with another torpedo.

There was more to come, but not for a week or two, after some violent storms. When the weather eased slightly, Grider's patience was rewarded with the sight of a group of oil tankers, but the sea was still rough enough to make a torpedo attack inadvisable, so he waited. After a time he was convinced that he had missed his chance and that the convoy was gone. Then the boat's radar picked up the echo of an island, Tortue Island, which seemed to be moving. It was, in fact, five large oil tankers, three escorts and a destroyer. Twelve hours later, after a cat and mouse fight with the escorts, the convoy comprised two large tankers, a sinking destroyer and three despondent escorts.

Grider and *Flasher* made a major contribution to the eventual destruction of the Japanese merchant fleet – indeed, American submarines totally destroyed Japan's ability to import oil.

During the First World War German U-boats did not penetrate the Gulf of Mexico or the Panama Canal area but when the Second started it was not long before they were active in the Caribbean, which made the Americans grow extremely nervous. They decided to establish a submarine base on the Virgin Islands and before long had established a patrol area around it.

Thomas B. Klakring began the sea war in the Atlantic as commander of S-17, action coming quickly when the submarine's listening equipment picked up the sound of another boat in the area. The periscope showed nothing on the surface which meant it must be another submarine.

Klakring called 'battle stations' and his immediate thought was to ram the intruder, but his first attempt came to nothing. The following day a U-boat was seen on the surface and, just as quickly it seemed, it saw S-17 and submerged. S-17 followed suit and for a time there was a game of 'blind man's buff' as the two tried to pick up each other's echo. There was a scare on S-17 when something like a torpedo seemed to pass close by, but in the event nothing happened and the submarines lost each other.

Six months later, in August 1942, Klakring was sent to command *Guardfish* in the Pacific, his first assignment in the new battlefield being a solo attack, the first, on Honshu, one of the main islands of Japan. What made it even more difficult was that, this early in the war, American submarines were not fitted with radar, although *Guardfish* still recorded over 70 sight contacts.

When Klakring made his first attack it was the first episode in what became a long-drawn-out, boring story of malfunctioning torpedoes – he fired three at his target, heard three explosions, hoisted his periscope and saw his prey sailing serenely on its way.

A frustrated Krakling then saw three small vessels, so surfaced and sank two of them with gunfire. Then he found a 3,000-ton vessel outside Kinkasan Harbour and sank it, sending a shiver of fear among other ships in the harbour, which refused to leave.

More attacks, more failed torpedoes followed, but another success came a week later when his torpedoes blew up a vessel. Then followed a period when it seemed that all the Japanese patrol boats in the area were looking for him, luckily without success. There was, however, an incident which lifted the crew's morale – *Guardfish* was so close to the Japanese mainland that they were able to watch a horse race through the periscope. They even photographed it so that sceptics at home, when told the story, could see the proof, although there is no record that any member of the crew offered odds on any of the horses.

The submarine was awarded the Presidential Unit Citation, then Klakring's and *Guardfish*'s reputation received a further boost when patrolling off the harbour of Rabaul on the island of New Britain near Guadalcanal. They sank a destroyer whereupon Klakring decided to go into the harbour and have a look round. Having crept in he saw two groups of ships, but when he raised his periscope to fix his position for an attack, bombs rained down from aircraft which had spotted him so he decided that discretion was the better part of valour and withdrew.

Late in 1942, when the US Navy was planning the first full-scale carrier-air attack on the Japanese mainland, Klakring was put in charge of a seven-strong wolf pack assigned to patrol and clear a corridor through which the carrier force would pass. Bad weather dogged the operation and so did the Japanese, who threw aircraft and patrol boats into the area to make life impossible for the submarines. The operation was a failure, but it was valuable because it taught the Americans several lessons – in future operations they had to have better communications, better protection and more ammunition.

As an example of courage and tenacity of a high degree there can be few, if any, finer examples, than that of Cdr Boris Karnicki and the crew of the Polish submarine *Sokol*.

In the first four months of 1942 the island of Malta was under constant attack by German and Italian bombers, attacks that went on for more than 12 hours out of every 24. The submarine shore messdecks, officers' quarters and base hospital were totally demolished; most of the population were intent on staying in the rock shelters. Four submarines at the base were severely damaged and all the other boats were under orders to remain submerged during daylight hours, except for one at the base repair wharf.

The British U-class submarine *Sokol*, with a Polish captain and crew, had returned from patrol on 17 March to be greeted by yet another air raid. At 1600 hrs five heavy bombs fell within 30 yards of *Sokol* damaging battery cells, air and water pipes and gauges, and shifting torpedo warheads.

The following day, under continuous attack, the torpedoes were unloaded and the batteries tested. The next day the submarine was moved from the Lazaretto base to Grand Harbour, during its passage being attacked by two German fighters with cannon and machine guns.

On 20 March it was planned to change the damaged battery cells but because of considerable dockyard casualties, the dockyard workers refused to work during the continuous air raids, so the work could not be carried out. However, the captain and his crew did work during the raids over the next two days and repairs on No. 2 battery were completed. During the night *Sokol* returned to Lazaretto.

On 23 March there was a likelihood of even more trouble because a convoy was expected and sure enough, the next day Grand Harbour came under very heavy attack. The German bombers came in waves of 70 aircraft and every ship in the convoy was hit. Work in the dockyard came to a standstill, not least because the SS *Talbot*, carrying ammunition, torpedoes and bombs was on fire. Two days later the Germans turned their attention on the submarine base. The submarine P-39, lying in the same creek as *Sokol* had its back broken by a bomb which missed but exploded underneath it. Dive-bombers continued their relentless attack with about 15 bombs falling in the creek where the *Sokol* lay, including a 1,000-lb bomb which failed to explode.

There was a brief respite on 27 March because the weather was so bad that bombers could not operate, which meant a lot of work could be done on *Sokol*. By 30 March all work on the submarine was complete and it was moved to French Creek for degaussing (demagnetising) ready for a resumption of patrolling. But the heavy raids restarted with 40 bombers attacking French Creek, during which three one-ton bombs fell within 10 yards of *Sokol* damaging battery cells and filling the boat with chlorine gas. Repair work had to be carried out with the crew wearing gas masks or escape breathing equipment. All the damaged cells were removed but there was no power, no telephones, no workers in the dockyard and no tugs available to move *Sokol*.

On 1 April it was possible to move the submarine back to the dockyard to remove the damaged batteries, but work had to stop again when a series of air raids were directed at the submarine base, and all the crew was sent to the shelters. The following day all work was at a standstill again, and at a conference held by Commander Submarines it was decided that as the dockyard workers would not work at night and work was limited during the day, the batteries had to be removed by the crew and any volunteers willing to help. These came from military personnel on the island; no dockyard worker volunteered.

By 4 April the crew was once again able to get 31 cells out, but no power was available and no work in the dockyard was possible. When all the batteries had been repaired they had to be loaded again by the crew and volunteers. It was thought advisable that *Sokol* should be moved from the dockyard, camouflaged and tied up against the hull of the *Essex*, an 11,000-ton motor ship in Bighi Creek. But this had been spotted by German reconnaissance planes and during the afternoon bombs fell all around the *Essex*.

Undeterred, it was decided that *Sokol* should be moved again, back into the dockyard where the remaining 66 cells of Battery No. 1 were removed in $4\frac{1}{2}$ hours, thanks to help from the crew of P-39.

On 6 April *Sokol* was moved again, to Marsa Creek, where it was surrounded by barges, camouflaged and parked with its stern aground. But the Germans had watched this operation too and they plastered Marsa Creek with bombs sinking nine of the surrounding barges. On the following day another 12 barges were sunk, but no damage was sustained by the Polish submarine. When army experts were called in to perfect the camouflage, it proved to be a waste of time because on 8 April the camouflage was burned away by an attack by 300 bombers which destroyed all the buildings around the creek. Bombs fell within three to five yards of *Sokol*, which was heavily damaged with 400 holes in the casing and conning tower, including small holes in the pressure hull which was found to be leaking in several places; water and air pipes were badly ruptured.

It would be reasonable to think that the captain and crew, and anyone else with any common sense, would have given up at this stage, but not Karnicki. On 9 April the submarine was moved back to the *Essex* and camouflaged again. Although the batteries were not ready it was decided to replace the broken cells so that *Sokol* could at least submerge. That night it was transferred once again to the dockyard and 66 cells loaded into No. 1 battery; then back to the *Essex* and the camouflage.

Heavy raids on 10 and 11 April meant that nothing could be done, and on 12 April it became obvious that the Germans knew where the submarine was, for the attacks were restarted on the *Essex*, which caught fire. That night *Sokol* was moved back into the dockyard – it was almost like playing 'find the lady' – and No. 1 battery was completed and connected up. The submarine was then submerged at the bottom of Bighi Bay. That night it was moved to the Lazaretto base and spent the following day on the bottom of Marra Muscetto Harbour. Then on 15 April, at night, *Sokol* was taken to the dockyard for periscope adjustments following damage from a bomb splinter.

Trouble was not yet over for Commander Karnicki and his crew. While entering Grand Harbour *Sokol* fouled the booms and bumped heavily on rocks for about two hours during which it broke its starboard propeller.

On 16 April *Sokol* surfaced, entered the dockyard, loaded provisions and the next day sailed out on patrol, with one useable propeller, and a battery section which gave off an embarrassing amount of chlorine.

Sokol continued patrolling in the Mediterranean off Naples, East Calabria, Bari and Malta; while carrying out one of six patrols in the Aegean Sea it sank an anti-submarine patrol boat, an E-boat and three schooners, killing 200 Germans and taking no prisoners.

CHAPTER SIX

The Undaunted –
The Axis Powers

Doenitz, Von Arnauld, Hersing, Topp, Gysae,
Liebe, Bleichrodt, Merten, Hardegen, Emmermann,
Schultze, Luth, Brandi, Schutze, Lehmann-
Willenbrock.

I N a similar way to the British and Americans the Germans had their submarine heroes. The major difference in the Second World War was that the Germans had many more submarines and therefore many more submariners, partly because the U-boat campaign was a major part of the German offensive, and partly because their losses were so huge. More than 1,170 U-boats were commissioned; more than 28,000 of the 37,000 U-boat men lost their lives in action or were missing, while around 5,000 were taken prisoner.

In the First World War two U-boat commanders were outstanding – Arnauld de la Periere and Korvettenkapitan Otto Hersing, commander of U-21.

Lothar von Arnauld de la Periere, was the German ace of aces. Lothar von Arnauld, as he preferred to be called, sank a total of 200 ships and over 500,000 tons, a prodigious effort in the days when the size of ships could not be compared with those of later years.

By the Second World War tallies such as his were recognised by an award of a Knight's Cross of the Iron Cross, which became the highest award a U-boat commander and his crew could achieve. The Knight's Cross could be recommended for sinking 100,000 tons of shipping but it could also be awarded for a single outstanding action or a particularly successful patrol. Oak Leaves, Swords and Diamonds could be added for further achievements. For example, Lehmann-Willenbrock was awarded the Oak Leaves to his Knight's Cross for sinking 16 ships in 12 days. Altogether 29 U-boat commanders won the Knight's Cross with Oak Leaves, five had the Swords added and only two, Brandi and Luth, achieved the outstanding Diamonds.

Von Arnauld's great-grandfather, a French Protestant Huguenot soldier of fortune, gave his sword to Frederick the Great and founded a German family. He began his naval career as a torpedo officer on the famous battleship *Emden*, became aide-de-camp to Grand Admiral Tirpitz and took his first submarine command in January 1916.

In the days when submarine activity had moved temporarily into the Mediterranean and on his first patrol in U-35, von Arnauld sank 51 vessels, totalling 91,000, tons. His record cruise lasted just over three weeks from 26 July to 20 August 1916, during which he sank 54 ships. Returning to base he described the patrol as routine with no adventures, although this was not strictly true. For when attacking one convoy he had had to fight a tense battle with the British submarine chaser *Primola* before he was finally victorious and sank it.

Among his most important targets were the French troopships *Provence* and *Gallia*, the latter carrying 3,000 troops and artillery destined for Salonika. Although he had only one torpedo left von Arnauld attacked the zigzagging ship and fired at precisely the right moment; over 1,000 men died when she sank.

In the spring of 1918 Arnauld was given command of the new U-139, named *Commander Schweiger* in accordance with the practice of the day, after a U-boat commander who had gone down with his ship. Schweiger was the man who sank the *Lusitania*. It was a modern boat of nearly 2,000 tons, 400 feet long with two decks, two 15mm guns and four torpedo tubes, two in the bow and two in the stern. It had a surface speed of 13 knots and could dive in two minutes. It was in this boat that von Arnauld fought his last great battle of the war.

On 1 October 1918, off Cape Finisterre, on a dark and stormy night, he saw a tell-tale plume of smoke on the horizon. Keeping careful watch he saw the smudge develop into a ship, then several ships and eventually a large convoy escorted by two auxiliary cruisers.

U-139 closed up to attack, fired a salvo of torpedoes and then dived deep to avoid the expected counter-measures. Nothing happened, the torpedoes missed and it seems that no one in the convoy even noticed their tracks. So von Arnauld decided to attack with guns. He surfaced in the middle of the convoy and discovered that every one of its ships was equipped with at least one gun. He came under a hail of fire, so U-139 dived again and the escorts immediately hurled depth charges in every direction. Having waited until the sounds of battle had died down, he returned to periscope depth and saw the convoy disappearing in the distance.

U-139 gave chase and, when in range, fired shells at a steamer, recording some hits. An escorting auxiliary cruiser was quickly on the scene, attempting to ram the U-boat, but von Arnauld dived to avoid the ramming, and then began another torpedo attack. When it was impossible to miss he fired and blew up a ship, but was so close to it that when it sank it did so right on top of him. The German boat found itself being forced deeper and deeper as the wreck sank towards the bottom.

U-139's skipper ordered all ballast tanks to be blown but at first nothing happened, and the U-boat continued downwards. When it was almost too late the wreck above suddenly heeled over, freeing the U-boat which slid away at last. It then shot straight to the surface, where von Arnauld found that the upper structure had been almost completely destroyed and that his periscope was gone. Enemy ships were still in the area so the U-boat dived again until it was all clear. Undaunted by the lack of a periscope von Arnauld continued his patrol, attacking a Portuguese gun boat, which fought back with great ferocity before being sunk. He was still on patrol when the war ended and Germany surrendered.

On 27 February 1941, von Arnauld was reported 'killed in an accident' in Brest. It is believed he was still fighting the underwater war, directing U-boats from the French port, when it was bombed by the RAF, after it was reported that the cruiser *Hipper* was in harbour.

Korvettenkapitan Otto Hersing, as already mentioned, achieved fame and a place in submarine history by torpedoing the British light cruiser *Pathfinder* in 1914 – the first major warship to be sunk by a submarine's torpedo. Sent in November 1914 to cover the shipping lanes in the English Channel that were being used to supply the British Expeditionary Force in France, he intercepted the steamer *Malachite*. Following the then rules of war, he fired a shot across her bows to make her heave to. A U-boat commander was still under orders to find out what the ship was carrying before he could attack, and having confirmed that the *Malachite* carried a valuable cargo, he ordered the crew to abandon ship before sinking her using the deck gun. Three days later he sank the merchant vessel *Primo*. Although these attacks were nothing compared with what was to come, they had the desired effect of bringing home to the British that the sea, which they had dominated for so long, was no longer their exclusive property.

Hersing then proceeded to ram the message home by patrolling the Irish Sea where he had the nerve to bombard an airfield on England's north-western coast at Barrow. He then sailed southwards and sank a British collier, his actions being sufficient to close the important port of Liverpool for several days.

Hersing, as will by now be obvious, was a trail blazer. He was sent to the Austrian port of Cattari in the Mediterranean, first hugging the Danish and Norwegian coasts before swinging round the Orkney Islands and, then south to the coast of Spain where he met the supply ship *Marzala* and refuelled. Unfortunately for U-21 the fuel taken on board proved to be unsuitable for the submarine's engines, but despite this set-back Hersing decided to press on with his assignment.

On 5 May 1915 he passed through the Straits of Gibraltar, home ground for the Royal Navy, at night and on the surface. By morning

U-21 had broken through into the 'English lake' and although there was a moment of crisis when his fuel ran out this quickly passed when an Austrian destroyer came out of port and towed him in. Hersing then went on to emulate the British by joining in the Gallipoli campaign.

When he arrived on 25 May he was greeted by what, to a U-boat commander, would have been a glorious sight – a mass of British and French battleships lying at anchor. Unfortunately for Hersing his arrival was quickly spotted by the British trawler *Minoru* and other patrolling escorts. Undeterred he pressed home his attack, first sinking the battleship *Triumph* and then the battleship *Majestic*.

Now a national hero and awarded the Iron Cross – also awarded, incidentally, to every member of his crew – Hershing took U-21 through the Dardanelles to Constantinople to be warmly greeted by the Turks.

After these two pioneers from the First World War it is time to turn to the Third Reich, beginning with Cdr Eric Topp, aged 26, an ace U-boat commander who was most notable in that he sank the first US warship of the war.

Topp took command of U-57 in May 1940, but faced early difficulties when he was rammed by a Norwegian steamer in September while entering a lock in the Kiel Canal. Six men died and the submarine sunk, but it was later salvaged. After this sticky start he was assigned to U-552 and, based at St Nazaire, carried out a series of tough patrols in the North Atlantic, during which he sank 14 ships.

But that was only the overture to the main event. Sent to Canadian waters in December 1941, he sank his first ship there in January 1942, but experienced problems with his torpedoes, taking 13 torpedoes to sink two ships and miss a destroyer. Topp went home very angry.

In March he was off to North American waters again and quickly sank six ships, including five oil tankers, before he ran out of torpedoes. Already a holder of the coveted Knight's Cross, he was awarded the Oak Leaves and offered any assignment he wanted. He chose to remain in action at sea in the North Atlantic and had soon added more sinkings to his growing scorecard, although he endured further malfunctions. He enhanced his reputation as both a pack leader who could find and stay in contact with convoys, and as a destroyer of enemy ships.

In August 1942, he led an attack on convoy Outbound North 10 but was damaged by a British destroyer and had to withdraw home. On the way he was bombed and damaged in the Bay of Biscay, but managed to get back to base. The Crossed Swords were added to his Oak Leaves.

After April and May 1943, when the Germans lost 58 U-boats, the time had come for them to reconsider strategy and Eric Topp was one of the leading commanders who thought that the battle to sink as much Allied shipping as possible should end because of the appalling losses. Doenitz listened but had no choice in the matter, for Hitler demanded that it continue, no matter what the cost. In May 1943 Topp was assigned to command a training flotilla.

Thirty-year-old Robert Gysae, given his first patrol in the new U-98, sank two freighters, the first victims of an eventual total of 10 in the same U-boat. Gysae was assigned to be part of a hastily formed 'submarine curtain' which Doenitz threw round the battleship *Tirpitz* when it was being hounded by the British fleet, his role being to act as 'lookout' and guide other boats to the enemy. The operation, as history records, was a failure and the *Tirpitz* escaped up a Norwegian fjord. In March 1942 he was transferred to one of the new U-cruisers, U-177. On 10 November 1942, U-98, pride of the German Navy, was bombed off Cape St Vincent and sunk with all hands.

Gysae served on U-177 – a 1,600-ton boat with extra fuel tanks and a range of 24,000 miles at 12 knots submerged and a surface speed of 19 knots – in Southern African waters until November 1943 during which time he sank a further 17 ships. During this period he was injured in an Allied raid on Bremen and when he returned to his ship on crutches, the crew decided to paint some on the boat's conning tower as their emblem.

While on patrol off Mozambique Gysae sank the unescorted British troopship *Nova Scotia* which was homeward bound carrying

765 Italian civilian internees, 134 South African soldiers and nearly 900 passengers. He signalled Doenitz for instructions telling him that he had sunk the ship carrying 1,000 Italian civilians from Ethiopia, had two survivors on board but that some 400 survivors were still on rafts and boats. Doenitz replied that there should be no rescue attempts, that waging war came first and he was to continue on his patrol. He did, however, notify the Mozambique authorities who sent ships to the rescue. Only 192 survivors were picked up.

On his second trip to South Africa, Gysae created something of a precedent by carrying a new search device – a one-man, three-rotor, motorless helicopter which could be stowed in a deck canister, assembled in ten minutes and dismantled in five. The idea was that the helicopter was tethered to the U-boat by a 1,000ft cable on an air-powered winch giving the pilot a 25-mile all-round view. In case of trouble both helicopter and pilot were expendable. Neither the U-cruiser concept nor the helicopter proved very successful. The three U-cruisers sent on patrol sank only seven ships.

Gysae was given a staff appointment and was able to see out the war. Altogether he had sunk 139,000 tons of shipping, including one 10,000 tonner and was awarded the Knight's Cross.

Heinrich Liebe, the 31-year-old son of an army officer, got his commission in 1938 and joined the new U-38. He had an early shock in September 1939 while on patrol off Lisbon when he fired a warning shot across the bows of the British freighter *Manaar* with his 4.1-inch deck gun and the British ship fired back with a gun of a similar size. He dived U-38 and torpedoed his attacker, fearing that the *Manaar* was one of the dreaded 'Q' ships – merchant vessels armed with hidden guns.

Shortly afterwards he torpedoed the *Inverliffey*, a 9,500-ton tanker which exploded into a massive fireball. Despite the risk to his submarine, Liebe saved the crew by towing their lifeboats away from the blazing sea.

During his 21 months in command of U-38 he carried out ten patrols in the North Atlantic, Arctic, North West Approaches, Norway, south and west Ireland and west of Africa.

Heinrich Bleichrodt's big chance came after the wolf pack of which he was part had a poor time attacking a convoy and sank only 5 ships out of 53. Doenitz was not happy.

A few days later, the 30-year-old U-boat commander of U-30 intercepted another convoy and, on his own, sank four ships and an escort. He then attacked another convoy as part of a wolf pack and sank two more. Doenitz was much happier.

After a short spell on U-67 he was posted to U-109 in June 1940. Patrolling off Cape Hatteras on America's east coast, as part of the 'Mordbrenner' wolf pack of four U-boats he added five more ships to his growing score sheet. The group as a whole was not very successful and then U-109 suffered from mechanical problems and had to withdraw to make repairs while still at sea.

In January 1943 he was one of six boats sent to American east coast waters but only managed to record two ships sunk. His luck had not really changed by July when, diverted to the African Gold Coast, he sank two but missed another two.

Feeling tired from the strain of 18 months perpetually at sea, and with deteriorating health, Bleichrodt set off for the Bay of Biscay on yet another patrol. After clashing with some British destroyers he finally requested permission to abort the patrol. The reaction at Submarine Headquarters back in Germany was one of horror – this was just not done by U-boat commanders; he could be shot. His request was refused by Doenitz who understood the possible consequences; a second request was also turned down. Such was Bleichrodt's state of mind that his second in command decided to take command and did abort against orders. Bleichrodt was taken home, hospitalised and then assigned to a training command.

The 35-year-old Karl Frederick Merten started uncertainly in U-68 in June 1941. When tracking a convoy he was chased away by a British corvette and then, on his first patrol in the South Atlantic in September when his companion Hessler in U-67 had four malfunctioning torpedoes, he thought he had sunk two ships and damaged a tanker, but later investigation showed he had only damaged a freighter.

He took part in a wolf-pack attack on another convoy of 11 ships. They sank six and after a rendezvous with another U-boat and reloading with torpedoes and stores, life got really exciting. He was involved in a vicious battle with the British submarine *Clyde,* captained by David Ingram, in which U-111 was also involved. After a skirmish with the British submarine, U-111 dived to avoid a possible ramming, and so the *Clyde* turned on U-68 and fired six torpedoes. Fortunately a lookout on the U-boat saw them coming, and Merten was able to take avoiding action by turning U-68 to steer a parallel course before crash-diving.

Still in the South Atlantic, and after being resupplied by another U-boat, he bravely took U-68 into Jamestown Harbour at St Helena and sank an 8,000-ton tanker. While being revictualled yet again by the supply ship *Python* he was almost caught on the surface by the British cruiser *Dorsetshire.* With no time to trim the boat he carried out an emergency dive which sent U-68 out of control, sinking too steeply and too fast. After a frantic struggle Merten only just managed to avoid a disaster. The cruiser, which had already sunk the German raider *Atlantis*, refrained from attacking the *Python* because there was a danger that she might be carrying British prisoners of war.

U-68 and U-A, commanded by Carl Eckermann, then restarted their attack on the *Dorsetshire* but were driven off by heavy fire. The crew of the *Python* however, terrified by the close presence of an enemy heavy cruiser, decided to scuttle their vessel. The two U-boats surfaced to rescue the survivors of the *Atlantis* and the *Python*, U-68 taking on 100, U-A another 100 while 214 were put in lifeboats and set out to try and make the 5,000 mile journey back to France; happily for them, U-124 and U-129 came to their rescue and took all 214 on board. It was the proud boast of the Germans that not one of the 414 survivors from the two German ships lost their lives. The story became a legend in the submarine service.

Merton was next despatched to Freetown in Sierra Leone and Lagos in Nigeria, where he sank several ships, and then to the Panama Canal area. There he nearly met his destruction when he fired on a ship carrying 5,000 tons of dynamite. It exploded and U-68 was literally blown out of the water before crashing back into the sea with a shuddering impact, but little damage was done and he was able to withdraw.

The peripatetic Merten was then sent to South Africa where he sank another six ships – a total of 36,000 tons in 24 hours.

Richard Hardegen began as a naval aviator, but when he was hurt in a crash he hid his injury so that he could join the submarine service. Having qualified, he was very soon given U-123 to command, and it became one of the most successful U-boats in the Atlantic, enduring many counter-attacks including one in which the escorts plastered U-123 with 126 depth charges.

Although dedicated to his work he was not that enthusiastic about obeying orders to the letter. On patrol as part of the 'Schlagetod' wolf pack he sighted a convoy, reported it, and was then ordered to return to his patrol area, but he ignored the order and damaged a White Star liner before following instructions.

Hardegen again ignored an order, or 'showed initiative', whichever way you look at it, when told to investigate a broken-down vessel, provided he was not more than 150 miles from it. He was, in reality, nearly 300 miles away, but set off to investigate. When he arrived on the scene he found that the crippled ship was surrounded by escorts so he had second thoughts about an attack. The delay and waste of time was not appreciated by his superiors.

Later, as part of a group of three U-boats, U-123 moved to America's east coast, off Long Island, New York where Hardegen sank a tanker in shallow waters and then spent 24 hours on the seabed resting his crew and saving fuel. The next day he took U-123 into the outer reaches of New York harbour, so close that they could see the lights of Manhattan. He gave most of the crew the opportunity to see New York by night, through the periscope.

After a short rest U-123 was again sent back to American waters as part of a 26-strong group and, of course, sank more ships, although Hardegen very nearly came unstuck when he attacked what he thought was an innocent freighter. It turned out to be one of the notorious 'Q' ships – freighters with hidden guns and a Royal Navy team on board – which fought back forcing him to temporarily withdrew before returning to sink the ship.

At the end of this patrol, his 27th, he left U-123 for a post in training command.

Carl Emmermann, aged 27, had a tough baptism in submarines as First Officer of U-A when it was enthusiastically attacked by a British destroyer and other escorts. He was partly responsible for its successful escape by suggesting to his commanding officer that the best way to get away was to surface at night and creep quietly away using the boat's electric motors.

On patrol off Cape Town, as commander of U-172, he took part with Merten in what was supposed to be a surprise attack on British ships inside the harbour. Creeping in to avoid mines which had been laid earlier by his own countrymen, he was disappointed to find that it was almost empty and that it was brightly illuminated by searchlights and surrounded by radar stations, making a surface attack impossible.

He reported this to Doenitz who, determined to surprise the British, told Emmermann to wait 24 hours to see if more ships came in. It was an impossible situation for Emmermann so he claimed the signal was difficult to read, and thought it told him to use his own discretion. He did not wait 24 hours but sank a freighter on its way out and another on its way in, for which he was severely reprimanded for making a premature attack and losing the advantage of surprise.

While on patrol off America, Emmermann and U-172 went to the aid of U-508 which had been badly damaged by air attack and was unable to submerge. Despite the obvious dangers, he stood by for several days while U-508 made temporary repairs to enable it to limp home.

During this period of hectic activity Emmermann was awarded the Knight's Cross; when he finally arrived home he was given command of a training flotilla and instructed to develop tactics for a new type of U-boat.

Herbert Schultze was one of Germany's leading U-boat aces, being the one with the highest number of ships sunk, 54, and the greatest tonnage, 320,429. He was also an officer and a gentleman (see page 60). He built up his amazing record during twelve patrols in the North Atlantic, Norway and Shetlands, off Spain, north of Ireland and in the North Western Approaches, becoming a national hero when he had sunk 12 ships totalling 77,500 tons. He was then despatched to England's south coast where he laid mines and sunk four more vessels which took him to what was for Doenitz the magic total of 100,000 tons.

He continued to wreak havoc among Allied shipping, but he also had his moments of bad luck – for example, he had the British battleship *Warspite* clearly in his sights when his torpedoes failed him. He took part in Doenitz's great attempt to protect the battleship *Bismark* by setting U-boat traps to catch the Allied hunting fleet, using 15 U-boats. But by June 1941 both he, the crew and his submarine were tired and worn out and this was recognised at U-boat HQ, so he was ordered to Germany to take up an appointment as a flotilla commander. On the way home, of course, he sank four more ships.

Wolfgang Luth recorded 47 ship sinkings totalling a massive 221,981 tons. He and U-181 also made the longest submarine patrol of the war – 203 days at sea between March and December 1943.

His actions towards survivors was enigmatic. On 26 May 1943 he sank the 1,600-ton Swedish steamer *Sicilia* after stopping to examine her papers and helping the crew to depart safely. On 18 July he sank the British collier *Empire Lake* and left the survivors clinging to bits of floating wreckage. A month later he sent a British merchantmen to the bottom, helped the wounded survivors and, when he had left the scene, signalled their position to Allied authorities in Mauritius so they could be rescued.

This book is full of sad stories of submarine heroes of all nations who lost their lives as a result of enemy action, but the death of Wolfgang Luth is probably one of the saddest. On 13 May 1945 as commandant of a Navy Cadet school at Flensburg-Murvic, he failed to respond to a challenge by one of his own sentries and was shot dead.

Albrecht Brandi, aged 28, and on his maiden patrol in command of

U-617, made a good start when he sank three ships as part of a wolf-pack attack on a convoy in which the other 20 U-boats only destroyed two ships.

Brandi's was one of five boats sent by Doenitz to reinforce the Mediterranean group when the Allies launched Operation Torch, the invasion of North Africa. He made a number of claims about hitting Allied warships, but none of them were confirmed and the operation to thwart the Allies failed. Then on his second Mediterranean patrol he claimed eight ships sunk but again they were not confirmed.

For his work on U-617 he was awarded his Knight's Cross followed by the Oak Leaves. In 1943 when the future of the U-boat campaign was being discussed by the hierarchy he and Luth were two of the few commanders who believed the campaign should be continued with enthusiasm. Although a number of his claims for sinking warships could not be confirmed, there was no doubt about his destruction of an American destroyer escort off Gibraltar, at a time when the Allies were busy invading Italy in 1943. Later U-617 was attacked by aircraft and escorts off Oran and ran aground before being destroyed by gunfire, but Brandi was taken ashore and interned in Cadiz. He was released in due course and given command of U-380, but that did not change his luck. The submarine was caught in Toulon harbour in an air attack and badly damaged, then destroyed in a further air raid.

Undeterred, Brandi moved to U-967 and had the Swords added to his Knight's Cross. After an attack on a convoy he sent the American destroyer escort *Fechteler* to the bottom and the Diamonds were added to his Knight's Cross in November 1944.

Life was no holiday for 25-year-old Viktor Schutze and the crew of U-25 patrolling off northern Norway early in 1940. The long days and four- or five-hour nights meant that there was little time for surfacing and recharging batteries; this had to be done largely in daylight, hopefully using bad weather under which the submarine could hide from enemy aircraft.

An attack on a British destroyer had not helped the crew's morale when the torpedoes proved to be faulty. A second attack also failed for the same reason when U-25 ventured up a Norwegian Fjord to attack British warships – and a third one.

A change of boats, to U-103, changed Schutze's luck for a time when he sank a 7,000-ton Norwegian tanker, then another merchant ship. On one occasion Schutze tried a 'down-the-throat' (head-on) shot, later adopted by US submarine commanders, but the torpedo ricocheted off the ship's hull. After sinking a British freighter, the last of three ships from one convoy consigned to the deep, Schutze found that one of their lifeboats had capsized. He rescued the survivors, righted their boat and stocked it with food and water, some spirits and cigarettes and then set them on course for Freetown, before going on to sink three more ships.

By mid-May 1941 his score was 12 ships and 60,000 tons, but he then went on a 32-day patrol and returned without a single success, although he eventually sank 35 ships during his time as commander of U-103, ending up as the fourth most successful U-boat commander behind Kretschmer, Luth and Prien. He took command of U-404 for a short time before being sent to command a new training flotilla.

Heinrich Lehmann-Willenbrock is the man on whom the author Lothar-Gunther Buchheim based the U-boat commander in his exceptional book *Das Boot*, the basis of the outstanding television drama series. In December 1940 he and U-96 sailed on weather reporting duty in the North West Approaches, but while on their way came across a big in-bound convoy and before long he had torpedoed and sunk a 10,000-ton British freighter.

A U-boat commander could spend days, often weeks, without sight of the enemy or without a success. Sometimes, as in this case, they had the luck to find a convoy when not even looking for one. The same kind of luck could hit the whole U-boat fleet at the same time, which meant flush periods, described as 'Happy Times', when they sank almost everything in sight. They also had 'Unhappy Times', such as the first few months of 1941 when bad weather, which stopped convoys forming and sailing, played a major part in spoiling their operations. But Lehmann-Willenbrock, after sinking five ships on his first patrol in U-96, sailed from Lorient at the beginning of January 1941, and was back in 14 days having sunk two more ships totalling 29,000 tons. His luck continued the following month when, operating alone, he sank several ships and was awarded his Knight's Cross for reaching the magical 100,000 tons.

His luck was not a permanent feature, however. Finding a convoy of five ships he attacked and sank one carrying troops. The response of the escorts was a total of 26 depth charges dropped on him with a high degree of accuracy, forcing Lehmann-Willenbrock to abort his patrol because of serious damage.

Repaired, U-96 was soon back in action off Greenland as part of a wolf pack. He spotted a convoy and immediately called up his colleagues, who caused considerable damage.

Again on his own, he found a 34-strong convoy with 6 escorts. Although weather conditions were not in his favour, the sea was rough and the night sky was clear with a full moon, but he decided to attack on the surface. He fired at two ships, sinking one, and when the escorts pounced on him he dived to safety.

He was less successful with his next venture, being caught on the surface by enemy aircraft and almost bombed into submission. Although badly damaged, he managed to limp back to France.

Awarded the Oak Leaves to his Knight's Cross at the end of 1941, he was promoted to command the 9th Combat Flotilla. His total number of ships sunk was 25 with a tonnage of 183,000 tons, placing him sixth in the list of the top ten U-boat commanders. He slightly blotted his copybook in February 1942, however, when, patrolling off Cape Hatteras, he sank two more ships, both Brazilian neutrals. Brazil was not happy and there was a flurry of diplomatic activity.

When, in June 1943, it seemed that the U-boats were losing the war at sea Lehmann-Willenbrock was one of the flotilla commanders who met Grand Admiral Doentiz to tell him so. Doenitz was forced by Hitler to continue the U-boat war at full spate.

Commanding the 9th Flotilla based in the ruins of Brest, Lehman-Willenbrock was ordered to evacuate to Norway and after a dreadful 45-day journey thanks to the weather and the enemy, he arrived safely in Bergen where it was found that his boat, U-256, was badly damaged and beyond saving. It was decommissioned and Lehman-Willenbrock was eventually taken prisoner.

CHAPTER SEVEN

War in the Pacific

Pearl Harbor, the pioneers,
'Down the throat', 'Up the kilt', the patrol
of the USS Bowfin, *the 'tanker killer', wolf packs,*
Japanese bombard the US, the Hashimoto incident.

WHEN Japan made the fatal mistake of attacking Pearl Harbor on 7 December 1941 and dragging the world's greatest industrial nation into the war, the United States only had 55 submarines in commission, from old short-range boats through minelayers to the latest fleet submarines. One of the major problems facing the fleets engaged in the Pacific war was the huge distances that had to be travelled. It took many days for US submarines, travelling on the surface as far as possible, to reach Japanese waters.

Built in 1938 the fleet submarines displaced some 1,459 tons, with eight torpedo tubes, four forward tubes, four astern, and a 3-inch deck gun. They could carry enough fuel for the long patrols necessary in the Pacific and their diesel-electric propulsion gave them a surface speed of 20 knots. The hull was strengthened to dive to 400 feet. Both boats and crews were highly efficient, sinking an average of 50,000 tons each month in 1943 and boosting this to a massive 200,000 tons a month in the first half of 1944. After that there was not very much Japanese merchant shipping left to sink. Their record against the Japanese Navy was also outstanding, sinking 1 battleship, 8 aircraft carriers, 15 cruisers, 42 destroyers and 25 submarines. By contrast, the United States lost a total of

55 boats, the equivalent of one for every state in the Union, many of them simply disappearing into the vast wastes and deeps of the Pacific Ocean.

When battle commenced following the attack on Pearl Harbor almost everything the submarine service did was an historical first. Lt Cdr S.P. Mosley's *Pollack* pioneered the night periscope and the night surface attack. Chasing an enemy destroyer he began with a daylight surface approach but then decided to submerge for a periscope attack, as at first he found he could not see the target sufficiently clearly to make an accurate estimation of course and range. He fired two torpedoes but missed with both. A few days later he stalked a Japanese freighter in a daytime submerged approach but again missed. Dogged determination being his by-word, he carried out a night surface attack on another freighter and sank it.

Gudgeon, captained by Lt Cdr Grenfell, created history by becoming the first US submarine to sink an enemy warship (see page 195), while *Plunger* had the dubious honour of being the object of the first depth-charge attack on a US submarine after attacking a Japanese destroyer, which resulted in several useful discoveries. First that Japanese underwater listening gear was highly efficient, that their sonar was on a par with American equipment, that Japanese depth charges had an explosive power of around 230 lb and that Japanese destroyers carried some 30 of them – not really the sort of discovery you want to make about your enemy. On the other hand, *Plunger* not only proved that it could take it, but that it could hand it out, by sinking a Japanese freighter using the traditional daytime submerged attack.

American heroes have often had a distinctive ability upon which their reputations were built. In the Wild West, for example, it was 'the fastest draw'. In the submarine service during the war in the Pacific the marine equivalent was 'down-the-throat' torpedo attacks – meeting the enemy head on and firing a salvo of torpedoes at the last moment. This gave the target vessel almost no chance of escape and as the Japanese flatly refused, in the early days, to adopt the convoy system for their merchant shipping, the method was very successful.

Tradition dictated that the best defence against a head-on attack by the enemy was to dive deep and wait. It was also thought to be much easier to hit a target broadside on rather than when it was a narrow target heading straight for you. Then it was thought that if a fan-shaped salvo of torpedoes was fired at an oncoming vessel, whatever avoiding action he took, he would be hit by at least one. Several submarine commanders had, in fact, attempted the procedure but failed to make a hit. The first successful attack was made by Lt Cdr J.W. 'Red' Coe in *Skipjack*, with a reputation for being an outstanding captain who could think and act quickly.

In May 1942, on a clear moonlit night which discouraged a surface attack, he sighted a Japanese freighter ahead of him but, in an attempt to draw level for a broadside shot, he underestimated his speed and found himself some 300 yards ahead of the enemy vessel. It was approaching at 11 knots so he didn't have much time in which to respond. Using the submarine's Torpedo Data Computer he found he just had time to set up the firing procedure, decided to go ahead and fired three torpedoes, one of which struck a fatal blow on the freighter.

The procedure was followed by Lt Cdr E.T. Sands in *Sawfish* on its third patrol off Nagasaki when he spotted a small convoy escorted by a single destroyer. As he was about to attack the largest freighter, the whole convoy altered course because the presence of a submarine had been detected. The destroyer meanwhile stayed on its course heading directly at the submerged submarine. Sands decided on a 'down-the-throat' attack and fired four torpedoes with a one degree spread. Twenty-five seconds later there was suddenly a massive explosion. He thought his torpedoes had prematurely exploded, but there was no immediate counter-attack An hour later, when he decided to surface, he was just in time to see the stern of the destroyer disappear into the ocean.

Whether or not it was a question of 'one-upmanship' (probably not), Lt Cdr Dave White of *Plunger* had earlier invented another type of attack which he called 'up-the-kilt'. This, a shot from astern was not as likely to be spotted as one from straight ahead.

White had seen a convoy and decided to attack the largest ship with four torpedoes, all of which missed for one reason or another. Night was about to fall and, as there was a strong moon, he felt that if he surfaced the submarine would present a clear silhouette. He decided, therefore, to chase the freighter and reloaded his forward tubes. Slowly he crept up behind the target and from a range of 400 yards fired one torpedo which hit the stern and blew it up. He then turned his attention to the other ships, sank one, missed the second through a faulty torpedo, and damaged the third. Therefore, it was generally agreed that a rear attack was feasible and from then on the Japanese kept one eye over their shoulder.

In the early days of the Pacific War, when submarine warfare was still at the low point of the learning curve, and based on traditional precepts, most submarines spent the daylight hours submerged. There were plenty of potential targets but they were nearly all small vessels such as trawlers, fishing boats, sampans – none of them really worth a torpedo. It eventually dawned on higher authority that these small vessels may not be what they seemed – innocent ships going about their unimportant business. They could, in fact, be lookouts or anti-submarine pickets.

The discovery called for a change of tactics. Attacking these vessels with deck or machine guns would achieve two important objectives: it would remove positive observers and pickets; and would be a boost for the submarine crews, thus enabling them to take offensive action and attack the enemy.

Lt Cdr Bruton and *Greenling* were the first team to adopt the new tactics when he fired a salvo of torpedoes, which failed to function, at a Japanese freighter. Angry and frustrated, he decided to surface and follow the ship. It was a moonlit night so visibility was reasonable, and lookouts on the Japanese ship sighted the submarine which was then fired upon. When in range Bruton fired six shots which straddled the Japanese ship. The duel continued for some time and ended in stalemate but, four days later, he fired a single shot at another freighter, which hit and sank it.

When America was drawn into the war, only a few submarines had air research radar which, as its name implies, was purely for the detection of aircraft. The first set of underwater equipment was taken into action by Lt Cdr Taylor in *Haddock*, but it was not until the summer of 1942 that submarines were fitted with radar that could locate surface vessels and determine their direction and range. Its arrival facilitated a blockade of Japanese home waters with a necklace of submarines posted around the approaches to the Empire. They included *Pompana* with Lt Cdr W.H. Thomas, *Growler* commanded by Lt Cdr Howard Gilmore, *Narwhal* with Lt Cdr C.W. Wilkins, and *Guardfish* commanded by Lt Cdr Thomas B. Klakring.

In August 1942 Taylor in *Haddock,* using the underwater equipment for almost the first time, tracked a Japanese freighter and sank it. From that moment the fate of the Japanese merchant fleet was sealed.

For a long period early in the Pacific War, Japan's rapid advance through the Pacific islands meant the South China Sea was almost out of bounds to the US submarine service. There was in any case a lot of work to be done elsewhere, there was a shortage of torpedoes and the long distances that had to be travelled meant that there were only sporadic infiltrations into areas dominated by the enemy – just enough to remind Japan that there was another presence. However, it soon became clear that more concentrated efforts had to be made to disrupt Japanese merchant shipping routes there.

On 1 September 1943 *Bowfin* commanded by Lt Cdr W.T. Griffith was sent to reconnoitre the area and sank a couple of small ships without any drastic reaction.

Of one thing a sailor can be sure. When the weather is at its worst, and thoughts of home and comfort are foremost in the mind, that is the time to be most alert to danger and opportunity.

It was on just such a night when *Bowfin's* radar picked up several 'blips'. Thought at first to be a group of small islands, there was a rapid change of mind when the submarine was almost rammed by a huge tanker, and five ships were suddenly identified on the radar screen. Griffith did not hesitate and fired three torpedoes at the leading vessel. One hit and disintegrated the bow of the enemy ship, the second torpedo struck her amidships so that she veered sharply and almost struck *Bowfin*. A second merchantman was also damaged and Griffith finished her off with a torpedo.

Looking for the rest of the convoy *Bowfin* came across a 5,000-ton freighter which he sank the next day. Shortly afterwards *Bowfin* received a signal from another submarine indicating that there was a second convoy in the vicinity. It comprised five ships which was quickly reduced to four after *Bowfin* attacked. Four minutes later Griffith put another ship out of action, wallowing in heavy seas, but quickly found himself under fire from the 5-inch gun of another merchant vessel which hit *Bowfin*'s superstructure – two torpedoes soon ended that aggressive vessel's activities. With only two torpedoes left Griffith targeted the largest vessel still afloat, but one torpedo exploded prematurely and this deflected the second.

The result of this frenetic and successful patrol was 12 ships totalling some 30,000 tons sunk in the region. Not a bad 'reconnaissance' patrol.

The US submarine *Jack* joined the Pacific fleet early in 1943 and her skipper, Lt Cdr T.M. Dykers, was inordinately proud of her and her state-of-the-art equipment. Immediately he was able to demonstrate by sinking 16,000 tons of enemy shipping. But like many other submarine captains, Dykers found a successful first patrol was almost invariably followed by a complete failure. It was as if the 'Powers that Be' were proving that it wasn't that easy.

Sent to Fremantle, Australia, to join the south-west Pacific force *Jack* was assigned to the South China Sea. There his lookouts picked up an object on the horizon, quickly identified as an oil tanker. Hearts began to beat faster when a second one came into view, and even faster when a third joined them. Crew members were beginning to doubt their own powers of observation and sanity when a fourth and a fifth appeared.

The tankers were sailing serenely and without a care in the world in two lines – one of four ships, the other of one tanker and three escorts. Christmas had come early!

Dykers decided to concentrate on the tankers and by four o'clock in the morning was in position to attack, lining the *Jack* up so that the silhouettes of the four targets overlapped. He fired a spread of three torpedoes at one tanker as its silhouette overlapped with the second, then fired another torpedo at the last tanker in the line, which hit its target and the enemy vessel blew up. Two of the other torpedoes hit something but the smoke from the first obscured the view.

The sight of a Japanese destroyer racing towards him firing her guns frantically persuaded Dykers to withdraw and move to another position to attack again. When dawn broke he saw four tankers moving together slowly but, bafflingly, with no escorts in sight; so he put the mystery to one side and fired another four torpedoes from the stern tubes at two tankers whose silhouettes were in juxtaposition. Two hit the leading tanker and one hit the other; 15,000,000 gallons of fuel went up and two tankers went down.

After an hour submerged Dykers surfaced to find only two tankers, one stationary with an escort, the other fleeing into the distance, so he set off in pursuit of the second tanker and soon caught up with it, firing three torpedoes. But his luck had run out – one torpedo missed, one failed to run and the third went astray astern of the tanker. Nevertheless it came as something of a surprise when the tanker opened up with its 5-inch gun but, undeterred, Dykers once again fired a salvo of four torpedoes, three of which hit their target, blowing it up.

Despite his amazing success he was disappointed that he could not find the last remaining tanker and complete the set.

American submarines had to travel huge distances to get to the main battle area – it is, for example, 3,400 miles from the US submarine base on Hawaii to Japan, and 6,000 miles from the base at San Diego on the American mainland. A submarine going on patrol in the Sea of Japan would sail on a 52-day voyage and spend only eight days in the patrol area. Added to this was the fact that the Japanese did not, and probably could not, go in for the huge convoys used by the Allies in the Atlantic.

In 1943 when the American attack on Japanese shipping began in earnest their submarines worked alone, but in September that year they started adopting the 'wolf-pack' technique used so successfully by German U-boats in the Atlantic. The wolf-pack idea had occurred to the Americans early in the war but, as with the Germans, a lack of submarines and difficulties with torpedoes made it impossible. When they did get round to it they chose a different approach from the Germans which was sensible in view of the distances involved. A group of three or four submarines, it was decided, would patrol together controlled by a senior officer using Very High Frequency radio, which the Japanese, at that time, could not intercept. The patrols were to concentrate in areas known to be widely used by Japanese shipping.

Rewards from this new strategy were slow in coming, with little success from the first two wolf packs. But as the Japanese adopted the convoy system more and more, the number of wolf packs increased, and rewards quickly followed. One pack sank 35,000 tons of shipping in one convoy when it was found that the best method was to allow submarines to attack individually with only the broadest of directions being given. A submarine sighting a convoy would alert its companions and then shadow the convoy. After attacking, submarines would use their surface speed to get ahead and prepare to attack again.

Before long the practice of having an independent senior officer in charge of a group was revised when it was decided that a commander in one of the submarines in the group would be more efficient.

One of these groups, led by Commander G.R. Donahu and nicknamed 'Donk's Devils', set a wolf-pack record working in a patrol area called 'Convoy College'. In 15 days, between 25 August and 8 September 1944, the group comprising *Picadu*, *Redfish* and *Spadefish* sank 13 ships, totalling 64,448 tons.

One of the most spectacular operations carried out by US submarines, 'Operation Barney', came towards the end of the war and undoubtedly made an important contribution towards shattering Japanese morale. The aim of the operation was to break into the well-defended Sea of Japan, right into the enemy's 'front garden', and sink as many ships as possible.

Nine submarines were chosen for the attack and, as is the way with the flamboyant Americans, the group was nicknamed 'Hydeman's Hellcats', after their leader Cdr E.T. Hydeman. The nine submarines were divided into three groups of three boats – 'Hydeman's Hellcats' with Hydeman himself in *Sea Dog*, Cdr E.H. Steinmetz in *Crevalle* and Cdr W.J. Germerhausen in *Spadefish*; 'Riser's Bobcats' led by Cdr R.D. Rise in *Flyingfish* with Cdr A.K. Tyree in *Bowfin* and Cdr R.C. Latham in *Tinosa*; and finally, 'Pierce's Polecats' led by Cdr G.E. Pierce in *Tunny*, Cdr R.B. Lynch in *Skate* and Cdr L.L. Edge in *Bonefish*.

The flotilla left the submarine base on the island of Guam on 27 May 1945 and headed north for the Taushima Strait which separates South Korea and the Japanese island of Kyushu, around 100 miles wide at its narrowest. On the way there *Tinosa* deviated slightly to pick up the crew of an American B-29 bomber which had crashed 18 miles north-east of the island of Safu Gan, but apart from that the journey was made without incident. Crossing the East China Sea and passing through the heavily-mined straits between Korea and the island of Tsushima, they arrived safely in the Sea of Japan. The Americans were able to negotiate the minefield largely with thanks to special equipment which could 'sense' objects in their path, one example of the technical superiority that contributed greatly to their ultimate victory over Japan. As this also included shoals of fish, life on board the submarine could, at times, be extremely exciting.

The 'Hellcats' were in the north-west of Sea of Japan near Honshu Island, the *Sea Dog*, *Crevalle* and *Spadefish* working from Wakassa Wan to Hokkaido. The 'Polecats' were given the area in the south-eastern waters with *Tunny* even venturing right into the harbours of Etomo Ko and Uppuri Wan, where it had an inconclusive fight with two destroyers. *Skate* was even more successful, catching the unsuspecting Japanese submarine I-222 on the surface and sinking it. While its colleagues were enjoying themselves *Bonefish* was sinking two large merchantmen. In the western part of the Sea the 'Bobcats' were also creating havoc with *Flyingfish* and *Bowfin* sinking two vessels each while *Tinosa*, in Korean waters, destroyed four.

For 12 days the flotilla carried out its programme of death and destruction and when it had completed its work 27 vessels totalling over 57,000 tons had been sent to the bottom, including one submarine.

It was planned that the flotilla should leave the Sea of Japan on 24 June after a rendezvous at an assembly point in the La Perouse Strait, but when they met at the agreed time *Bonefish* was missing. The flotilla departed at the scheduled time leaving *Tunny* to wait in case *Bonefish* turned up needing help. It waited in vain for two more days and then returned home. On 18 June *Bonefish*, on its eighth patrol, rendezvoused with *Tunny* and Commander Edge requested permission to patrol Toyama Wan Bay submerged in daylight. Permission was given and *Bonefish* sailed off never to be seen again. It was learned later that Japanese anti-submarine surface vessels had attacked a submarine on the day *Bonefish* disappeared, shortly after it had torpedoed a 5,500-ton vessel, *Konzan Maru*. The Japanese attack took place in roughly the same area in which *Bonefish* was working, it had to be assumed that this was how it met its end, becoming the last American submarine to be sunk during the Pacific War.

During the 12-day attack the largest Japanese ship to be destroyed was the 6,892-ton *Oshikayama* – by the *Bonefish*. Thus ended an episode which confirmed beyond doubt the superiority of the American submarine in the Pacific. It had been a long, hard battle.

The Japanese were not too concerned about keeping accurate records of what happened to their merchant shipping fleet during the war, so when the conflict was over and Japanese papers were examined there was nothing to show how many ships were sunk or damaged by the amazing attack by *Barb* in the East China Sea in February 1945 (see Chapter 12).

The stories recounted in this chapter and in Chapters 4 and 5 testify to the patience, skill and fortitude of their commanders and crews.

As Ernest J. King, chief of the US Naval Staff, said: 'United States submarines played an important role in bringing the Japanese to submission. Sixty-three per cent of Japanese ships over 1,000 tons were sunk by submarines; the remainder by other armed forces.'

CHAPTER EIGHT

France, Russia, Italy and Japan

The tragedy of the French, the failure of the Russians,
the daring of the Italians. The dismal story of the Japanese.

Bᴿᴵᴛᴵꜱʜ, American and German submarines loom largest in the
story of the Second World War, but the parts played by submarines of other major combatants must not be forgotten.

The French fleet was one of the biggest and best equipped in the
world. At the outbreak of the war it included 5 battleships, 2 aircraft carriers, 15 cruisers, 32 super destroyers (or small cruisers),
44 destroyers and 59 submarines.

When France finally capitulated to the German military machine,
and the armistice was signed, Article 8 of the agreement declared:

The French war fleet, with the exception of that part permitted to the
French Government for the protection of French interests in its colonial
empire, is to be assembled in ports to be specified and disarmed under
German or Italian control . . . The German Government solemnly declares
to the French Government that it does not intend to use for its own
purposes in the war the French fleet which is in ports under German
control, with the exception of those units needed for coastal patrol and
minesweeping. Furthermore, it solemnly and expressly declares that it has
no intention of raising any claim to the French fleet at the time of the
conclusion of the peace. With the exception of that part of the French
Fleet, still to be determined, which is to represent French interests in the

colonial empire, all war vessels which are outside French territorial waters
are to be recalled to France.

It is hardly surprising that the British gave little credence to the
promises made in the convention.

On 21 June 1940, the French battleship *Courbet,* a destroyer
and three submarines were at Portsmouth, and a destroyer and
two submarines at Plymouth. There were also a large number of
smaller ships at both ports. British Admirals were instructed to
'grant all facilities to French ships for their departure to North
Africa' where a large proportion of the French fleet was based.
The following day that order was countermanded and an appeal
was made to French Naval C-in-C Admiral Darlan, pointing out
the vital importance of not allowing the fleet to fall into enemy
hands, and requesting he put it under the control of the Royal
Navy.

There was little doubt in the minds of the British Government
that if the Germans, who were expected to attempt the invasion of
Britain at any moment, were reinforced with French ships, the outcome would be disastrous for Britain. The French, on the other hand,
were in a difficult position trying to get the best armistice they could
and were fully aware that their fleet was a very powerful bargaining
tool.

On 2 July the British gave the French an ultimatum and the French
fleet at Oran and Mers-el-Kebir was given four choices: sail their
ships to British harbours and continue the fight against the Germans;
sail their ships to British ports from which the crews would be
repatriated where desired; sail their ships with reduced crews to
French ports in the West Indies; or scuttle their ships. At about the
same time the Germans made their demands: all French ships must
return to France immediately or 'the entire terms of the armistice
will be reconsidered'.

As far as the British were concerned, time had run out and it was
decided that 'Operation Catapult' should be put into action; this
included the takeover of all French ships in British ports.

When the Armistice was signed there were around 20,000 French
sailors, 1,200 of them on ships in British ports, but only a few of

them joined the Free French Naval Force. Among the French submarines to join the FFNF in its early stages were *Narval* and *Rubis*. Two others, apart from *Surcouf* (see Chapter 12), eventually went back into service with the Royal Navy after maintenance and repair.

On 8 August 1940, Churchill issued a directive emphasising the importance of the Vichy port of Dakar and the ships lying in harbour there, ordering that Operation Menace, either to destroy these ships or immobilise them, should be put into action.

When the British force approached Dakar at dawn on 23 September one of its first signals to the French was that if any submarines left harbour they would be sunk. The 1,400-ton Redoubtable-class *Persee,* with a crew of 76, was given little chance to disobey this instruction for it was sunk in the opening bombardment, but the return fire from the French ships in port was both heavy and accurate so the British temporarily withdrew. That night they received the order from Churchill to go back and finish the job.

The following morning the battle recommenced, one of the first casualties being another submarine, the 600-ton Diane class *Ajax* which, after being attacked and blown to the surface by the British destroyer *Fortune,* surrendered and its crew of 48 was taken prisoner.

Intermittent bombardment continued and eventually the only serviceable submarine remaining at Dakar was the 1,400-ton *Bevezier*. Its captain, Cdr Pierre Lancelot, while at periscope depth, watched the approaching British battleships *Barham* and *Resolution,* and once they were in range fired five torpedoes. Their tracks were quickly spotted by the battleships' escorting aircraft but their warning came too late for the old *Resolution* and one of the torpedoes blew a large hole in her side, flooding her port engine room. *Bevezier*, attacked by aircraft and destroyers, managed to escape and eventually made its way to Diego Suarez in Madagascar.

The British force, its work done, eventually moved onto the port of Libreville to gain control of French Gabon. At Port Gentil the French naval defences depended on a sloop and the 1,400-ton submarine *Poncelet*. The submarine moved to attack the British but was sighted, attacked and brought to the surface by a patrol vessel. Its commander, de Suassine, put his men over the side to safety, deliberately opened the sea cocks and went down with his ship.

But it was not only the British forces that the French were defying during this unhappy period. At the French naval base at Bizerta in Tunisia, Admiral Darrion was ordered by the German General Gause to hand over his ships, including eight submarines, otherwise, he threatened, all French ships and troop barracks would be attacked and no quarter given. Admiral Darrion's immediate reaction was to defy the order but, on reflection, he decided that he had no right to send hundreds of men to their deaths for no good reason, and yielded. Two submarines were subsequently sunk by Allied aircraft during bombing raids the following month, two more were scuttled and three towed to Italian ports where they were eventually destroyed by the retreating Germans. The other boat, *Poque*, did join the Italian Navy but was sunk by Allied aircraft before it could carry out a mission.

Unfortunately, Royal Navy attacks on French ships had not yet ended. On 8 June 1942 the British, again fearful of German infiltration, attacked Vichy possessions in Syria and Lebanon, the result being the loss of the submarine *Souffleur*. Then, worried that the Japanese would move against Madagascar after the invasion of Malaya, the British made a surprise attack on the island and the port of Diego Suarez. The submarines *Bevezier*, which had earlier escaped from Dakar, *Monge* and *La Heros*, all returning from patrol, were caught by the attacking force and sunk. Three others, *Casabianca*, *Marsoun* and *Le Glorieux* managed to make their escape and returned to Dakar.

The final assault on the French by Britain and the Allies came on 8 November 1942, with successful landings on the coast of North Africa in Operation Torch, at Casablanca, Oran and Algiers simultaneously. When the Allied fleet approached Casablanca three 600-ton Diane class submarines, *Meduse*, *Antiope* and *Amazone* put to sea and sailed towards the American transports and escorts, barely managing to escape. *Antiope* and *Amazone* were able to reach Dakar, but *Meduse,* hit and badly damaged, eventually had to beach at Cap Blanc. Three other Diane class submarines, each with a crew of 48, *Oreade, Amphitrite* and *Psyche* were bombed and destroyed in the early attacks.

Sybille, another small Diane class submarine, commanded by Lt Cdr Henri Kraut and operating off Fedala was sunk en route to Casablanca. The 1,300-ton *Siddi-Ferruch,* with its crew of 67, was bombed and machine-gunned on the surface and sunk on 11 November. Meanwhile a sister ship, *Conquerant,* was in floating dock at the time of the assault but put to sea without torpedoes or periscopes. It, too, made for Dakar but never reached its destination, being spotted by patrolling Catalina aircraft, attacked and sunk.

A third submarine of the same class, *Le Tonnant,* was bombed and depth-charged for two days, during which time it made an unsuccessful attack on the US aircraft carrier *Ranger.* Its executive officer, Lieutenant Pierre Corre, who took command when his captain was killed, tried to make for Spain but his submarine was too badly damaged. On 15 November, he brought his boat alongside a French fishing vessel and, after transferring the crew, scuttled his ship. The only Vichy submarine left, *Orphee,* stayed at sea and returned to Casablanca when the battle was over.

At Oran, French ships steamed out of harbour to meet the invasion fleet with the submarines *Acteon, Argonaute* and *Fresnel,* which had been in action against the British almost two years before. The *Acteon* and *Argonaute* were sunk by British warships *Westcott* and *Achates* while *Fresnel,* after being chased into Spanish territorial waters, escaped to Toulon.

The reunification of the French fleet began in 1942, and was started as the result of further treachery by the Germans. On 11 November they broke the terms of the Franco-German armistice and entered the unoccupied Vichy zone in France in some force.

The French port commander at Toulon, Admiral de Laborde, on his flagship *Strasbourg,* suffered the same indecision and inability to understand German intentions that had seemed to characterise many French naval officers during 1940. It was not until German tanks had actually crashed through the gates that he gave orders to scuttle 80 warships in the harbour.

Fortunately, the Germans did not seem to realise how quickly a ship could be scuttled and also had difficulty in finding their way around the massive and complicated dockyard. Battleships, cruisers, super-destroyers and destroyers, and many small vessels were scuttled or burning by the time the Germans reached them. Among the first to be destroyed were the submarines *L'Espoir*, *Acheron*, *Pascal*, *Galathee*, *Naiade*, *Sirene*, *Thetis* and *Eurydice* which had been decommissioned and only had skeleton crews. Sixteen more were blown up or scuttled including *L'Aurore*, *Redoubtable*, *Vangeur*, *Henri Poincare*, *Fresnel* (which had earlier escaped from Oran), *Saphir*, *Requin*, *Caiman* (which had escaped British attacks after attempting to sink the British cruiser *Phoebe* during the Syrian campaign and later escaped from Algiers), *Dauphin*, *Espadon*, *Diamante*, *Circe* and *Calypso*.

From the Mourillon docks five submarines – *Casabianca*, *L'Hermione*, *Iris*, *Venus* and *Le Glorieux* got under way when the Germans attacked and tried to make their escape. *Venus* got no further than the outer roads, where it was scuttled in deep water. The three others all survived to join the Allies in Algeria.

After Toulon the only task facing Admiral Darlan, who had, at last, joined the Allies, was to reorganise what was left of his fleet. But on Christmas Eve 1942, after he had called upon the French to unite against the Germans, he was murdered.

The last of the French fleet to join the Allied cause were the ships which, in 1940, had been demobilised at the request of the British at the latter's base in Alexandria. Admiral Godfrey's return to the fray brought the submarines *Casabianca*, *Archimede*, *Perle*, *Curie*, *Arethuse*, *Orphee* and *La Sultane* into the Mediterranean fleet, and they operated with great credit carrying out 45 patrols and sinking at least eight enemy ships. *Casabianca* especially, commanded by Lt Cdr L'Herminier, was credited with sinking three enemy vessels on its own, landing secret agents on the Corsican coast in June 1943, and by the end of August that year had carried out half a dozen other missions. In the middle of 1943, *La Vestale* commanded by Lt Cdr Raymond Attane, was mistakenly attacked by the British *Wishart* and an ensign aboard was killed. On 8 July 1944 *Perle*, commanded by Lt Cdr Marecel Tachin, was sunk when it was mistakenly attacked by a British warship. The only French submarine to be lost in action against the enemy in the Mediterranean was *Protee* which failed to return from a patrol off Provence in 1943.

It was not all gloom and despondency for French submarines during the war. As mentioned earlier there were several which joined the British fleet at the time of the fall of France and carried out many successful patrols. One of these, *Narval,* commanded by Lt Cdr Francois Drogue, was stationed with his division at Sousse, Tunisia, at the time of the armistice. While many of his colleagues were trying to make up their own minds as to their future actions, he sailed his boat to Malta where he declared his allegiance to the FFNF, and was put under Royal Navy command. *Narval* patrolled in the Mediterranean but, on its third voyage it failed to return. In October 1957, sixteen years later, Italian divers found its hull split open by a mine, near Kerkenna Island, off the coast of Tunisia.

Minerve had been towed to Britain from Brest and was based at Dundee in Scotland. *Junon* was another submarine which escaped from Brest under tow at the same time as the *Minerve* but it took longer to get it seaworthy. It took part in the search for the *Tirpitz* and was used on several expeditions to land agents and commandos on the coast of Norway. It was *Junon* which landed a British commando force that blew up the German heavy water production plant near Glomfjord on 15 September 1942 (see page 156).

Rubis was one of half a dozen submarine minelayers being built for the French Navy before the war. Four of them were incomplete when war broke out and were destroyed, but *Rubis* was serving with the Royal Navy before the armistice was signed and continued to do so afterwards.

The story of the French fleet during the war was not a happy one, yet it could have been so different. If the French naval High Command had made a quick decision to throw their forces into the battle against the Germans at the time of the armistice, the history of the war at sea would have been very different, and possibly the loss of life, particularly in Atlantic convoys, would have been much smaller.

The performance of the Russian submarine fleet was disappointing although their failure was mostly due to obsolete submarines and uncertain management.

Russian submarine activity in the First World War was largely confined to laying mines in the Gulf of Finland and the mouth of the Gulf of Riga, and was very much the same in the Second World War. As explained on page 35 the Russian submarine fleet was joined by two British submarines in 1914, E-1 and E-9 which, on the whole, were more successful than their Russian allies.

By the time the Russians were forced into the Second World War they had 65 submarines in the Baltic, 47 in the Black Sea, 15 in the Northern Fleet and 91 in the Pacific, all of them built between 1930 and 1938.

In the Baltic the tactic of laying minefields was repeated. The main trouble was that the Germans and Finns, under an agreement, laid over 10,000 mines in the Gulf of Finland making Russian submarines more or less ineffective. Their operations in the Baltic were generally considered, even by themselves, to have been below what could reasonably have been expected.

In the Black Sea their work was devoted to cutting the German Army's sea supply routes and protecting Russia's own supply routes, particularly those used by oil tankers. Their work was restricted because most of the submarines were old and needed constant repair or maintenance and for a considerable amount of time they were out of action.

Again, the North Sea fleet of submarines, around eight boats, seem never to have been used effectively and were mainly involved in cutting supply routes or defending their own and Allied convoys.

Italian submarines did not play a vitally important role in the final outcome of the Second World War at sea, but their submarine captains lacked neither skill nor courage, and their submarines, like many of their warships, were fine vessels. They could have posed a major problem for the Allies in the Mediterranean and at the beginning of the conflict almost 100 submarines were in commission. But very heavy losses and damage soon reduced the effective number to around 20; by the end of the war they had lost 86 boats. By the time the Germans moved some of their U-boats into the vicinity to help them, in November 1941, they had sunk only 11 unescorted Allied supply ships, but they had accounted for 2 British cruisers and a destroyer while losing 21 of their number.

When the Mediterranean war began Italian submarines were dispersed in seven bases from Cagliari in the west to Laros and Tobruk in the east, and were largely used for the defence of the central area and for reconnaissance. Italian crews, unlike their German U-boat allies, were trained only for daylight submerged attack, and had not developed any tactics for use on the surface at night.

The major successes of Italian submarines during the whole war were confined to the sinking of the British cruiser *Calypso* by *Bagnolini* on 12 June 1940, south of Crete, the cruiser *Bonaventure* by *Ambra* on 31 March 1941, in the same area, and the destruction of the destroyer *Escort* by *Marconi* east of Gibraltar. The sinking of the *Calypso* was the first success of the war for the Italian Navy as a whole, happening less than two days after Italy entered the war on 10 June 1940.

Bagnolini's captain, Lt Cdr Franco Tasoni Pittoni, was one of the most experienced of Italy's submarine commanders, having been in the service for ten years. It was this experience that led him to stay on the surface and chase his target, even though the cruiser had a strong destroyer escort, rather than submerge immediately as most of his colleagues would have done. He again established an Italian precedent by attacking at night, when he was able to get within a few hundred yards of the British squadron before releasing his torpedoes and diving. Thirty seconds after firing their salvo *Bagnolini's* captain and crew heard tell-tale explosions which indicated that they had struck the target. *Calypso*, a 4,000-ton light cruiser, took the full force of Pittoni's salvo and was sent to the bottom within minutes. A counter-attack by British escorts developed at once but by then Bagnolini was already deep and safe and able to creep away.

The Battle of Calabria was fought off the south-east coast of Italy on 9 July 1940. The British were covering a convoy from Malta to Alexandria while the Italians were escorting a convoy to North Africa. In the action that followed the use of torpedo bombers and long-range guns dominated, but the result of the action was inconclusive as both naval forces withdrew to complete their convoy duties. On the way back to Gibraltar, however, the British ships were attacked by the Italian submarine *Marconi* and the destroyer *Escort* was sunk.

On 30 March 1941 the submarine *Ambra*, commanded by Lt Arillo, was patrolling on the surface when it sighted the new British light cruiser *Bonaventure*. While still on the surface, the gallant Arillo took the *Ambra* straight into a torpedo attack, hitting the cruiser which quickly sank. However, for over 12 months after this victory Italian submarines were unable to sink another British warship and delivered only a few blows to merchant shipping.

Ambra saw little more activity until December 1942 when it left Spezia for Algiers for an attack with Italy's famous human torpedoes, known as *Il Maiale* or The Pig (see page 222). The plan was that *Ambra* would take them to a rendezvous point off the port of Algiers to attack British warships, but the plan went awry and they had to withdraw.

When the Allies landed in Sicily in July 1943, *Ambra*, now commanded by Lt Cdr Fellini, took part in the island's defence, again carrying The Pig. The submarine arrived off Syracuse harbour on 25 July but was caught on the surface by Allied aircraft. Bombed and strafed, *Ambra* dived to safety, but it had already been hit several times and sustained damage. Fellini decided nevertheless to carry out the attack on Allied shipping in the harbour, but when it came to releasing The Pig it was found that the bombing had buckled the release door which could not now be opened, so he crept slowly back to base.

When the Italians entered the war, it had already been agreed with their German allies that their larger submarines would be sent to the Atlantic to join the U-boats in an attack on British shipping. The Italians, it was agreed, would patrol areas south of Lisbon (see Chapter 9).

Cappellini under Captain Salvatore Todaru, having made an adventurous trip through the Straits of Gibraltar in the summer of 1940, was by now in the middle of a boring and uneventful patrol. Few ships had been sighted and the Atlantic weather was, as expected, variable and unpredictable. Most of the patrolling had to be carried out on the surface because, with targets few and far between, they could easily be missed by a periscope watch. The submarine had been in the Atlantic for two weeks when a dark blob appeared on the horizon, sending the crew to action stations for the first time.

Although, of course, Todaru did not know what vessel he had sighted it was, in fact, the Portuguese freighter *Cabalho* which was under charter to the British with a cargo of crated aircraft. He attacked in what was his normal manner – on the surface with the deck gun. There was a short sharp bombardment with the inevitable result that the *Cabalho* received a mortal blow and was sent to the bottom. The action thus far was typical of many such fights in the Atlantic at that time, but after the ship's sinking it becomes most untypical.

The *Cabalho*'s crew had taken to the boats and Todaru, who had a reputation for consideration in such matters, was concerned for their safety. He had the choice, he told himself, of leaving them to the capricious weather of the Atlantic, or taking them aboard. The second solution was in reality completely untenable as there was no way he could take on board, and feed, a dozen or so extra men in the already cramped quarters of the submarine. But he was certainly not happy about abandoning them so he adopted a tactic which was contrary to all the tenets of submarine warfare, which left *Cappellini* open to the dangers of enemy attack and himself to the criticism of his superiors – he took *Cabalho*'s lifeboat in tow and pulled it 600 miles across the Atlantic, only dropping the tow line when they were in sight of land.

Todaru, as expected, earned himself the anger of his superiors and the scorn of the Germans. What he did as a submarine commander was quite obviously wrong, yet what he did as a human being restored some confidence in the human race at a time when there was not a lot of it about.

Cappellini's next task was to patrol off West Africa where, up to that time, no Italian or German submarines had operated. It was soon in action fighting and sinking the 7,000-ton armed merchantman *Aeumas*.

Another armed merchantman, the *Shakespeare*, was the next opponent. Fighting started early in the morning with the *Cappellini* on the surface, and lasted for over four hours. The *Shakespeare* was equipped with three 4-inch guns and was a powerful and determined adversary, but eventually had had enough and turned away to escape. Todaru gave chase and the battle continued with *Cappellini* suffering a number of casualties, with almost every member of the submarine's crew trying to get on deck and join in the fight, manning the machine guns or replacing wounded or dead colleagues on the deck gun. Just after noon *Cappellini* struck the fatal blow, firing a torpedo at point-blank range.

Before sinking, the *Shakespeare* had radioed an SOS which brought both aircraft and anti-submarine vessels to the scene, ensuing the hunt for *Cappellini* lasting more than 48 hours. Todaru, however, eventually managed to manoeuvre the boat clear of the attackers and make his way back to Bordeaux where the boat arrived in a very sorry state.

Todaru and *Cappellini* carried out three more Atlantic patrols and sank some 25,000 tons of Allied shipping, before he transferred to the naval commandos and to the task of training a flotilla of midget submarines.

The submarine *Torelli*, under Lt Cdr Cocchia, spent three years in the Atlantic and if it did nothing else it won a reputation for bringing its crew back to base safely, no matter what happened, and surviving the war. Several times the submarine was badly damaged by Allied air attack or the cruel Atlantic weather, but it always got back home. Later, commanded by Lt Cdr Bruno Miglierini who had taken over from Cocchia, it was bombed by aircraft, stranded when its batteries burnt out, attacked by aircraft again and seriously damaged, escaped internment by the Spanish authorities through a last-minute dash for freedom, and sailed through a hurricane.

When Antonio de Giacomo took over *Torelli* it was sent on patrol off the Brazilian coast and again was caught by enemy aircraft, this time shooting one down and then sinking a tanker.

The high spot of its exciting career came in January and February 1941 when it attacked a small convoy of four ships and sank the lot. Then, with yet another new commanding officer, this time Lt Grapallo, who had been a member of the crew since the beginning, it made an 11-week journey from Bordeaux to Singapore.

Another Italian submarine destined to spend its career in the south Atlantic was *Tazzoli* under the command of Lt Cdr Carlo Facia di Cossato. Taking over the submarine in March 1941, by December he had sunk a cruiser, four freighters and a tanker, besides shooting down a plane. Of these feats the most difficult was the sinking of the 8,000-ton *Alfred Olsen* which involved an 11-hour chase, over 100 rounds of 4.7 inch ammunition and all of *Tazzoli's* remaining torpedoes.

When Di Cossato finally left the submarine service for torpedo boats in February 1943, he had been responsible for sinking more than 100,000 tons of Allied shipping. Meanwhile *Tazzoli* then went back into dock for a major refit, its war virtually over.

La Pallice, a minor port north of Bordeaux, saw a strange sight on 11 May 1944 – that is, if anyone bothered to look out into the small harbour. At first sight it might have appeared to be a small hump-backed camel making its way across the water. In fact, it was the Italian submarine *Cappellini,* whose story has already been told, beginning a 13,000-mile journey to the Far East.

Under an agreement with the Germans, signed before the September 1943 surrender, five large Italian submarines had been converted into cargo-carrying vessels capable of making the long journey on the surface, the aim being for them to go first to Abang in Sumatra and then on to Singapore. Leaving La Pallice at spaced intervals, *Capellini* sailed first followed by *Tanzeli* on 16 May,

Giuliani on 23 May, *Torrelli* on 14 June and *Barbarigo* on 15 June; they carried neither guns nor torpedoes.

All the submarines left the French port under German names for this was a German operation, the agreement being that the Germans would use the big Italian submarines, in exchange for the same number of more efficient U-boats, which were no longer fit for commercial raiding. They would take out U-boat supplies to the base at Penang and bring back desperately needed supplies of tin, cotton and rubber. The maximum amount of cargo the submarines could carry was in the region of 150 tons on the outward journey and 190 tons on the return journey, not a lot when it is considered that a small freighter could carry between 3,000 and 4,000 tons of cargo. It did, however, show how desperately these cargoes were needed.

Only three submarines successfully made the journey to the Far East, for *Tazzoli* and *Barbarigo* disappeared without trace, *Tazzoli* probably being sunk in the Bay of Biscay by Allied aircraft on the first day out.

Cappellini carried 92 tons of rubber, 54 tons of tin, 5 tons of tungsten and 4 tons of opium and quinine on the return journey. The crew were under strict instructions that even if they saw an American or British troopship they were to let it go without reporting the sighting, as the task of getting their cargo home was more important. They could not have taken any offensive action even if they had wanted to, for their only armament was an anti-aircraft gun. All the torpedoes had been removed and the space used for stacking cargo, the ammunition lockers had been converted to carrying fuel, crew bunks had disappeared and even two of the three toilets had been removed leaving just one for fifty crew for the three-month journey.

During the long and tedious voyage all the surviving submarines were spotted by Allied aircraft but managed to take evasive action and reach their destination, *Cappellini* on 9 July, *Giuliani* on 30 July and *Torrelli* on 26 August. There *Cappellini* reloaded with 155 tons of rubber, tin and other raw materials for the return journey but on 8 September 1944 Italy signed the armistice with the Allies and for the Italian submarine the war was over.

All three were interned by the Germans. *Giuliani* was recommissioned as UIT-23 and lost on 14 February 1944 after being torpedoed in the Malacca Channel by the *Tally Ho*. *Torelli* and the famous *Cappellini* were handed over to the Japanese and both of them were sunk by US forces off Kobe in 1945 – a sad end, particularly for *Cappellini* which had served its country well.

Japanese submarines were a dismal failure in the Pacific War. They started hostilities with 53 boats, 22 of which were ocean-going cruising boats of some 2,000 tons mounting one or two 5.5-inch guns and six 21-inch torpedo tubes; 20 more were fleet submarines with a 4.7-inch gun and six 21-inch torpedo tubes. A steady building programme only just managed to balance losses. At the end of the war the Japanese had lost 130 boats and had very little to show for it.

Three submarine flotillas, 27 boats in all, were strategically placed around Pearl Harbor when the attack started in December 1941, the aim being that they would sink any American warship that tried to escape from the inferno. They had with them five midget submarines and these were to be sent right into the harbour to create, it was thought, even more mayhem than the air attack. But not one American ship was destroyed or damaged by a Japanese submarine, the midgets failing to break their way into the harbour, foiled by impenetrable anti-submarine nets, and were all sunk.

The nearest a Japanese submarine could be said to have come to a major success in January 1942 was when I-165, patrolling off the Malaysian peninsular, sighted and reported the British battleships *Prince of Wales* and *Renown*, which led to the eventual sinking of the two mighty warships by air attack.

A month after Pearl Harbor the Japanese adopted a picket line strategy, which initially worked well. Set up near Johnston Island they were ordered to reconnoitre westward and I-6 soon found a target, an aircraft carrier with a cruiser and two escorts. Its attack resulted in the sinking of the US carrier *Saratoga* in March 1945. Although this was a major success, it must be recalled that there were no other hits by Japanese submarines in an area where the

Americans had a large number of aircraft carriers, cruisers and destroyers using Pearl Harbor on a regular basis. The story remained very much the same with picket lines off Wake Island and Fiji.

In the Indian Ocean the Japanese planned air attacks on Trincomalee and Colombo in Ceylon (now Sri Lanka), and to send submarines to reconnoitre the waters around Ceylon and the west coast of India. A squadron of six ocean-going submarines sailed on this assignment but, again, did not achieve very much. I-7 was supposed to use its seaplane for a look at the two targets, but could not get anywhere near because the strong air defences reduced the seaplane pilot's enthusiasm.

Fifty Japanese submarines were active in the Indian Ocean in 1942 and 1943, and managed to sink 80 ships during the two-year period, but none of them were what could be described as a large and important vessel. Two Japanese submarines were sunk in the same area during this period.

The Eastern flotilla of five submarines patrolling around Australia and New Zealand, the 3rd Squadron of five boats covering Fiji and Samoa, and the 7th Squadron of two submarines in the Port Moresby-Santa Isabel area were able to sink ten vessels without loss.

Widely used for reconnaissance purposes around Midway Island and the Aleutians submarines provided vital weather information and were valuable, both when the invasion was taking place and, shortly afterwards, during the withdrawal. Picket lines were used by the Japanese ostensibly to warn them of the presence of major US warships, such as the seven-strong line set up off Malaila Island north-east of Guadalcanal, put there to intercept US carriers en route to the support areas in Guadalcanal.

Picket duty fell again to Japanese submarines during the battle for Midway Island in May 1942. The decision to do this followed the disastrous loss of four aircraft carriers, and was inspired by the hope that they would be able to strike back at the US carrier force. All fleet submarines in the area were established on a 200-mile line east of Midway, but uncertainty about what the

Americans would do led to a change of decision and they moved the line to the west of the island. It was a mistake, for bad weather delayed the re-establishment and when it was complete it was learned that the American carriers were still east of Midway. So they were all sent back to the original line, but it was too late – the American ships were safely on their way back to Pearl Harbor.

American operations to reinforce Guadalcanal were watched by Japanese submarines whose task was supposed to stop supplies reaching the island. This turned out to be mainly a reconnaissance operation with the base at Espirito Santo being observed by the seaplane from I-21 mentioned earlier.

In 1943, when the Japanese were aware that the US was about to begin an assault on Wake Island, and were concerned about what sort of strength the Americans were building up at Pearl Harbor, they sent several submarines with seaplanes to find out. I-36 was deterred by radar surveillance, but managed to launch the plane from a point 150 miles away, reporting that four aircraft carriers and four battleships were in the harbour. However the plane could not find its parent ship on return and disappeared. Meanwhile I-19's aircraft saw a battleship and an aircraft carrier, and made it back to the mother ship, the news making the Japanese even more nervous.

After the Japanese withdrawal from Guadalcanal between January and November 1943, 26 submarines covered the area, managing to sink only 20 ships while losing 7 of their number in the process. By contrast, aggressive patrolling and depth-charging by American destroyers and anti-submarine patrols largely nullified Japanese submarine attacks, while American submarines played an important role in bringing the Japanese to submission, not only sinking almost every Japanese merchantman and nearly half the Japanese fleet, but also destroying 25 of their submarines.

Cdr Mochitsura Hashimoto survived the war despite the horrific casualties sustained by the Japanese submarine service. By July 1945 it was a beaten force, but he played a leading role in what was a deeply tragic episode in the history of the US Navy. While patrolling in the Philippine Sea area in I-58, much to his surprise he sighted a large warship sailing unescorted ahead of him, seemingly without any concern that there might be an enemy submarine in the vicinity. Getting over his surprise he manoeuvred into an attacking position and fired a salvo at what was, in fact, the American heavy cruiser *Indianapolis*. Through his periscope he saw his torpedoes strike their target followed by plumes of water and smoke, and then fire.

On 16 July 1945, the *Indianapolis* had been sent at high speed to Tinian Island in the Marianas carrying parts and nuclear material to be used in the atom bombs subsequently dropped on Hiroshima and Nagasaki. After completing the assignment she had called in at Guam and was on her way to Leyte in the Philippines when she was attacked.

It was an hour before Hashimoto surfaced but he could see no sign of either a damaged cruiser or wreckage, so he sailed to the north and only submerged when an aircraft came into view. Later, surfacing, he radioed headquarters in Tokyo reporting that he had sunk an American battleship.

His report was intercepted by a US Navy radio unit, deciphered and given to the Commander-in-Chief some 16 hours after the *Indianapolis* had been sent to the bottom. Naval headquarters viewed the intercepted signal as another example of the Japanese propensity to exaggerate and, anyway, no one knew where I-58 was or even that a US ship was missing.

In fact the *Indianapolis* went down at 12.14 hrs on 30 July, sinking in 12 minutes with some 300 of the 1,196 officers and men aboard going down with her. The remaining 900 were left floating in the shark-infested sea, with no lifeboats and little food and water. By the time the survivors from the *Indianapolis* were found, completely by accident, four days later, only 316 of the original 900 were alive.

It later transpired that the Navy knew that there was a Japanese submarine in the area but had not found it necessary to warn the captain of the *Indianapolis* or send the cruiser to sea with an escort. The captain, Charles McVay, survived and was court-martialled and found guilty of 'hazarding his ship by failing to zigzag'. This, despite evidence from Hashimoto that zigzagging would have made no difference.

Although some 700 US ships were lost during the Second World War, McVay was the only captain to be court-martialled. Strangely, no account was taken of the negligence of failing to warn him of the submarine's presence or to give him an escort; nor indeed of failing to notice that the *Indianapolis* had not arrived in harbour when she was due.

CHAPTER NINE

Dangerous Missions

*Minelaying, supplying guerrillas, landing agents,
reconnaissance, evacuating refugees, rescuing troops,
defending the Aleutians. Italians break into the Atlantic.*

THE role of the submarine, used first as a defensive weapon,
expanded rapidly as the conflict developed, being quickly
identified as a superb weapon of attack, especially by the Germans.
Other roles were then adopted – minelaying, supplying guerrillas,
landing agents, reconnaissance, evacuation and rescue – each with
great success.

Minelaying by submarines was tried by the Germans in the First
World War when in May 1915, submarine minelayers were sent to
lay new minefields off Scotland's Firth of Forth, Cromarty and Scapa
Flow to catch British warships entering and leaving harbour. They
followed this up in August using a new, smaller U-boat, which
carried 12 mines and laid fields in the Thames Estuary in total
secrecy, sinking a number of ships. Further activity, in the southern
North Sea, reaped a harvest of between 12 and 15 ships a month
sunk. By contrast, the British, who carried out mining activities in
the Heligoland and German Bights, did not achieve such good
results.

Britain's first mining operation of the Second World War was in
April 1940, when the Heligoland Bight was mined by the submarine
Narwhal and almost immediately sank a small ship and a trawler.
Narwhal was one of five built in 1933 with the specific purpose of
laying mines, only one of which survived the war. Early in the conflict

a mine was developed that could be laid through a normal torpedo tube, so specialist minelaying submarines were no longer required since all could carry out the task.

The waters of the Kattegat and the Skagerak at the entrance to the Baltic are generally shallow, and so not a good place or time for a submarine to loiter in. Nevertheless the work of mining them was carried out with courage and determination, and some close shaves.

The Italians were enthusiastic minelayers and with some success. Of the 45 British submarines lost during the Mediterranean campaign 22 are believed to have been due to mines.

The Japanese laid large numbers of mines as an anti-submarine measure, but they were so thinly spread they had little effect and are believed to have been responsible for the loss of only two American submarines, although the mine barrier around the Sea of Japan did keep American submarines out for some time.

It was a shortage of reliable torpedoes that encouraged the adoption by the US submarine service of what was, to them, a new tactic. In the autumn of 1942 there was a period when not all submarines could be loaded with a full complement of torpedoes, which meant that there was space left for mines, these being laid in strategic Japanese shipping lanes in October and November 1942. They had been regularly patrolled by submarines, but a crisis around the Solomon Islands forced the submarine force to be largely withdrawn. As submarine minelaying had a distinct advantage over a surface-laid minefield, because of the element of surprise, the procedure could not be observed, so a second patrol was sent out in December, including Lt Cdr John B. Azer's *Whale* on its maiden patrol. It headed for the Kii Suido passage, one of the main routes for Japanese traffic. Despite his orders to sow the mines near the fields laid earlier, Azer noticed that the Japanese vessels were, in fact, hugging the coast in shallow waters. After watching the ships and plotting their routes, and despite the fact that he was going through a Japanese defensive minefield, he decided to go inshore. The irony of going through a minefield to set a minefield did not escape him.

He went in carefully on a moonlit night and laid the first field directly on the shipping route; the second field was also laid close inshore. No sooner had he completed his task than he saw a convoy approaching. This, he was sure, would enliven the proceedings and he attacked with torpedoes but without any evidence of success. Later, when he surfaced in the moonlight, he saw a scene of total chaos with damaged ships either running aground or turning into the minefield.

Trigger, commanded by Ltd Cdr Benson, followed suit and, again in bright moonlight, sowed his first field. As he started on the second, he saw a large freighter approaching but let it pass because he did not want to disclose his position. Shortly after the vessel passed him, it hit a mine, blew up and sank. Moments later he heard another massive explosion, which he could not identify but watching Japanese activity through his periscope he decided that another vessel had been sunk.

As a result of these efforts it was decided that minefields would be laid regularly in the shallow waters of harbour approaches so that shipping would be driven into the deeper water where submarines could lurk.

Britain's Royal Navy had discussed the value of submarines as supply ships in 1941. Discussion became a fact when the Germans decided that to safeguard their army in North Africa they had to capture the Mediterranean island of Malta, the first part of this plan being to bomb the hell out of the island – in February they dropped 1,000 tons of bombs, in March 2,000 tons and 6,000 tons in April in a total of 233 air raids.

German E-boats laid some 500 mines around the island and as all the minesweepers at the base had been sunk, submarines based at Malta had to be withdrawn to Alexandria. As a result supplies began to flow again to Rommel's army and with the Germans firmly believing they had neutralised Malta, they withdrew many of their aircraft.

With the fall of Crete in June and the British Army's withdrawal to the Egyptian frontier it was almost impossible for British supply ships to reach Malta. Despite the incredible difficulties and dangers, submarines therefore had to be loaded with aviation spirit, ammunition, stores and some passengers and taken to the supply-starved island; it cost the Royal Navy six submarines. *Cachalot* was one submarine that had to make regular trips. In June alone, it made four – with 120,300 gallons of white oil, $12\frac{1}{2}$ tons of stores, 359 bags of mail, kerosene, benzine, ammunition, torpedoes, dehydrated vegetables and other food stores.

The Germans also found the value of U-boats as supply ships, but in their case it was an act of desperation as all other routes were virtually closed to them. They sent their U-boats to the Far East ostensibly to sink ships, but more vitally to bring back much needed strategic supplies. In the first half of 1944 some 16 U-boats were despatched to the Far East carrying supplies to the U-boat base at Penang, and to bring back vital supplies such as rubber, tin, tungsten, quinine and opium. Only 8 of the 24 submarines completed their assignments, sinking 19 ships totalling around 115,000 tons. Only 2 returned to France with about 300 tons of supplies. Of the 600 men involved 423 were killed and some 117 were taken prisoner.

In September 1942 the US submarine *Amberjack*, Lt Cdr A.J. Bole, was on patrol successfully sinking several ships before being recalled to Pearl Harbor, and then sent to Espirito Santo, the US base in the New Hebrides, where marines were fighting a last-ditch battle on Guadalcanal. They had no fuel except that remaining in the tanks of planes which had reached the outpost.

Amberjack was ordered to load 9,000 tons of high-octane fuel, 15 army personnel and two hundred 100-lb bombs to go to Guadalcanal. Bole was almost at his destination when he was ordered to Tugali off Florida Island, as Japanese destroyers had started bombarding Guadalcanal.

The USS *Trout*, commanded by Lt Cdr F.W. Fenno, was early into the supply business when it was sent to Corregidor on 12 January 1942 with ammunition for anti-aircraft guns, and other supplies. *Trout* refuelled at Midway Island and on its arrival at Corregidor found that it was being bombed, so the submarine groped its way to the South Dock and unloaded shells, grapefruit, cigarettes and canned food as fast as it could. Fenno had expected the ballast necessary for the return journey would be sand or cement, but was told that this was not possible. In the Manila Bank there was a large store of gold bullion, currency, and securities which had to be moved out quickly before it fell into enemy hands. After some frantic, secretive loading *Trout* eventually took out 2 tons of gold bars, 18 tons of silver pesos, vital documents and US mail as well as currency. Submerging at dawn the submarine crept out through three mine-fields. Despite his precious cargo Fenno still spent time looking for enemy shipping to attack on the homeward journey, finally reaching Pearl Harbor 52 days after leaving.

In July 1940, Operation Anger was one of the first of what was to become a routine occurrence for submarines in most theatres of war – landing agents and reconnaissance parties on enemy coasts. It was carried out by the British submarine *Seawolf*. Lt Cdr H.R. Colvin took on board an officer of the Guernsey Militia at Plymouth on 6 July and landed him unseen near Icart Bay on the night of 7/8 July, re-embarking him the next day. It was a tricky operation organised at short notice and with no rehearsal, and was carried out in waters which were generally regarded by submarine officers with considerable distaste because of the tide rips and strong currents. But the militia officer got vital information about the German defences on Guernsey.

The French submarine *Junon*, now serving with the Royal Navy, was tasked with landing a party of Combined Operations personnel on the Norwegian coast in September 1942 to blow up a power station. After carrying out this task the party was scheduled to make its way home through Sweden.

The landing place was to be Tennholm Fjord, but on the evening of departure, 11 September 1942, one of the Norwegian guides declared the area to be unsuitable because of the number of Germans in the vicinity. The landing point was altered to Bjaering Fjord, reported to be sparsely populated. It was an uneventful passage via Lyngvaer Fjord, Ottraer Fjord, Skars Fjord to Bjaerangs Fjord, some 30 miles up the coast, on 15 September. There was a lot of traffic in the area so the submarine had to remain submerged until nightfall. It was clear and calm when the Combined Operations party was disembarked in 55 minutes and the power station was blown up. They all escaped to Sweden.

Junon's next job was to land stores in northern Norway for a coastal watching and reporting organisation established by British Intelligence.

On 13 November *Junon* went to Me Fjord where the landing was scheduled to take place, but bad weather delayed it until 17 November. The submarine dived into the fjord, in order to settle on the bottom at the head of the fjord. But the rocky nature of the bottom made settling impossible so the submarine had to move to deeper water.

In the evening it surfaced to find calm water and soon a boat with four agents and crew was on its way ashore, only to find a rocky beach which made landing almost impossible, although it was eventually achieved with difficulty and the boat returned for the second load, but by that time a party of ten Germans had arrived in the village, so landing was no longer practical. Unfortunately, because of a misunderstanding, two Norwegians, who were meant to have been collected, and two sailors had remained ashore and could not be recovered because of German activity, so *Junon*, assisted by a strong wind which had suddenly blown up, went out to sea for the night. It surfaced in daylight but a rescue attempt was unsuccessful so it dived again out in the fjord, and signalled a report on the situation. The weather however remained so bad that they could not attempt any further rescues and was not until the 28th that *Junon* could land the remaining stores, but there was no sign of the four men left behind.

Nevertheless the story has a happy ending. *Junon* returned in 1943 when snowstorms in Me Fjord forced Captain Querville to surface because the coastline was blotted out by the weather. At 19.00 hrs a boat with two Norwegian guides left for the shore but it was 21.00 hrs before the operation was complete and the castaways were recovered. Capt Querville was awarded the Distinguished Service Cross and congratulated by the British Admiralty.

While many submariners of all maritime nations became known as aces because of their ability to sink enemy shipping, several earned the title because of their ability to rescue evacuees from enemy territory, acting as marine 'Scarlet Pimpernels'.

The American submarine *Narwhal* became very practised in the art of rescue. Commanded by Lt Cdr F.D. Latte it left Australia in October 1942, bound for the Philippines and carrying 45 tons of stores plus two specialist parties. After a short chase by two Japanese anti-submarine vessels, it moored alongside an unmanned Japanese registry schooner and unloaded part of its stores, before going on to Naspit Harbour in Mindanao where it ran aground in 20ft of water. Fortunately it managed to float off and unload supplies.

Latte agreed to take on 32 Australia-bound evacuees, including a baby. *Narwhal* set off a second time for the Philippines, loaded with 90 tons of ammunition and stores, where it picked up another party of eight, and then on to Aluinbijid, Majacalas Bay, where it took on three women, four children and two men. The captain and crew were beginning to feel that they were running a bus and supply service, and it was a good feeling when they could momentarily return to the war and sink an enemy ship with their deck guns.

In the middle of 1944 it seemed that the main task of the US submarine service was keeping the Philippines supplied with guns, ammunition and supplies and collecting evacuees. *Narwhal* was at it again dropping ammunition and stores to guerrillas on Panay and, shortly afterwards, evacuating 28 men, women and children to Australia. In March she delivered more guerrilla supplies and again evacuated 28 people from Mindanao before going on to Tawi Tawi.

Lt Cdr J.S. Titus took over command of *Narwhal* and with *Nautilus*, *Stingray* and *Redfin* continued the difficult task of keeping the guerrillas on the Pacific islands supplied with ammunition and stores, struggling through shallow waters, unpredictable seas, mines and, of course, with enemy patrols always possible.

At Bougainville in the Solomon Islands, *Nautilus* took off 14 nuns, 3 married women with children and 9 men, all of whom faced the alternative of an horrific future in a concentration camp. Probably one of the most satisfactory operations carried out by the *Narwhal*, was the evacuation of 81 prisoners of war and a doctor from Sindangau Bay, north-west Mindanao; the men were survivors from a Japanese ship which had been sunk by the US submarine *Paddle* on 7 September 1944.

In July 1941, under the command of 29-year-old Lt Cdr P.J. Cowell, the Royal Navy's *Thrasher* sailed from Alexandria under orders to reconnoitre the beaches at Limni in Crete and then patrol in the southern Aegean Sea. Having carried out its reconnaissance duties, it then received reports that 50–60 British soldiers were still hiding on Crete after being left behind during the recent evacuation. They would be gathered on the beach on the night of 27/28 July to await rescue.

Cowell returned to the island in the dead of night on a comparatively calm sea and nudged *Thrasher* to within 75 yards of the beach with its nose aground, to be suddenly greeted by a mass of excited men, British and Greek, with only one thing on their mind – escape. The problem immediately facing Haggard was unlike any other he had met in his submarine career. Much to his surprise, he found that most of the men were naked, which made it impossible to tell who were British soldiers needing rescue, and who were Greeks anxious to escape. With extreme patience and authority Haggard slowly organised the rabble and loaded the men aboard *Thrasher*, before finally sailing with 62 British soldiers, 5 naval ratings and 11 Greeks on board and returning safely to Alexandria.

Lt Cdr R.I. Olsen, skipper of the US submarine *Angler*, was sent on a similar 'fishing trip' to pick up 50 Americans off the north coast of Panay. Submerging *Angler* near the rendezvous point at daybreak, he surveyed the scene through his periscope and saw a large group of people behind some trees. After an hour he spotted the pre-arranged signal from along the water's edge.

At sunset, with the crew of *Angler* at battle stations he moved towards the beach, Olsen was informed that there were, in fact, 58 evacuees. Even though this number almost equalled the total number of his crew he agreed to take them aboard, temporarily putting aside the multitude of problems that would arise. It took an hour for the refugees, who included 16 women and children, to board *Angler* and as soon as the task was complete Olsen headed the submarine out to sea on a 12-day voyage to Darwin in Northern Australia.

The first problem was one of accommodation, and this was solved by putting all the crew in the after battery compartment. The two torpedo rooms were assigned to the other refugees – men and boys aft and women and children forward. Special arrangements – officers' cabins – were made for an eight-month pregnant woman, one with a two-month-old baby, a seriously ill girl and two elderly women.

When *Angler* had stopped off the coast of Panay, unbeknown to the crew, it also took on a host of cockroaches, fleas, body lice and other obnoxious creatures, while the atmosphere in the submarine had 'seriously deteriorated'. Food was strictly rationed with soup the main part of the daily diet. The state of the heads (toilets) which, in a submarine are extremely complicated to use, beggars the imagination. But despite all these handicaps *Angler* made it back to safety and the passengers were unloaded.

The Aleutians is a chain of 14 islands extending westwards from Alaska, which are foggy, rainy, mountainous, treeless and subject to rapid changes in the weather, rarely for the better. Shortly before the war the Americans, after some uncertainty, had decided to establish submarine bases at Dutch Harbour and Iliuku, because the American naval authorities had become nervous at the proximity of an increasingly aggressive Japanese nation, periscopes of Japanese submarines and seaplanes in the area confirming these suspicions.

The Japanese sent a strong force to the Aleutians and by 7 January 1942 had landed and occupied Attu and Kiska. The battle in the islands became fast and furious, with US submarines used extensively in the foul seas to cut enemy supply lines. It was, in fact, a three-way battle, between the Americans, the Japanese and the weather. But the tide turned, as it always does, and the Japanese hold on Attu and Kiska became more and more tenuous, reaching the stage when they were totally dependent on submarines for supplies of ammunition and food.

The Americans decided that April 1943 would mark the end of the occupation of the Aleutians by the Japanese and planned a substantial invasion force. Two submarines, *Narwhal* and *Nautilus* were earmarked to land 214 scouts at Dutch Harbour, in advance of a massive naval strike force, but a mixture of snowstorms and fog delayed the operation for three days while the submarines tried to keep out of the way of surface shipping. Life on board the two submarines became almost impossible, as each was carrying over 100 extra men, however the boats eventually made their way to a point off Blind Cove and disembarked their passengers into rubber boats; although the coast was partly obscured they made it to the shore. Nearly two hours later, the task complete, *Narwhal* and *Nautilus* made for the open sea and safety.

Attu was eventually secured and when the relieving forces reached Kiska the Japanese had completely disappeared, having used the murky weather and fog to escape by ship and submarine.

When the Italians entered the war it had already been agreed with their German allies that their larger submarines would be sent to the Atlantic to join the U-boats in an attack on British shipping. The Italians, it was agreed, would patrol areas south of Lisbon.

On 13 June 1940 the Italians began to keep their part of the bargain when the submarine *Finzi*, under the command of Lt Cdr Dominici, passed safely through the Straits of Gibraltar, the first of 27 Italian boats to be despatched to the Atlantic; within six months 4 of them had been destroyed.

Cappellini, commanded by Lt Cdr Salvatore Todaru, a captain with very little submarine experience at that time, was scheduled to follow *Finzi* and *Calvi* into the Atlantic but on his way through almost collided with a British destroyer. It was far too late for Todaru to dive, so he had little choice but to stay on the surface and fight it out. The Straits echoed to the sound of gunfire as the two vessels bombarded each other with guns and torpedoes without, at first, doing any serious damage. Then *Cappellini* was badly hit and Todaru had no alternative but to dive and try to escape. With great skill he managed to evade the destroyer and sail into the neutral Spanish port of Ceuta for repairs – not a moment too soon for when he arrived it became clear that *Cappellini* would soon have sunk. In the 24 hours allowed under International Law, rapid repairs were carried out to make the submarine seaworthy and it was able, at last, to join its colleagues in the Atlantic.

At about the same time that Todaru was having his difficulties Lt Cdr Buonamici was creating a precedent, albeit a minor one. Italian submarines delegated to Atlantic duty were under strict instructions to travel through the Straits of Gibraltar on the surface because of underwater traps laid by the British.

Buonamici would have none of this, believing the British traps a danger preferable to British destroyers and, off Europa Point, decided to disobey orders and dive. Probably no one was more surprised than the Veniero's captain and crew to find that the passage through the Straits, under water, was difficult but certainly not as impossible as everyone in the Italian High Command had thought.

On 8 September 1940 *Torelli* under Lt Cdr Cocchia started a voyage through the Straits that took a total of 24 hours and was also largely carried out submerged. The submarine had reached its starting point off Alboran Island at dawn the day before, when it dived to spend the day on the bottom awaiting nightfall. As darkness fell *Torelli* surfaced and by 02.00 hrs found itself two miles south of the Rock of Gibraltar. Suddenly Cocchia picked up the sound of an approaching boat so he took the submarine down and decided to continue the passage submerged. No attack developed, so he never did find out what sort of ship he had heard approaching but, anyway, the decision was now made.

Torelli now got caught up in the very strong currents that flow through the main channel at certain times. Cocchia knew it was a lateral current but had no idea whether his submarine was being carried northwards or south. Eventually he saw the lights of Tarifa through his periscope and realised that they had been drifting south, but he still could not fix his position as the soundings being made by the boat's ill-functioning echo-sounder were completely baffling, showing shallow water where he thought it should be deep, and deep water where shallow was expected.

Cocchia now faced another problem – *Torelli*'s engines were running flat out, but it was clear that the boat was making no progress against the current; in fact all they were doing was keeping the submarine almost exactly where it was. After over four hours of struggle Cocchia at last found a favourable current which carried the submarine safely through the Straits and into the Atlantic.

CHAPTER TEN

The Unexpected

K-boats in WW1, Umpire–the victim of friendly action,
Spearfish–first in action, Enright's biggest success,
a survivor–two years late, Silversides' torpedo problems,
Britons rescued by US sub, POWs rescued, sickness aboard,
Shindo's surprise, Japanese bombard the USA,
the Hashimoto Incident, bombarding the USA,
capture – Seal, O'Kane, Kretschmer,U-boats captured,
Italy's Perla captured.

ALTHOUGH this book is specifically concerned with submarines that took part in action against the enemy, this seems a good time to discuss Britain's famous K-class submarine, which can certainly be described as unusual in that they did little damage to the enemy but they had a hell of a time attacking each other.

In 1916, pursuing an obsession that the Royal Navy should have a submarine which could keep up with other ships of the fleet on the surface when travelling at the normal battle speed of 24 knots, the Admiralty authorised the construction of HMS *Swordfish*. This had powerful 3,750 horsepower steam engines with boilers, furnaces and a funnel which could be collapsed and sealed when the submarine submerged. The designer seemed to have forgotten the previous experiences with submarine steam engines which had proved that boilers create far too much heat for a confined space when submerged, and need a prodigious amount of air to remain functional. A year later *Swordfish* was converted into a surface vessel but it gave birth to the ill-fated K-class submarine.

For harbour and coastal propulsion these new boats used their diesel-electric meters, but for cruising at the required speed of 24 knots they used oil-fired steam turbine engines, and took an inordinately long time to dive.

On 31 January 1918, ten K-class submarines set out to join the Grand Fleet, sailing from Rosyth to a rendezvous off Norway. Leaving harbour at the same time were destroyer flotillas, cruiser squadrons, battleships and battlecruisers, spaced according to orders, and sailing in line ahead at a speed of about 20 knots.

The whole mini-fleet was well under way when suddenly, and for no obvious reason, K-14 turned out of line with its helm jammed and struck K-22; before the two submarines could disentangle themselves the battlecruiser *Inflexible* rammed K-14. Up sailed another group of ships and K-17, which had turned to try and help K-14 was rammed and cut in half by the cruiser *Fearless*. K-4, seeing what the *Fearless* had done, turned out of line to avoid her and stopped engines, only to be rammed and cut in half by K-6 which had also turned out of line but not stopped. Both K-17 and K-4 sank with all hands; the K-22, K-14, K-6 and a light cruiser were badly damaged.

In July 1941, a convoy from the Thames estuary was heading along the east coast of Britain bound for the Clyde, escorted by armed trawlers and gunboats. *Umpire,* commanded by Lt Cdr Mervyn Wingfield, was travelling as an escort to the convoy simply because, although destined for service in the Mediterranean, it had first to go to the Clyde for sea trials. The small 600-ton submarine had been travelling on the surface but an attack by a German aircraft had forced it to make its first-ever dive. All went well and when the attack was over it surfaced again, however, during the night *Umpire* developed engine trouble and had to stop for repairs, while the convoy continued its journey.

As luck would have it at the same time, a south-bound convoy was making its way through the same waters. *Umpire*'s alert officer-of-the-watch sighted the ships and was slightly perturbed when half a dozen of them, disobeying the maritime regulations which meant that they should have turned to starboard to prevent a collision, in fact turned to port and passed down the submarine's starboard side. Disgust at the mariners' ignorance of the law was replaced by alarm when the officers and crew on the bridge of the *Umpire* saw an armed trawler bearing down on them. According to maritime law the trawler had the right of way and *Umpire* should have turned to starboard to avoid it, but this was impossible because the ships that were breaking the law were passing down that side of the submarine.

Wingfield did the only thing possible and ordered his boat to go hard-a-port. At the same time the men on the bridge of the trawler saw the submarine and correctly ordered an emergency turn to starboard – straight towards *Umpire* again. There was an appalling crash as the trawler's bows cut into the submarine, throwing Wingfield and two lookouts into the sea. *Umpire* was sinking quickly and a desperate rescue operation was then started but only half of the crew were saved.

It was a sad end to the career of a submarine that never really got started. But a much chastened Wingfield was eventually given command of another submarine, *Taurus*, and by December 1943 was serving in the Far East where he sank the Japanese submarine I-34 (see page 192).

Spearfish was probably the first Royal Navy warship to see action in the Second World War. There could hardly be another claimant. At 11 a.m. on Sunday, 3 September 1939 British submarines received the signal to commence hostilities against Germany. *Spearfish*'s captain, Lieutenant J.H. Hardy, hardly had time to read the Admiralty signal and digest the news before a torpedo fired by an enemy submarine flashed past his boat – a near miss and a fortunate baptism of fire.

The second engagement was not long in coming, and did not have such a happy ending. Operating close to the enemy shore, off the coast of southern Norway in the approaches to the Skaggerak, *Spearfish* was severely damaged by depth charges and, after evading this attack with some difficulty, had to be escorted home by a destroyer.

In April 1940 the Germans were intent on invading Norway and their convoys were making significant use of the waters in the

Kattegat and Skaggerak. On 10 April *Triton* attacked a large convoy and managed to sink three ships before being attacked itself. *Spearfish,* whose captain was now the redoubtable Lt Forbes, was not far away from the scene and the enemy's attention was turned to it as well.

German anti-submarine vessels and aircraft dropped over 60 depth charges around *Spearfish* which spent the best part of 24 hours trying to avoid destruction, eventually being able to creep away from the scene and surface to recharge batteries. However, the respite was short lived because after only an hour on the surface Forbes saw the bow wave of an approaching destroyer. Not wishing to submerge without the batteries fully charged, he turned away hoping to avoid detection and was in the middle of this manoeuvre when he realised that the bow wave was not that of an approaching destroyer but a very large ship. He did not know it at the time but the potential target was the German battleship *Lützow*, later renamed *Deutschland*, on passage for Kiel to prepare for raiding in the Atlantic. Forbes managed to launch a salvo of six torpedoes, one of which found its mark smashing the *Lützow*'s propellers and rudder, leaving her a wallowing hulk. Luckily for the German warship Forbes did not realise that she was travelling without escort, so he withdrew before the expected barrage of depth charges, leaving *Lützow* to be towed to safety.

Spearfish returned to her base in triumph, but it was a joy that was not to last long. On 1 August, on patrol in the North Sea, it was attacked on the surface by U-34 and destroyed; all but one of the crew lost their lives.

While other submarine commanders could claim a larger number of ships and a greater tonnage, Commander Enright in the USS *Archerfish* could claim the biggest prize of all – a Japanese aircraft carrier. In November 1944 *Archerfish* was one of a number of American submarines strung out like a necklace of pearls across the sea lanes south of Tokyo, and round the Japanese mainland, their task at this time being to pick up the crews of American aircraft that had crashed in the sea following air raids on the Japanese capital.

Enright's radar picked up approaching ships. Racing towards the targets he quickly realised that one of them was an aircraft carrier, the only difficulty being that it was screened by four destroyers. Although he was easily detectable on the surface, Enright pressed on for having to submerge would have lost valuable time and, probably, contact. Realising that somehow or other he had to get ahead of the convoy in order to deliver his attack, but thinking this might not be possible, he sent out an 'enemy sighted' signal in the hope that another submarine in the area might be better placed.

The chase continued throughout the night and although the convoy altered course several times it still kept well out of range. With engines running flat out *Archerfish* gradually began to make progress and slowly overtake it. Enright had almost given up hope of being able to position himself for an attack when the convoy suddenly, for no apparent reason, altered course again, right into the path of the submarine.

Enright submerged *Archerfish* and took up an attacking position. Slowly the carrier and its escorts approached the waiting submarine and at 15.15 hrs a salvo of six torpedoes left the submarine and sped towards the target. It was an agonising wait as the torpedoes closed the gap but suddenly there was an explosion, then another, and another, then three more in quick succession. Every torpedo had hit their target.

Enright had no difficulty in taking *Archerfish* to safety for the escorting destroyers were too busy with their stricken aircraft carrier to search for him. Although the 59,000-ton *Shinano* was the only Japanese ship sunk by *Archerfish,* it was enough.

In far too many cases submarines simply disappeared without trace while on patrol, although in a few instances subsequent examination of German records, after the war, revealed what had really happened. But the end of the Royal Navy's *Perseus* was eventually explained by a survivor – two years after the event.

On 26 November 1941 *Perseus,* under the command of Lt Cdr E.C. Nicolay, left for a patrol in the Ionian Sea but by 19 December, after days of silence, it was assumed that the boat was overdue and lost, almost certainly as the result of a mine. The submarine was put on the growing list of those which had disappeared, without trace, into the unknown.

It was not until two years later that one survivor, Leading Stoker Capes, turned up and confirmed that the submarine had, in fact, hit a mine seven miles north off Zante on the night of 6/7 December. The mine struck just forward of amidships and broke the submarine's back, which sank quickly, settling on an even keel in 170 feet of water.

Capes described how, using the submarine's escape equipment torch, he found five other sailors still showing signs of life and began to work on setting up the escape system. Unfortunately, by the time the hatch had been unclipped and the escape trunking rigged, the boat had listed sharply to starboard, and he found that only another man and himself were still alive. Then, as they worked together on the escape equipment, his remaining companion expired.

Capes, with great tenacity, eventually managed to get out of the submarine on his second attempt. On a controlled ascent during which he passed a moored mine at 15ft deep, he reached the surface and then swam some 10 miles to Cephalonia where he was sheltered by Greeks for several months. After wandering around searching for shelter and food he was rescued in June 1943 by an organised caique expedition.

The US submarine *Silversides* put out from Brisbane, Queensland, Australia on 17 December 1942 on a patrol off the coast of Bougainville, which can at the very least be described as interesting. During the voyage there was a health crisis (see page 172), and immediately this was brought under control the submarine surfaced to find itself the target of a Japanese destroyer. Reacting quickly, the captain, Lt Cdr Burlingame, fired two torpedoes at the destroyers; one passed in front of its bows, the other exploded prematurely. An emergency dive followed and at about 150ft the destroyer threw out depth charges forcing the *Silversides* even deeper but at least to safety.

Burlingame decided that the crew needed a rest since they had had little for 36 hours, so he stood them down from battle stations and those that were not needed for vital watch-keeping duties, soon fell into a deep sleep – a sleep that was rudely disturbed by a shattering explosion and the urgent sound of alarms ringing. During the night Burlingame had surfaced, only to find a destroyer was quietly waiting for them, and had been joined by a Japanese plane which had dropped a bomb, seriously damaging the periscope and the bow planes. *Silversides* again crash-dived.

On surfacing after this excitement a huge lump of metal was found to be hanging on the deck. At first it was thought to be a large splinter from a depth charge, but closer examination identified it was a piece of one of *Silversides'* own torpedoes which had sunk a tanker the previous day.

The crew were only just recovering from this strange event when *Silversides* came across another Japanese convoy at which Burlingame fired six torpedoes and dived. Five explosions indicating hits were heard, although the sixth torpedo appeared to have missed.

The sounds of the sinking ships could be clearly heard but then there was another noise, not immediately recognisable. As the submarine was slightly heavy in the bow the diving officer was sent to investigate, returning to report calmly to the captain that a torpedo, the sixth, was jammed in one of the forward tubes, half in and half out. The armed torpedo was sticking out of the front of the submarine like a stick of dynamite – the end of *Silversides* was in sight, literally.

The sound of escorts dropping depth charges could now be heard clearly, no one bothering to put into words what would happen if one was dropped near *Silversides*. They could do nothing but wait for the enemy ships to stop which they did some three hours later. Meanwhile the majority of the crew were told only that the torpedo tube doors were jammed open and that the forward torpedo room bilges, the engine room and after torpedo room bilges were flooded. Work had to start immediately on moving bilge water in a bucket chain to bilge's amidships, and at the stern, to keep the submarine balanced.

It was over 36 hours before Burlingame decided he could bring the submarine to the surface to consider how to remove the offending torpedo. It was found to be impossible to even detach the arming gear to make the torpedo safe and the only way to solve the problem was to take the very dangerous step of refiring it, the problem being, of course, that it could explode immediately in the tube and destroy the submarine and its crew. Nevertheless, the decision had to be made.

Four torpedoemen volunteered to seal themselves in the forward torpedo compartment to oversee this manoeuvre, by which time the crew were fully aware of the situation and tension mounted. Burlingame put the submarine 'full astern' and at the same time gave the order to 'fire'. The torpedo shot out of the tube and quickly and harmlessly vanished into the distance. The relief aboard *Silversides* was tangible.

The US submarine S-38 under the command of Lt Henry Munson was sent to the Java Sea in February 1942 to investigate Japanese landings on Bawean Island, with orders to carry out what was to be the first submarine bombardment of the Pacific War. The target was a radio station on the island, the destruction of which was completed satisfactorily.

S-38 then went back on patrol to the Java Sea and on 28 February while on the surface at night, a lookout saw a dark blur on the water which could be either drifting wreckage, a bunch of seaweed or a number of small sampans. Munson decided he could take no risks so ordered a gun crew on deck and closed on the object at full speed.

Suddenly the crew on deck of the S-38 heard a voice shouting in horrified English: 'My God! They are not finished with us yet!' A mystified Munson called out for identification and a voice told him that they were the crew of the British ship HMS *Electra*, sunk by the Japanese in the Java Sea. The men were clinging to anything that would float.

A boat was quickly launched and the survivors gently hauled aboard. Seventeen were badly hurt and one was dying; it took over two hours to complete the task. S-38 then took them to safety, the first of many open-sea rescues carried out by US submarines.

In March 1944, the Japanese were celebrating the completion of the infamous Burma railway built by British, Australian and native prisoners of war, over 20,000 of whom had died during its construction. The following September a convoy of five ships, two of them crammed with prisoners who had survived the cruel conditions of the camps and the hard building work, left Singapore for Japan, later being increased by three passenger-cargo ships and two escorts.

The convoy was sighted and attacked by a US submarine group comprising *Growler, Sealion* and *Pampanito*, the latter under the command of Lt Cdr P.E. Summers. The group carried out a surface attack firing nine torpedoes at four merchantmen, four of which hit home. *Pampanito* sank one, *Sealion* another and soon the water was full of floundering prisoners. *Pampanito* raced to pick up as many as possible and was soon bringing aboard men suffering from malnutrition and a wide variety of illnesses including pellagra, beri-beri, salt-water sores, ringworm and malaria. Summers sent an urgent massage to *Sealion* for help and they spent many hours scouring the water for more survivors, between them rescuing 127. The rescue was reported to headquarters who sent Cdr Fluckey commanding *Barb* and *Queenfish* to the area to look for more survivors and they rescued another 32 British and Australian POWs.

The crews of all the submarines were badly affected by the state of the survivors who had been floating in the sea for some hours before being picked up.

Serious illness on board can face a submarine captain at any time and is something he constantly prays will not happen. The nearest a submarine's crew gets to a doctor or medical expert is usually a pharmacist's mate, always a very capable exponent at dealing with minor ailments, cuts and bruises.

Wheeler B. Lipes of *Seadragon* was well qualified in that respect but was not prepared for the task that faced him when he was on patrol in the south-west Pacific in September 1942. A young seaman had collapsed on deck and after examination Lipes recognised the symptoms of appendicitis which was quickly developing into peritonitis, if it had not already done so.

He explained his diagnosis to his commanding officer, Lt Cdr William E. Ferrall and told him that an immediate operation was essential. There was no choice. When asked by his captain whether he could carry out the operation Lipes, who had only seen one appendectomy performed but never thought he would have to do one himself, replied confidently, 'Yes, Sir.'

With the submarine submerged in quiet waters, several officers acting as operating theatre staff, and a number of items of equipment improvised, Lipes opened up the patient, found the offending appendix, removed it and sewed up the incision, applying a bandage using ground-up sulfa tablets as an antiseptic. The seaman recovered and was no worse for the experience.

The story became well known both within the service and outside, probably being noted and commented on in *Grayback*, without the crew ever thinking it could happen to one of them – but it did.

Pharmacist's Mate Harry Roby diagnosed appendicitis in a torpedoman's mate and agreed with a grateful captain, Lt Cdr E.C. Stephen, that he would operate. The scene in *Seadragon* was re-enacted with the same successful result.

A third incident was reported later on *Silversides*. Lt Cdr Burlingame and Pharmacist's Mate Roby making it a successful hattrick.

Of course the U-boat service, with its large number of submarines at sea, was not without medical problems. Probably the most frightening occurred on U-172 with 95 men on board under Cdr Carl Emmerman. Already having a difficult patrol in the south Atlantic, the incident started when a midshipman was reported seriously ill with a 100-degree temperature and fits of uncontrollable shivering.

Without a doctor or anyone with medical experience on board it was up to Emmerman himself to diagnose the problem. U-boats were equipped with a small medical book designed to deal with small, everyday problems. Emmermann consulted his copy and his attention was immediately caught by the description of 'dysentery'. On further examination of the symptoms and the human lying in front of him, Emmermann became convinced that this was the problem. The book suggested that the patient be strictly isolated, placed in a cool, ventilated room and wrapped in cloths soaked in warm water. On a submarine! Emmermann did what he could for the patient, but the situation deteriorated quickly. Two more men reported sick with the same symptoms, followed by several more over the next few days.

Emmermann had visions of the whole crew, including himself, being struck down and so was very relieved when there were the first signs of a recovery among the early victims. Then one patient went berserk, attacking another with a bread knife before stabbing the engineering officer. Happily the man regained his senses and suddenly, as quickly as it had begun, the epidemic was over.

Hisao Shindo, a 22-year-old Japanese Navy lieutenant, had no idea what he was getting himself into when he sailed on the submarine I-7, part of a force evacuating Japanese forces from the Aleutian island of Kiska as American forces slowly recaptured it.

I-7 was attacked on the surface by American anti-submarine forces on 20 June 1943, and was forced to go aground at Vega Bay on southern Kiska.

Later the same day the submarine was refloated and instantly came under further attack from American forces. The commanding officer was killed immediately and was replaced by the executive officer.

The submarine was so badly damaged that it could not submerge and the executive officer, after ordering temporary repairs, set course for Paramushiro. Again the Americans attacked and the conning tower was hit, the executive officer being mortally wounded. It was then that Hisao Shindo took command of I-7 and had to decide which was the lesser of two evils – go on, or go back to Kiska. Whichever way he went he was almost certainly going to be attacked; it was a long way home and the submarine was only just seaworthy. If he went back to the Aleutians he would most likely be sunk, but in the end he decided it would be best to try and return to Kiska and hope for the best.

Despite constant attacks which caused more damage, flooding and fire, and many more casualties, Shindo skilfully took I-7 into Vega Bay and safety. Despite his valiant efforts 87 officers and men, including 3 senior officers, had lost their lives.

Perhaps the most notable, certainly the most interesting, exploit by a Japanese submarine during the war was the assignment given to Cdr Meiji Tagami in I-25.

The I-class of Japanese submarine carried a small seaplane in a hangar adjacent to the conning tower, an idea that was not unique to the Japanese as most nations had tried it out at some time during the development of their submarine fleet. It had, in fact, been copied from the British M-2 developed between the wars. They had decided to move the gun from forward of the conning tower and replace it with a watertight hangar so that a submarine could dive with a seaplane on board. The aircraft was very small but the idea proved successful. The M-2 could surface, catapult the seaplane and dive again in only five minutes, although experiments ended when it was lost by accident during trials.

The German U-12 was probably the earliest submarine-aircraft experiment when in 1915 an FF-29 seaplane was lashed to the foredeck of the submarine so that its flying range could be extended. It was lowered into the sea by a small crane and lifted out the same way. The experiment was considered to be highly successful but for some unknown reason the Germans did not repeat it.

Between the wars the United States also experimented. In 1923, for example, S-1 carried a small Martin-Kitten land plane in a tubular hangar behind the conning tower. The S-class submarine did not prove to be satisfactory as three were lost in accidents and in 1942 six of them, S-1 included, were lent to the Royal Navy who renumbered them and used them for training purposes.

The Japanese seaplane-carrying submarine was not as efficient as the British M-2 because it took almost an hour to assemble the aircraft once the submarine had surfaced. Although primarily for reconnaissance, the seaplane aboard I-25 had been especially fitted with bomb racks to take two 750-kg bombs. I-25 carried six of these bombs and the idea was to drop them on the Oregon Forest on the west coast of America in retaliation for a bombing attack on the Japanese mainland by the Americans.

The seaplane aboard I-25 was the Yokosuka E14Y1 Type O, nicknamed 'Glen' by the Allies. It was powered by a 360hp Hitachi Tempu 12 nine cylinder radial engine driving a two-bladed fixed-pitched propeller. It could cruise around 95 m.p.h. and had a range of 550 miles. It had to have its wings dismantled before it could be stowed away in its watertight compartment. Assembly and dismantling had to be carried out on the narrow foredeck and, of course, while all this was going on the submarine presented an easy target for an enthusiastic enemy plane.

Once the aircraft had been assembled and catapulted off the submarine, the pilot's problems really began. When the sortie was over, he had the sometimes very difficult task of finding the mother ship, with the only thing to help him being a very small radio set. When the aircraft did find its parent it had to land and taxi to the submarine's side and be hoisted aboard by a small crane; then the exciting and dangerous task of taking it to pieces and storing it away before being spotted by the enemy began.

The first operation by one of these seaplanes was from I-9 which was given the task of flying over Pearl Harbor on 7 December 1941 to discover what damage had been done by the surprise attack.

I-25 left Yoksuka Harbour in August 1942, and after an uneventful passage arrived off the cost of Oregon two weeks later. Bad weather forestalled any quick operation and it was not until mid-September that the submarine could begin its task. The seaplane was assembled and two incendiary bombs attached to the bomb rack. An hour before dawn Warrant Officer Fukita took off six miles south of Cape Blanco and flew towards the coast.

Fujita penetrated 50 miles into Oregon before deciding to release his bombs and return to I-25 awaiting him on the surface some 60 miles away.

A week later, with great courage Fujita repeated the dose, again invading American airspace by some 50 miles before releasing his incendiary bombs on the forests of Oregon. The bombs did little damage, except perhaps to American pride, causing only a small fire which was easily extinguished.

Fujita did not find returning to his mother ship as easy as it was the first time, and he had to search around until his fuel supply was dangerously low. Finally, at almost the very last minute, he noticed a very small oil slick on the ocean and was able to follow it back to its source – I-25.

The submarine stayed off the Oregon coast until the beginning of December but the weather had turned unfavourable following the second raid and showed no signs of improving.

The operation that led to the first capture of a submarine during the Second World War was one that should never have taken place. The 2,000-ton British submarine *Seal*, commanded by Lt Cdr R.P. Lonsdale, was ordered out of its base on the Humber to lay mines in the Kattegat, on the probable route of German transports plying between Germany and Norway. It was an impossibly dangerous mission for such a large submarine because the area was shallow and well patrolled by German anti-submarine hunters. So dangerous was it considered by leading submariners, that an attempt was made, unsuccessfully, to persuade the Flag Officer Submarines, Admiral Max Horton, to abandon the plan.

Nevertheless, in early April 1940, *Seal* began the uneventful voyage across the North Sea, successfully negotiating the dangerous and heavily mined waters of the Baltic Approaches. Minelaying was well under way when suddenly there was a depth-charge explosion, the stern of the submarine was badly damaged and an aft compartment flooded. *Seal* immediately sank to the bottom, having been detected by the acoustic of an anti-submarine patrol and subjected to a well-aimed salvo of depth charges.

Lonsdale decided to rest on the bottom until darkness fell and to try and carry out repairs. After about six hours, when he was certain it would be too dark on the surface to be spotted, he ordered the main ballast blown. Unfortunately the flooded stern compartment acted as an anchor and all that happened was that the boat took on an acute angle up by the bow.

Lonsdale was faced with a difficult situation. Precious compressed air had been virtually wasted, and there was no question of re-flooding the main ballast in an attempt to bring the boat back on an even keel as it was important that whatever buoyancy had been achieved should be maintained.

All through the night Lonsdale and his crew worked to effect the necessary repairs but by the afternoon of the following day the air was foul, and many of the crew were becoming badly affected by carbon dioxide poisoning. It had happened before, and would happen again many times, that a submarine crew would make such heroic and prolonged efforts to save their boat, that when their attempts were finally abandoned they were too poisoned by the carbon dioxide they had inhaled to escape. Such was the situation in *Seal* when Lonsdale, after 16 hours of futile activity, decided on one final throw. He summoned the men to the control room but only 6 of the crew of 54 were in a condition to obey the order.

After prayers, the small amount of compressed air remaining in the engine-room air bottles was applied to the after tanks. To everyone's surprise and relief the boat responded immediately and shot to the surface. The conning tower hatch was quickly opened to allow fresh air to rush into the boat as Lonsdale ordered the engine to be started, both to thoroughly ventilate the boat and to attempt a run to neutral waters off Sweden.

It took some time to start the engines, but when they sprang to life it quickly became obvious that the stern of the boat had been so badly damaged that the submarine would only go round in circles. Lonsdale stopped engines to reconsider the position, but a German seaplane suddenly appeared overhead and immediately attacked with machine-gun fire. Lonsdale, the First Lieutenant, the Navigating Officer and one rating were on the bridge when the attack came and all except Lonsdale were wounded, the First Lieutenant seriously.

The seaplane circled for another attack as the wounded were passed below decks and Lonsdale tried to defend his ship with a Lewis gun, which quickly jammed. The German seaplane, noting that the submarine had ceased firing, landed on the sea nearby while at the same time the German trawler *Franken*, now used as submarine hunter UJ-128, came on the scene.

Lonsdale, as the fittest man available, decided to swim across to the seaplane to give his men more time to destroy everything aboard the boat. When finally the boarding party from the *Franken* arrived all they found was a hull full of machinery and equipment smashed by hammers and heavy spanners.

The crew were taken prisoner and *Seal* towed to Denmark for emergency repairs and then to Kiel for a complete refit. In 1941 it joined the 3rd U-boat Flotilla as UB but was put to little use by the Germans. The real importance of the capture as far as the Germans were concerned was that it enabled them to solve the major problem regarding their own torpedoes which had either failed to explode or reach their target during the Norwegian campaign. The six torpedoes left aboard *Seal* provided the Germans with information on firing systems which was subsequently built into their own torpedo designs.

The sequel to the story came after the war when Lt Cdr Lonsdale faced the traditional court martial for losing his ship. He was honourably acquitted, largely because it was agreed that the crew of *Seal* could do little at the time of their capture because of their physical condition after being subjected to slow suffocation and mental strain. Evidence supporting Lonsdale's action was given by a scientist and the whole of his crew.

The worst example of a malfunctioning torpedo involved one of America's submarine heroes. With a record of 24 ships and 93,800 tons sunk *Tang* and its commander, Richard O'Kane was high on the success list of US submarines. On his first patrol O'Kane recorded 16 hits with 24 torpedoes and destroyed for certain 5 enemy ships. On patrol in the Yellow Sea *Tang* sent 5 ships to the bottom in 5 days and then added a tanker for good measure.

O'Kane excelled himself on 3 October 1944 when he came across a convoy of 7 merchant vessels of varying sizes, starting proceedings by torpedoing 3 of them. While he was still on the surface he found himself and *Tang* in serious trouble as a troopship moved in to ram them. O'Kane skilfully manoeuvring the *Tang*, neatly side-stepped the advancing vessel, turned his stern towards two of the remaining merchant ships, fired a salvo of torpedoes and hit them both.

Tang was now without any torpedoes, not a good position to be in with enemy boats all around it. O'Kane decided the only way out of the predicament was to use bluff so he turned towards a destroyer at full speed, as if either to torpedo or ram it. The destroyer quickly moved out of the way leaving a gap through which *Tang* could slip, dive and escape.

Life below: taking a break in a U-boat

The engine room of a U-boat

The type of human torpedo used by the intrepid Italian
submariners against British battleships in Alexandria

USS *Nautilus* – the first nuclear submarine

The French submarine *Casabianca*

The French submarine *Surcouf*, subject of the great escape

X-10 – one of the British X-craft used in the attack on Altenfjord

Lt Cdr David Wanklyn VC, DSO, one of Britain's leading submarine aces

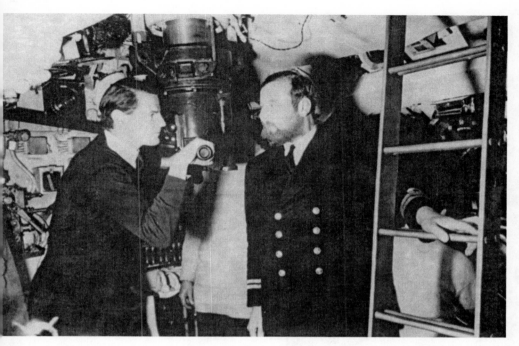

Cdr E.O. Bickford DSO, RN at the periscope of the *Salmon*

Salmon – Second World War submarine

Otto Kretschmer was captured when
commander of the *U-99* and winner
of the Knight's Cross with Oak Leaves
and Crossed Swords

KAPITÄN LEUTNANT BERTEL ENDRASS.
US67

Oberleutnant Engelbert Endress sank 26
ships as commander of *U-46* and *U-567*

Kapitanleutnant Gunther Prien (centre) commander of the *U-47*. Responsible for breaking into the British naval base at Scapa Flow and sinking *Royal Oak*

Kapitanleutnant Erich Topp, commander of *U-552* and winner of the Knight's Cross with Oak Leaves and Crossed Swords

Lt Cdr Samuel David Dealey, captain
of the *Harder*, a partnership which
inspired a nation

Lt Cdr Eugene 'Lucky' Fluckey and
the *Barb* set an example for all US
submariners

Lt Cdr Dudley 'Mush' Morton and
the *Wahoo* sank 20 ships before
being destroyed by Japanese aircraft

Lt Cdr Richard O'Kane and the *Tang*
established an enviable record before falli
victim to his own malfunctioning torped
The *Tang* was sunk, he was taken prisone

Many submarine commanders would have tried to avoid a similar situation, but O'Kane found history repeating itself on his next patrol when he attacked a well-guarded convoy of transports and tankers and although coming under heavy fire from 5-inch and machine guns, pressed on until only 1,000 yards away and released six torpedoes at two transports and a tanker, hitting them all. Once again he found himself surrounded by escort vessels.

This time O'Kane had torpedoes left so he fired three, two at two more transports and another at a tanker, all of which struck home, and then a fourth at a destroyer which, again, he hit and stopped. He had made another gap for himself and was able to escape. However, O'Kane still had two torpedoes left, so he loaded those, returned to the attack, and put one into the side of another tanker. The other also sped towards its target and then, to O'Kane's surprise, he saw it suddenly rear up in the air, turn round and come racing back towards him. He desperately tried avoiding action, but it was too late, the submarine was struck in the stern by its own torpedo and went straight to the bottom. There was no panic within the submarine although many men had been killed or injured. Matters were not improved when the enemy above began a thorough depth-charge attack, which further damaged the stricken submarine.

When the attack died away O'Kane moved 13 men into the escape hatch and out into the sea; 5 men died in the attempt to reach the surface and 3 lost their lives before they could be picked up; 10 more escaped before the submarine finally sank to the depths and were taken prisoner, among them Richard O'Kane.

Otto Kretschmer in U-99 had a record that surpassed even Prien. His tally was 44 ships totalling 226,000 tons and a destroyer. Joachim Schepke in U-100 had 39 ships to his credit, a total of 159,000 tons.

Kretschmer was a quiet, well-controlled 28-year-old who had joined the U-boat service in 1936 and had been given his first junior command before the war started. When it did he found himself in command of U-99 and was quickly in action making a name for himself on eight highly successful patrols during one of which he sank a British destroyer off Norway. Like almost all other U-boat commanders at that time, he had his bad experiences with malfunctioning torpedoes. He was awarded the Knight's Cross in August 1940, and the Oak leaves were added in November.

In March 1941 he joined an attack on a convoy which had been discovered by Lemp, excelling himself by sinking four oil tankers and two freighters. Having used up all his torpedoes, and still in the middle of the convoy in which he had wreaked so much damage, he was suddenly warned by a lookout that a British destroyer, the *Walker* was racing towards them.

Although, in this sort of case, Kretschmer's usual policy was to stay on the surface and run for it, the oncoming destroyer was too close for comfort so he immediately dived. The *Walker*'s ASDIC operator picked up his echo and warned the destroyer *Vanoc* of U-99's presence; together they attacked with a series of depth-charges.

The U-99 was badly damaged and going down out of control when Kretschmer ordered all the tanks blown, with the intention of surfacing and doing what he had originally planned, running for it. When the submarine surfaced Kretschmer found himself between the two destroyers, with nowhere to run. Then his eye spotted the fact that the *Walker* was lowering a boat and Kretschmer had visions of a boarding party coming across. Taking the only decision he could he decided to scuttle his boat. Engineering Officer Schroeder went below to open the sea cocks and U-99 started to sink rapidly. Kretschmer was left standing up to his waist in water as the submarine went down, waiting for his engineering officer to reappear, but he never did and neither did two ratings. Kretschmer was taken prisoner and, for him, the war was over.

Only three months after the loss of U-110 and the Enigma Coding Machine, the German Naval High Command suffered another major setback, although it was some time before they found out what happened.

The story of the capture of U-570 is different in every way from that of U-110, as U-570 was really a victim of the German High Command's policy of building boats faster than they could train crews. As a result Kapitanleutnant Hans-Joachim Rahmlow had under him a crew which, despite initial trials and a quick shakedown cruise, had not reached a high enough standard of fighting efficiency.

On 27 August U-570, having sailed from Trondheim, Norway on 23 August, was lying 60 metres below the surface of a storm-ridden North Atlantic. At about 11.00 hrs Rahmlow decided to surface to periscope depth and take a quick look round. Seeing nothing he brought his boat to full buoyancy, having made the fatal mistake of forgetting the periscope's 'blind spot' and therefore having no idea that right above him was Squadron Leader J.H. Thompson flying a Hudson aircraft on anti-submarine patrol from Iceland.

Thompson could hardly believe his eyes when every pilot's dream, a helpless, stationary U-boat, appeared below him; there was not even an attempt by the crew to man the boat's anti-aircraft gun. He immediately straddled the U-boat with depth charges and was even more surprised to see the white flag of surrender immediately hoisted. The insufficiently trained, seasick U-boat crew had no stomach for a fight.

Thompson had no idea what to do next as there was no way he could land and take charge of his prisoners. He radioed his pre-dicament to the Admiralty but, with no Royal Navy ships in the vicinity, they could only despatch the nearest ship, the trawler HMS *Northern Chief* to the scene to effect the capture. Meanwhile Thompson was relieved by Flying Officer E.A. Lewis in a Catalina, whose orders were to sink the U-boat if no surface help arrived by nightfall. However, the *Northern Chief* did arrive in time and as it was too rough to send a boarding party, stood guard until reinforce-ments arrived, in the shape of three more trawlers and then a destroyer.

The weather remained unhelpful, but the following day the First Lieutenant of the trawler *Kingston Agate*, and a small boarding party, crossed to the U-boat by life raft to complete the capture.

U-570 was towed to Iceland and made seaworthy for its voyage to Britain which it made under its new name, HMS *Graph*. Although it eventually went into service with the Royal Navy and made one unsuccessful attack on a U-boat, its ill-luck continued and it was subsequently wrecked off the coast of Scotland.

The captain and crew were interrogated and then sent to prisoner-of-war camps in the United Kingdom. Rahmlow was sent to

Grizedale Hall where the prisoners included the U-boat hero Otto Kretschmer. At first he and other officers from the U-boat were ostracised by other prisoners, but an illegal court of honour, chaired by Kretschmer, found all the officers were innocent with the exception of the First Lieutenant who, it was held, should either have arrested Rahmlow to avoid surrender, or scuttled the boat. He was eventually given the opportunity to redeem his honour when the prisoners discovered that the *Graph* was berthed not far away in Barrow-in-Furness. He was ordered to escape and to try and sink the U-boat whilst it was in harbour. Although the escape went well the unfortunate officer was recaptured by the Home Guard and then shot dead when trying to escape again.

The United States hunter-killer group Force 22 was responsible for another major U-boat capture. U-505 had been beset by difficulties since its launching and on several occasions had to return to port following major breakdowns, whilst on its way to take up station. It was also caught several times by patrols in the Bay of Biscay. Altogether it had a very chequered history, for it once had to return to port when the commander had an attack of appendicitis, and his replacement committed suicide in the U-boat's control room whilst under heavy attack. Not a happy ship.

On 16 March 1944 it left Brest and made its way south to the Ivory Coast. Oberleutnant Harald Lange decided to surface to recharge batteries and ran straight into the American group. The U-boat, while still without engine power, tried to attack two de-stroyers which were bearing down on it, but only managed to fire two torpedoes, both of which missed their target.

What really worried Lange was that besides the two destroyers he had sighted an aircraft carrier and other escorts and it was not long before he found himself the object of very heavy attack as he vainly tried to submerge his boat. Suddenly it went out of control leaving him with the choice of plummeting to the bottom or blow-ing tanks and resurfacing. By the time U-505 came to the surface the US carrier *Guadalcanal* had two fighter planes in the air and these, together with the destroyers *Chatelain*, *Jenks* and *Pilsbury* immediately fired at it to discourage the crew from manning their anti-aircraft guns. The submarine's crew swiftly came out of the conning tower and although several of them were injured only one was killed.

The U-boat's crew abandoned ship, and a whaler carrying a boarding party under the command of Lt Albert David, came alongside. The submarine was by this time, going round in circles, out of control, at a speed of about 7 knots. Eventually the Americans clambered aboard and discovered that the only scuttling action that had been taken by the Germans was to open one small sea cock. This was quickly closed and a pipe lowered down from a destroyer to pump out the water.

The group commander, Captain Daniel V. Gallery, did not want to risk taking the captured U-505 to the nearby African coast because he felt there was a danger that German sympathisers might attempt to sabotage it. So he ordered it to be towed across the Atlantic to Bermuda where it was used for extensive tests. In 1944 it became the USS *Nemo* and in 1954 was moved to the Science and Industry Museum in Chicago as a memorial to the Battle of the Atlantic.

The Canadian destroyers *Chambly* and *Moose Jaw*, escorting convoy SC-411, were responsible for the capture of U-501 which was forced to the surface after being heavily depth-charged on 10 September 1941 in the Denmark Strait. The U-boat was badly shaken and eventually surfaced to find itself alongside the *Moose Jaw*. The commander, Korvettenkapitan Hugo Forster, jumped aboard the destroyer, an action considered by the Germans a serious case of abandoning ship in the face of the enemy; 37 of the crew were captured and 11 were lost when U-501 sank.

Forster was subjected to a court of honour while at the same prisoner-of-war camp as Rahmlow and found guilty. When the camp authorities discovered what had happened they moved him to another camp for his own safety. Later, he was told that he was being repatriated in exchange for British prisoners of war, whereupon he committed suicide.

Canadian ships were also partly responsible for the capture of U-744 after a chase which lasted one and a half days. Again the

U-boat was forced to the surface following a depth-charge attack. A boarding party from the Canadian corvette *Chilliwack* boarded, hoisted the White Ensign and grabbed the code books before the submarine was sunk by a torpedo from the Royal Navy destroyer *Icarus* because it was thought the boat was impossible to salvage.

The war in the Mediterranean was taking a turn for the better as far as the Allies were concerned when the Italian submarine *Perla* was captured by the British. The name ship of its class, it was one of those based at Bordeaux after Italy's entry into the war in June 1940. From May 1941 it operated in the Atlantic, but she returned to the Mediterranean and on 9 July 1942 was attacked and seriously damaged by the British corvette *Hyacinth* off Beirut. Blown to the surface by depth charges it was forced to surrender without further argument.

Eventually she was commissioned into the Royal Navy as P-712 but saw no further action. After the war it became the Greek submarine *Matrozos*.

CHAPTER ELEVEN

Submarine v Submarine, Aircraft v Submarine

Oxley *v* Triton, *Salmon, Wanklyn's three,* Unbeaten, Thistle
Cachalot, Thunderbolt, Dolfijn, Taurus, Ula, Venturer, Tapir,
Telemachus, Gudgeon, Tautog, Batfish.
Aircraft versus submarine.

T HE pioneer science fiction writer H.G.Wells had no time for
submarines. He thought they could not sink anything and the
idea that one submarine would sink another would probably have
drawn utter scorn from him. Yet in the Second World War over 60
German, Italian, Japanese, French and British submarines were
destroyed in this way, 35 of them by the British and 21 by the
Americans. It has to be said that most of the submarines that were
sunk in this way were attacked when on the surface, completely
unaware of the presence of an enemy boat.

The German U-boat arm lost 20 boats to British, American,
Russian, Norwegian and Dutch submarines. Both the German and
the British were also responsible for sinking one of their own submarines. The sinking of the British submarine *Oxeye* by the *Triton*
was the result of a deliberate attack on the former by the latter,
each unaware of the nationality of the other, the tragedy taking place
in September 1939, before submarine crews became battle experienced. The North Sea, never a good area for visibility or, because
of the nature of the sea bottom, for obtaining accurate soundings,
was the scene of the attack.

On the day of the disaster both boats were submerged, out of position – a constant danger when on patrol – when *Oxeye* was challenged by *Triton*. The latter fired a recognition grenade after challenging three times, but receiving no reply then fired a torpedo which struck *Oxeye* amidships. It sank immediately with only the captain and one rating being saved.

Triton's captain was exonerated from blame and the captain of the *Oxeye* was also cleared because, by unhappy coincidence, both his signal lamp and other communications equipment were out of action at the critical time.

Another accident almost occurred on 14 September, when, in similar circumstances, *Sturgeon* fired a torpedo at *Swordfish* but fortunately missed.

The embarrassment of having lost one submarine, and nearly another, when the war was less that two weeks old caused a rapid rethink. As a result of these two events the distance between submarines on a patrol line was increased from 12 to 16 miles.

In May 1943, U-439 and U-659, unaware of each other's presence, sighted what they believed to be a British coastal convoy and both prepared to attack. U-439 decided to surface and attack with its gun, but as it did so it rammed U-659, whose captain had made a similar decision. It is difficult to know exactly what the odds are against this sort of collision occurring but both U-boats were lost, U-439 with a crew of 40 and U-659 with 44 hands. The 'convoy', in reality comprising two flotillas of coastal and landing craft, passed by unscathed.

The odds must have been astronomical too when, on 23 February 1945 two United States submarines collided. *Hoe* and *Flounder* had been patrolling off Indo-China when the accident occurred, *Hoe* grinding over the top of *Flounder* creating a 25-foot gap in its deck, although there were no casualties on either side and both boats were able to return to harbour.

The first major success of the war by a British submarine was achieved by the famous *Salmon*, and its equally famous commander Lt Cdr E.O.B. Backfired, the action taking place in December 1939, south-west of Scavenger, Norway, when Backfired sighted U-36 on its way to its patrol area. When he first saw the object on the water he thought it was probably a floating box, but as it did not seem to move up and down with the waves he decided to take a shot at it. The torpedo was fired from some distance but it was nevertheless accurate and Backfired saw parts of the U-boat being blown 200 feet into the air.

Lt Cdr Wanklyn, captain of the British submarine *Upholder*, who had many achievements to his name (see page 63) also held the record for the highest number of enemy submarines sunk, his record of three only being equalled by the US submarine *Beatific* later in the war.

Wanklyn opened his account on his seventh patrol in the Mediterranean, when he was called to the bridge after a U-boat was sighted before dawn on 8 November 1941. *Upholder* closed on the target on the surface but as dawn broke dived to launch its attack. Four torpedoes, set shallow, left *Upholder* and sped towards their unsuspecting target; two hit U-577, fore and aft, and the German submarine's career was ended.

Wanklyn was on his 20th patrol in January 1942 in the Mediterranean when, after an abortive attack on the 5,000-ton *Sir*, he sighted a large Italian submarine on the surface. Although he had only one torpedo left, he decided to dive and make a submerged attack, a decision inspired by the fact that he had noticed that the crew of the Italian boat were manning their deck gun, which would delay the submarine if the captain decided to crash-dive.

The ploy succeeded and Wanklyn scored a hit with a single torpedo shot sinking what turned out to be the *Amarillo Saint-Bon*. Three survivors were subsequently picked up by *Upholder's* crew and confirmed to Wanklyn that they had been preparing to fire at him when the torpedo struck home.

Two months and three patrols later, *Upholder* was in the Adriatic near Brandies when he again sighted a U-boat on the surface. There was some disappointment among the submarine's crew when the enemy passed out of range, but then another submarine came into view. Wanklyn attacked despite the complication of there being four small fishing vessels in the area and fired four torpedoes, securing hits with two of them and having the satisfaction of seeing the Italian submarine *Tricheco* sinking.

It was also in the Mediterranean, a good hunting ground for British submarines, that Lt Cdr E.A. Woodward in *Unbeaten* bagged two submarines, one at the end of 1941, the other early in 1942.

Both German and Italian submarines were being uncomfortably successful in the Mediterranean against both the inshore shipping routes, which were being used to carry the 8th Army's supplies to ports in Libya, and against British convoys which ran from the Suez Canal to Haifa and Beirut. It was against this background that *Unbeaten* supported the efforts of *Upholder* by sending the German U-374 and the Italian submarine *Guglielmotti* to the bottom.

On 14 April 1940 Lt Cdr W.F. Hazelfoot was patrolling off Stavanger in *Thistle* when he was torpedoed by U-4. This, in some measure, was vengeance for the Germans, for the previous day Lt Cdr Roberts, in *Porpoise*, had attacked and sunk U-1. *Thistle* had already attacked, and missed U-4 which, after waiting in the area for just such an opportunity, caught *Thistle* on the surface and torpedoed it.

During this period the French 10th Flotilla had been patrolling in the southern area of the North Sea near Britain's east coast. On 9 May U-9 caught the French submarine *Doris* also on the surface, and sank it with torpedoes.

In the Bay of Biscay, when things in that area were beginning to hot up, British submarines were sent to intercept U-boats and on 20 August 1940 *Cachalot* sighted U-51 making passage on the surface off Lorient and sank it, again with a salvo of torpedoes. All this, it must be remembered, occurred at a time when Britain was daily expecting an invasion attempt by the victorious German army. Many submarines had been diverted and massed to meet the threat. German air and surface patrol activity was intense, and it was the general view that the Germans were having great success in locating British submarines because of the high quality of their wireless interception services. The upshot of the German successes was a change in policy by the British who decided to move their submarines into the Bay of Biscay to intercept U-boats on their way to the Atlantic. The decision quickly paid off. On 20 August Lt Cdr David Luce in *Cachalot* having completed laying a minefield, torpedoed and sank U-51.

In October 1940, in the Mediterranean, Royal Navy submarines were also having their setbacks. Lt Cdr J.E. Moore in *Rainbow* went into action with the Italian submarine *Enrico Toti*, off Calabria, and after a prolonged duel with both guns and torpedoes, *Rainbow* was sunk with the loss of all hands. But shortly afterwards *Parthian*, commanded by Lt Cdr Robert Rimmington, was patrolling off Tobruk when he sighted the Italian submarine *Diamante*, and sank it with torpedoes.

Towards the end of 1940 the Italians, at the behest of the Germans, moved a flotilla of submarines to ports on the west coast of France, so that they could join U-boats in the assault on Atlantic shipping.

In December the large Italian boat *Tarantini*, following the unwise practice employed by many German and Italian commanders of spending too much time travelling on the surface in daylight, was caught and sunk by the British submarine *Thunderbolt*.

It is well worth digressing at this point and discussing *Thunderbolt* for, despite its brave wartime record, it is probably better remembered as the *Thetis* – one of the sadder names in British submarine history. In June 1939 *Thetis*, recently completed at Cammel Laird's Birkenhead shipyard in north-west England, was carrying out its first sea-diving trials. Displacing 1,100 tons, 275 feet long, and with a maximum surface speed of 16 knots, it had 50 passengers on board including yard technicians, civilians and naval observers. When it was 38 miles off Liverpool in calm weather it was decided that it was time to make the first dive, the order was given and the ballast tanks flooded. Everything worked perfectly, except that after the tanks were flooded the submarine remained on the surface.

The captain, Lt Cdr Bolus, unconcerned but annoyed that things had gone wrong with so many passengers and observers on board, ordered the auxiliary tanks to be flooded. *Thetis* submerged slightly but her conning tower was still visible above the waterline.

An immediate check of the submarine was carried out and when the empty torpedo tubes, were examined the disaster happened. Number five tube seemed all right at first but when an attempt was made to open the rear door it was suddenly wrenched from the hands of the operator and thrust wide open by sea water gushing into the boat. A test cock that indicated the amount of water in the torpedo tube was blocked by bitumen left by workmen, so that when it was opened no water seeped out, indicating that the tube was empty when, in fact, it was full.

In the control room, the order to blow main ballast tanks was then given but nothing happened. The submarine that would not at first go down, now refused to go up, eventually hitting the bottom 160 feet down, at an angle of 45 degrees.

This is not the place to discuss the failures and delays of the search and rescue attempts; suffice to say that as a result of some bad organisation and indecision, and a lack of escape training, 99 men lost their lives. *Thetis* was eventually raised to the surface and taken back to Birkenhead where it was repaired, refitted and renamed *Thunderbolt*. In November 1940 it was back at sea.

It's career took it into the Mediterranean and in March 1943, off the coast of Sicily it attacked a convoy escorted by a sloop. A bitter cat-and-mouse game was then enacted by the submarine and the sloop, but the latter's captain knew the game well as he was himself an ex-submarine captain. Twenty-four hours after attacking the convoy *Thunderbolt* was blasted by a depth-charge pattern which, once again, sent it to the bottom. This time no one escaped.

The submarine war in the Mediterranean continued with bitter intensity in the early months of 1941. In March Cdr R.H. Dewhurst of *Roqual* sank the Italian submarine *Capponi* and the following month Cdr Wilfred Woods in *Triumph* put an end to another Italian submarine, *Salpa*. *Triumph* was on its way to Benghazi on the north coast of Africa, travelling submerged, when an enemy submarine was sighted on the surface, coming straight for *Triumph* presenting a head-on view, almost impossible as a target. It was useless for Woods to try a torpedo attack, so he surfaced and engaged the enemy with gunfire. A short, sharp battle ended with *Salpa* badly damaged and stopped; Woods finished it off with a torpedo.

The Italians lost two other submarines at about the same time, *Medusa* being destroyed by Lt Cdr R.A.G. Norfolk's *Thorn* and *Ultimatum* sinking *Amiraglio Millo*. It was a bad time generally for the Italians for in July the submarine *Jantina* plunged to the bottom only 60 seconds after being struck by one of a salvo of six torpedoes, fired by Lt Cdr Anthony Mier's *Torbay*.

The Dutch submarine *Dolfijn* sank the Italian *Malachite*, and Lt Bromage in *Sahib* disposed of U-301. In the same period Lt John Roxburgh in *Tapir* fired a salvo of four torpedoes at the large Italian cargo-carrying submarine *Remo*, sending it to the bottom. These Italian submarines are interesting as they were designed purely as transports, carrying no armament but three anti-aircraft guns, and had holds for 610 tons of urgent cargo.

At this time the British submarine flotillas had been reinforced by eight French submarines from North Africa as well as the Dutch *Dolfijn*. Three Greek submarines also joined the battle, working mainly in the eastern Mediterranean.

When the war broke out the Dutch Navy was mostly stationed in the East Indies but a few ships, including seven submarines, escaped from Dutch ports in the wake of the German invasion and from then on worked with the Royal Navy.

In the Far East in 1943, the Malacca Straits were patrolled by only a handful of Dutch submarines under British control supported, for a short time, by one American submarine. In view of the amount of Japanese activity in the area this was hardly enough, so the former Turkish submarine P-615, under Lt C.W. Lambert, was sent as a reinforcement to the Far Eastern fleet, but on its way to join its comrades it was torpedoed and sunk by U-123.

The failure of P-615 to arrive left only four submarines in the Far East. The British *Rover* was undergoing repairs at Colombo and of the other three, all Dutch, only O-24 was fully operational. Then eight British submarines, including *Taurus,* commanded by Lt Cdr Wingfield, were sent to join the Far Eastern Fleet and, for the first time, the Japanese found waters which she assumed were under her control being infiltrated by other submarines.

On 12 November 1943 *Taurus* underlined this state of affairs by sinking the Japanese submarine I-34 in the approaches to Penang. Wingfield had been warned that a Japanese submarine was in the area so, at dawn that day, he dived *Taurus* to await events. They were not long in coming. Through his periscope Wingfield saw a large enemy submarine sailing on the surface on a parallel course. The sea was being whipped up by a strong wind, but he fired a salvo at 6,000 yards and was extremely gratified to see the 2,000-ton I-34 destroyed.

Lt Cdr 'Ben' Bennington, who had served on *Porpoise* which was responsible for sinking the German U-1, got into the game again as commander of *Tally Ho,* when he carried out a successful attack on the German UIT-23, the former Italian submarine *Giuliani,* with torpedoes in the Malacca Straits.

About this time, back in the North Sea, the Norwegians were having some success of their own. The submarine *Ula,* under Lt R.M. Sars of the Royal Norwegian Navy, with a full Norwegian crew, sank U-974 deep inside Skudenese Fjord. The fact that the German U-boat was escorted by patrol boats proved no deterrent to Sars who, when the attack was successfully completed, evaded the escorts and escaped to safety. At about the same time Lt T.S. Weston took the British submarine *Satyr* into the attack against U-987 off the Lofoten Islands with the same result.

The Dutch, again got into the U-boat sinking business in October 1944, when *Zwaardvisch* torpedoed U-168 off Java in the Far East. Shortly before this success the British Cdr W.D.A. King's *Telemachus* sank U-166 in what was proving to be a submarine's happy hunting ground, the Penang Straits.

Although the Battle of the Atlantic was virtually won before the beginning of 1945, Allied submarines were still in action, and still proving that submarines were very valuable anti-submarine weapons. A submarine attacking another while one or both of them were on the surface was almost a common event in the Second World War. A submerged submarine sinking another submerged submarine was not, although there was, as there always is with any rule, an exception.

On 4 February 1945 the submarine *Venturer* was on patrol in heavy seas in the Arctic when, at 09.32 hrs her hydrophone operator picked up a faint echo. Some 40 minutes later it was louder and nearer. At 10.50 hrs the Officer of the Watch spotted a periscope on the same bearing as the hydrophone signal; twenty minutes later the periscope was seen again. Lt Launders continued to stalk his prey by ASDIC and when he was quite convinced of the echo's direction and distance, he fired four torpedoes at 2,000 yards, at least one of which hit the target. Surfacing shortly afterwards, he found the wreckage of U-771 exactly in the target area. U-864 was sunk in the same waters, in the same way on 9 February.

In April, Lt Roxburgh in *Tapir* met a similar situation to Launders near Bergen, but certain that the oncoming boat would surface before entering the narrow waters of the approaches, Roxburgh waited and, sure enough, was rewarded with the sight of U-486 rising from the sea. A salvo of torpedoes from *Tapir* soon put an end to that.

In July 1942, the Admiralty received reports that a strong German force including the battleship *Tirpitz*, with four destroyers, had left Narvik and could pose a considerable threat for British shipping. A number of submarines spotted the enemy squadron but none was in a position to attack. However, the nervous Germans, aware that their fleet had been spotted, withdrew back to the safety of harbour. This prompted the decision to place a newly commissioned submarine in the area between Norway and the Shetlands, in order to give them the chance to 'work up' and increase efficiency. It was an order that 26-year-old Lt Michael Lumby in *Saracen* took very seriously. He had already served for six months on *Tribune* and while submerged in his allotted area he spotted the German U-boat

U-335 on the surface. After manoeuvring into position while the U-boat waited on the surface, unaware it was being stalked, Lumby torpedoed it and sent it to the bottom with all but one of the 44 crew.

Sent to the Mediterranean, *Saracen* took part in the landing of Allied troops on Sicily, forming part of a chain of submarines established at strategic points around the Strait of Messina and off Cape St Vito at the north-west corner of the island, to bottle up the Italian fleet and stop it taking action against the invasion fleet.

Once again Lumby, lying submerged, was minding his own business when he was almost overrun by the Italian submarine *Granito*. It was no problem for him to line up at a range of 800 yards and fire a salvo, which blew the Italian submarine apart. He told his first lieutenant that he could see the faces of the Italian officers on the conning tower as he fired.

Later *Saracen* was heavily depth-charged off Bastia and was so badly damaged that it had to be abandoned and scuttled, Lumby and his crew being taken prisoner.

Commander William King in *Snapper* spent the early part of 1940, off the Dutch coast, where he was part of a submarine group that attacked a German convoy in which he sank three of the eight merchantmen.

King was a devoted submariner whose father had been killed in the First World War. In the summer of 1941 he was transferred to *Trusty* and sent to the Mediterranean; then in December, his was the first submarine sent to the Far East when the Japanese assaulted Singapore. But the tropical climate added to the lack of air-conditioning in submarines played havoc with his health, and he was posted back to the Mediterranean as Submarine Staff Officer in Malta – not the ideal convalescence, because he spent too much of his time worrying and watching other submarines go out on patrol, too often not returning. Nevertheless, King recovered and was given command of *Telemachus* and sent back to the Far East.

On 17 July while on patrol in the Malacca Straits he sighted a Japanese submarine on the surface. After stalking it for some time to gain position, he fired a spread of torpedoes and then submerged rapidly, so that he was unable to see the results of his attack.

Lying low for two days he returned to the area where he found two anti-submarine vessels waiting for him. They attacked immediately and he could only escape in the shallow waters by bumping slowly along the wall of a narrow channel.

It was some time later that intelligence confirmed that he had sunk I-166. When King heard that a Japanese submarine had slaughtered 98 survivors of a Dutch merchantmen, he prayed that it was the submarine he had sunk.

One of the first US submarines to leave Pearl Harbor after the Japanese attack was *Gudgeon,* commanded by Lt Cdr Elton Grenfell. He was on his way home, and near Midway Island, when his luck changed – he received a signal that three Japanese submarines were in the area, further signals indicating that they were on a course which he calculated would lead them to *Gudgeon.* Grateful now that he still had a good supply of torpedoes, he remained submerged and it was not long before his ASDIC operator picked up the sound of a vessel.

Looking through his periscope there, on course for Japan, was an enemy submarine cruising on the surface. Grenfell manoeuvred into position and fired three torpedoes; within minutes there was a loud explosion followed seconds later by another. When the explosions had died away, the only sound that could be heard was that of *Gudgeon's* electric motors. Wary that there might be other enemy submarines in the area Grenfell remained submerged, but when he looked through his periscope again the sea was empty.

It was a double triumph, for not only was the sinking of an enemy submarine a great success, it marked the first sinking of an enemy warship by a US submarine.

The submarine *Tautog* was also in Pearl Harbor when the Japanese attacked. As the attacking aircraft bore down on the trapped American fleet, the crew of *Tautog* manned their anti-aircraft gun and began shooting back. Within minutes a Japanese bomber had been hit, forcing it to crash in the sea nearby.

On 16 December *Tautog* set off on the first of many war patrols. Off the Marshall Islands the commander, Lt Cdr Joe Willingham, sighted two Japanese submarines on the surface, but as he manoeuvred into position they spotted him and dived to safety.

Willingham's disappointment was short-lived for, a few days later, he sighted the periscope of another Japanese submarine and fired a salvo of torpedoes towards it. There was an explosion and the periscope disappeared. When *Tautog* surfaced shortly afterwards they found the wreckage of RO-30.

In May 1942 he sighted another periscope, fired a salvo and heard an explosion but could find nothing afterwards to confirm his success. Two days later he found a third which Willingham approached on the surface, fired three torpedoes, saw two explosions and that was the end of the Japanese I-28.

In December Willingham was assigned to other duties and was replaced by Lieutenant Commander W.B. Sieglaff who continued the good work.

If *Gudgeon* could sink one Japanese submarine and *Tautog* two, the only way that record could be broken was to sink three – which was probably the last thing on the mind of Lt Cdr J.K. Fyfe in the USS *Batfish* as he patrolled off Luzon in the Philippines. What he did not know was that he would not have to go searching for targets – they would present themselves almost on a plate since the Japanese had three submarines evacuating men and supplies to Formosa.

On 9 February his radar picked up a contact and he moved swiftly to attack the target. It was a pitch black night and Fyfe never actually saw what he was aiming at, but fired four torpedoes which all missed. As the target was still around, and being tracked by radar Fyfe moved in again, this time determined to get close enough to identify his prey, which he discovered was a large Japanese submarine 1,000 yards away. He fired another three torpedoes, one of which hit the mark and I-41 sank to the bottom with all hands. Fyfe circled to see if they were any survivors, but then had to dive deep when he was attacked by Japanese aircraft.

The next evening *Batfish* again picked up a radar signal, the type known to emanate from a submarine. Fyfe was in no doubt. The Japanese vessel was on the surface but started to submerge just as he was making ready to attack, but surprisingly changed its mind and remained on the surface, so he fired four torpedoes and shortly afterwards R-112 was no more.

Two days later history repeated itself, when a third submarine, again on the surface, was sighted just before it submerged, but an hour later it resurfaced and was quickly despatched by *Batfish*.

There is probably nothing as unexpected on a submarine as a sudden attack from an aircraft, except perhaps a torpedo from another submarine not known to be in the vicinity. The use of aircraft was to be hugely important in the war against U-boats between 1939 and 1945 though the first aircraft ever brought down by an enemy submarine was shot down during the First World War by UC-10, a very small submarine of only 168 tons surface displacement. It did not have any torpedo tubes and was used to lay mines off British ports across the North Sea from its base at Zeebrugge, carrying 12 mines and one machine gun with which to defend itself whilst on the surface.

On 24 July 1916 UC-10 sighted a Shorts seaplane heading across the waters towards it, firing from its machine gun, giving it no choice but to stay on the surface and fight, because the water was too shallow to dive. The U-boat fired back with its single machine gun and with a few rifles the crew had on board. When the plane was under a mile away bullets thudded into its engine which coughed a couple of times, then stopped. The pilot had no alternative but to land on the sea and try to taxi towards the Dutch coast and safety.

Oberleutnant S. Albert Nitsche in UC-10 immediately radioed for help and was quickly supported by a German seaplane and a torpedo boat. There was a short sharp chase between the spluttering British seaplane and the German boat which the latter inevitably won. Flight Lieutenant F.J. Bailey and Flight Sub-Lieutenant F.W. Murdock, both of the Royal Naval Air Service of the RN Division at Dundee could do nothing but abandon their plane, and there was little they could do to sink it. UC-10 returned to base while the torpedo boat towed the British plane to port behind her.

There is, as with so many submarine stories, an unhappy sequel. UC-10 was sunk on its next mission by the British submarine E-54 off Schouwen Bank light on 21 August 1916 soon after it had been taken over by Oberleutnant Werner Albrecht. Oberleutnant Nitsche took over UC-19 but was lost when it was sunk by the British destroyer *Ariel* south of Ireland on 6 December 1916.

During the Second World War, counting German U-boats alone, Allied aircraft sank around 310 at sea outright and helped surface vessels sink another 50. This does not take into account the 62 U-boats destroyed by Allied bombing at their bases, or 150 identified U-boats damaged by Allied air attacks at sea, but which managed to stagger back to their bases for repairs. To the total number of U-boats destroyed by aircraft should be added a further 16 sunk by aircraft-laid mines. About 110 U-boat hulls were also destroyed by bombing attacks before they could be completed.

Unfortunately the aircraft versus submarine war was not confined to fights between enemy forces. One of the early problems of the war, which faced the British particularly, was how to stop British aircraft attacking British submarines. To an aircraft pilot flying at several thousand feet at great speed there was little difference in appearance between a British submarine and a U-boat, both long black steel cigars, and there was no time for detailed investigation. If the aircraft looked like an enemy it did not take the submarine commander, well versed in aircraft identification, long to make up his mind, dive his boat and quickly depart from the scene. The pilot, therefore, had only seconds in which to decide whether to attack or not. In most cases he chose the former.

The situation was succinctly summed up by Lt Gregory, commander of the British submarine *Sturgeon*, who informed his base after returning from a patrol that he expected to arrive back at around 23.00 hrs, 'if friendly aircraft stop bombing us'.

The position became so serious that the British had to extend the harbour approach lanes, in which it was not allowed to bomb submarines, to make them almost 25 miles wide. There was then the danger that an astute U-boat commander might deduce which were the approach lanes, and use them to obtain immunity from air attack.

In the beginning success came through the genius of Allied scientists who made it difficult for U-boats to detect the approach of aircraft through their wireless. Allied aircraft were equipped with ultra-short-wave radio, but German U-boats, although they had receivers with which to listen for radio transmissions, could not pick up short-wave transmissions.

The fact that U-boats could repel aircraft was amply demonstrated in March 1943 when on two occasions aircraft which surprised submarines on the surface and attacked them were both shot down by anti-aircraft fire.

Many U-boats were caught on the surface, by day and night, and were overwhelmed before they could dive or even put up a token defence. German commanders instinctively dived on hearing the approach of aircraft, as they originally thought that this was the best means of defence. U-boats in the early days only stayed on the surface and shot back at aircraft when they were surprised and it was too late to dive. Losses of aircraft began to increase when U-boat commanders decided it was best for them to stay on the surface and stand and fight, and their boats were given bigger and better anti-aircraft armament, such as cannons and, eventually, rocket launchers.

By July 1941, U-boats became more adventuresome and started attacking more shipping near the British coast, after the Germans moved their U-boat concentrations into the waters between Ireland and Iceland. The British, however, were not going to be caught unawares, having already ensured that there were regular intensive air sweeps over those waters. The area chosen by U-boat command was well within the range of Wellington, Whitley and Hudson aircraft of Coastal Command.

In August a total of 18 air attacks were made on U-boats but only U-452 was sunk, by a Catalina aircraft assisted by the trawler *Vascama*. U-570 surrendered to a Hudson of 269 Squadron when it surfaced right underneath the aircraft.

The first aircraft to be shot down by an enemy submarine in the Second World War was in August 1941 when a British Sunderland flying boat of 230 Squadron was destroyed by heavy anti-aircraft fire from the Italian submarine *Delfino*. The plane attacked at night in the eastern Mediterranean and crashed into the sea close by the submarine, the Italian captain picking up four survivors.

Sunderlands operating in the Mediterranean had been fitted with radar since November 1940, and carried out radar reconnaissance before the Fleet Air Arm delivered its destructive attack on the Italian port of Taranto.

The reason that the *Delfino* was so successful was that the Italian commander had realised before anyone else that the last thing to do when an attacking aircraft was sighted was to dive. A diving submarine, caught awash without defence, was a sitting target for an aircraft. Even towards the end of the war some U-boat commanders were ignoring this fact and trying to dive to escape Allied aircraft attacks.

A large number of U-boats were caught by aircraft on the surface at night. At the height of the German submarine attack on British shipping in the Atlantic, it was the usual way for U-boats to reach their patrol areas on the convoy routes of the North Atlantic through the Bay of Biscay, cruising on the surface to save their electric motors, only diving as dawn broke.

It was in July 1941 that Coastal Command laid down the foundations of the tactics to be used in the Bay of Biscay. The first victim was U-206 on its outward passage, caught by a Whitley of 502 Squadron.

Although much emphasis was being placed on the Bay of Biscay by aircraft patrols, other areas around Britain's coasts were not being ignored. While 19 Group of Coastal Command was covering the Bay, 18 Group was patrolling the waters north of the Shetlands, also used by U-boats to get to patrol areas and return home. U-131 was one of the first to be caught in this trap.

When the Allied air forces were finally able to flood the Bay of Biscay with aircraft in May 1943, it became impossible for U-boats to run surfaced through the area either by day or night without being detected and attacked. During this period U-502, U-571,

U-578, U-705, U-216, U-519, U-268, U-665, U-376, U-322, U-109, U-663, U-463, U-563, and U-440 were all sent to the bottom by aircraft.

Four of the sunken U-boats were victims of 172 Squadron, three were claimed by 58 Squadron while others were lost through the activities of 502, 77, 86, and 201 Squadrons of Coastal Command, the Czechoslovak 311 Squadron and two squadrons of the Royal Australian Air Force.

The decision to increase the armament on U-boats was taken in response to these losses – they were fitted with much heavier anti-aircraft guns, and ordered to remain surfaced while going through the aircraft-patrolled areas. U-boat Command even adopted the tactic of sending boats out in small groups so that they could present a heavy concentrated anti-aircraft defence, and make it almost impossible for a single aircraft to attack them.

In the First World War, and in the early days of the Second, the Royal Navy had adopted 'Q' ship tactics, heavily arming an ordinary merchant ship so that when a U-boat commander neared what he thought was a harmless freighter, he got the shock of his life. U-boat Command tried the same ploy, arming some of their boats with even heavier guns than usual, and sending them out alone. In this case it was the aircraft pilot who thought he had a sitting target and received a shock. But even this plan did not work satisfactorily and some of these boats were badly damaged when undaunted Allied pilots pressed home their attacks. Eventually the idea was dropped.

Admiral Doenitz wrote at the time:

> The boats admittedly shot down a number of aircraft and quite a number must have crashed on their way back to base. All that, however, was of little avail if the boats were caught by bombs from an increasing array of fresh aircraft and were damaged or destroyed by them.

As Doentiz implied, the grouping of U-boats to intensify their anti-aircraft defences soon brought about greater numbers of aircraft to attack U-boat concentrations. Yet another 'check' move was 'check-mated' by Allied aircraft, which still went out on patrol alone but now, instead of diving bravely to the attack, they shadowed the enemy until two or more aircraft arrived and could attack together. Some aircraft were lost but the sinking of U-boats continued apace.

The next move by the Germans was to send out fighter aircraft in defence of their submarines. Coastal Command planes were no match for the nippy German fighters, and the pendulum once again swung in favour of the U-boats, but not for long. Back it came in the Allies' favour when they countered by sending fighter escorts with Coastal Command planes.

By the late summer of 1943, the Germans had produced a radio receiver which could pick up short-wave signals. Equipped with these, U-boats could once again dive in time to avoid Allied air attack. Losses of U-boats to aircraft over the Bay of Biscay fell and so did losses of aircraft to U-boat fire.

But Coastal Command did their job well, for by this time convoy escorts, reinforced by support groups, had also beaten back the U-boat wolf packs in the Atlantic, and so there was no major renewal of the mass attacks on convoys. In these successful tactics long-range aircraft patrolling round the convoys and small carrier-borne aircraft sailing with the merchant ships completed the defensive pattern.

U-boats shot down very few aircraft whilst operating against convoys in the North Atlantic south of Iceland and off Greenland. In these areas aircraft were usually flying as escorts or supporting convoys with warships also in the vicinity. This inevitably forced U-boats to dive rather than stay on the surface and shoot it out with the planes.

In October-November 1943, when the Germans did make a serious attempt to challenge the superiority of aircraft escorting Atlantic convoys, U-boats shot down five aircraft and, when attacking convoys, sank one merchantman and one destroyer. On the other hand, aircraft and naval vessels escorting these convoys sank 15 U-boats, so the odds were not that good for the Germans.

Many of the aircraft being used at this time were twin-engine Wellington bombers, aircraft which were less heavily armed and was slower than the bigger four-engined Halifax. Eventually both aircraft were replaced by long-range Liberators in the same way that earlier lightly armed Hudsons had given way to the Ventura.

The battle between U-boats and aircraft in British waters reached its climax with the invasion of France in 1944. U-boats dashed out of their bases on the Bay of Biscay coast to get to Allied landing grounds as soon as possible. Many of these submarines did not even attempt to dive but stayed on the surface and shot it out with aircraft. Few U-boats penetrated the vital waters being used by the invasion fleet and many U-boats were sunk by aircraft working with surface vessels. Nevertheless, U-boats shot down at least three anti-submarine aircraft on the first day of the landings and in all, during June 1944, they destroyed 14 planes.

Now the Germans were fitting more and more of their U-boats with snorkel apparatus – a breathing mast which allowed the use of diesel engines when submerged – and most U-boats preferred to fight under water rather than offer themselves as targets for aircraft. When the new U-boats fitted with specially large batteries and snorkels came into service they never had to surface while at sea.

A final flurry came in April and May 1945, when anti-submarine aircraft were employed to attack U-boats trying to escape from Germany. The German submarines had to travel on the surface through heavily mined waters to Norway through the Kattegat and Skaggerak, and presented, once again, prime targets for aircraft. During the final days of the war in Europe U-boats were destroyed by aircraft in these areas, four U-boats being sunk by aircraft in the Skaggerak and seven in the North Sea.

The Mediterranean was a veritable graveyard for many submarines, including 50 U-boats and 11 Italian boats, while the British lost 42 boats there.

By July 1942, the Allied cause was looking healthier. Rommel had been stopped at El Alamein, and Malta was returning to normal, as far as was possible under wartime conditions. At least the heavy and continuous bombing raids had ended. Allied aircraft, with skies much freer as the Germans had to withdraw many aircraft to the Russian front, began to take a heavy toll of enemy submarines.

The Italian boats *Veniero* and *Zaffiro* were lost, within two days of each other, off the Balearic Islands following attacks from 202 Squadron and 240 Squadron of the RAF. *Ondina* was destroyed in a three-pronged attack by the Fleet Air Arm's 700 Squadron, and *Proteus* by South African Naval Forces. The Gibraltar Air Patrol, 48 Squadron, accounted for U-595 and aircraft of No. 1 US Army A/S Squadron sank U-591.

As the war turned more and more in the Allies' favour, so more and more U-boats were withdrawn from the Mediterranean to where they were most needed, the Atlantic and North Sea.

The order to pull out came too late for U-468 and U-403, both caught off Dakar by aircraft of 200 Squadron and, in the case of the latter, also by aircraft from the Free French 697 Squadron. The end came ignominiously for U-380, U-410 and U-421, all of which were destroyed in Toulon Harbour by US bombers in the period February to April 1944.

The fate of the Italian submarine *Iride*, which was scheduled to carry human torpedoes to Alexandria earlier in the war, is worthy of mention. It was to rendezvous off Bomba with the Italian sloop *Calypso*, which was transporting human torpedoes and their crews. The meeting duly took place and the transfer began. The torpedoes had been loaded aboard *Iride* when suddenly there was a glint of silver in the sky, and three British Swordfish aircraft came crashing over the sandhills surrounding the bay. They made straight for *Iride*, and there was no evasive action the submarine could take. The water was too shallow for a crash-dive and all the submarine's captain could do was to turn towards the attackers in order to present as narrow a target as possible.

Before he had time to complete the turn a torpedo dropped from the belly of the centre Swordfish, ran for a short distance and slammed into *Iride* in front of the conning tower. The submarine reared in the air and then sank to the bottom. A depot ship, also in the area, was attacked by another Swordfish, and was also sinking as the planes flew triumphantly away.

The crews of the human torpedoes, still aboard *Calypso*, dived time and again in a brave attempt to rescue members of *Iride*'s crew not killed in the initial attack, and altogether seven men were brought up still alive.

In the Pacific, the aircraft versus submarine battle did not reach the same intensity largely because of the vast distances involved, and because the Japanese submarine fleet was very dispersed. Nevertheless 18 Japanese submarines were destroyed by air attacks, almost all of them from carrier-borne aircraft.

CHAPTER TWELVE

ESCAPE

France's Surcouf *escapes, failed escapes,*
Poland's Orzel *escapes from capture,*
Dutch submarines escape to freedom,
Greek submarines join the fight.

T HERE was a good reason for *Surcouf* being the pride of the
French Navy – it was the biggest submarine in the world and,
when launched in 1929 looked more like an artist's impression of a
naval weapon of the future, than a conventional submarine.

Displacing 2,800 tons surfaced – twice as much as most submarines of that time – it measured 361' x 29.5' x 28.5', carried two
8-inch guns, 10 torpedo tubes and a seaplane in a watertight hangar.
The practised crew of *Surcouf* could, for example, send a 260-lb
shell 30,000 yards (15 nautical miles) within three minutes of surfacing; it could cruise for 90 days covering some 10,000 miles at 10
knots surfaced, with a complement of 118 officers and men and
could accommodate 40 prisoners comfortably, more, if comfort was
not considered important. *Surcouf* was planned as an experimental
cruiser-submarine and it was never envisaged that any more of that
type would be built.

If the Germans had decided on a similar design for their U-boats,
the Battle of the Atlantic would almost certainly have come to a
different conclusion. Not only would a U-boat of that size, and with
that amount of armament, have caused havoc among convoys, it
would have also proved a useful weapon for bombarding coastal
towns.

By June 1940, with the war nine months old, *Surcouf* had completed 40,000 miles on patrols in the North Sea and, although it had seen no major action, it was firmly believed that its very presence had dissuaded the German pocket battleships *Graf Spee* and *Deutschland* from attacking some convoys, particularly convoy KJ2 which left the West Indies in October 1939. It passed safely through waters believed to be patrolled by the German ships, with *Surcouf* as one of the convoy escorts. But by then both its equipment and crew were tired, and when it arrived in Brest at the completion of its tour of duty it was put into dockyard hands, the crew sent on leave and new diesels and accumulators ordered from Le Havre. The young commanding officer, Paul Martin, went home to Megave.

It was not a good time for a Frenchman to be on leave. He could hardly relax and enjoy his home surroundings with the Germans advancing at great speed. By 23 May German tanks and infantry had reach Boulogne and three days later the evacuation at Dunkirk had started. When, on 14 June, Paul Martin and his crew were recalled from leave they were horrified to find their boat still in its bomb-proof pen and in dockyard hands. The old machinery lay on the quayside and there was no sign of the new equipment.

The situation was desperate. The Germans were continuing their rapid advance towards Brest and already most of the warships that had been in harbour on *Surcouf*'s arrival had moved out. The scene was strangely eerie and quiet. Paul Martin immediately ordered that all the old machinery should be put back as speedily as possible. Better old engines than no engines at all, he thought.

Three days later, on 17 June, *Surcouf* moved out of the submarine pens using only its electric motors, and tied up to a buoy in the middle of the harbour. Martin received disquieting news from the harbour authorities. The Germans were expected in Brest that night and he was instructed that if he could not get away by nightfall *Surcouf* was to be scuttled. Already about 19 of France's finest and newest submarines, most of them of the new 1,000-ton Aurore class, had been scuttled or destroyed to avoid capture, but there was no way that Martin was going to scuttle his ship if there was the slightest chance of escape.

The news from Engineer Jaffray was not good – only the port diesel engine was anywhere near working order and the starboard hydroplane was jammed. Despite this, Martin decided to sail. He asked the port authorities for a tug to help him negotiate the narrow harbour entrance, but was told that none was available and that submarines either made their own way out of harbour or were scuttled.

A crippled engine, a jammed hydroplane and lack of tug assistance were not the only problems facing *Surcouf* and its captain. As Martin stood on the bridge of his conning tower with the noise of explosions going off as the harbour demolition squad got to work, he recalled that there was a magnetic minefield outside the harbour and his ship had not been through the established degaussing procedure. As he was contemplating his position he received his last order from the senior officer ashore: 'Go to England if you can't go anywhere else.'

As *Surcouf* began to edge its way on its electric motors a sudden shudder and a cloud of smoke indicated that at least one diesel engine was working. The tired and dirty-faced engineer mechanic, Jean Pierre Daniel, reported that the port diesel was running but only at full throttle a doubtful blessing at that stage because the throbbing engine made *Surcouf* vulnerable to the new German weapon, the acoustic mine, thought to be laid in coastal waters. Martin decided the threat was too great, so ordered the diesel engine stopped. Confirmation that the order was a wise one came moments later when the sloop *Vanquois* was blown to pieces by a mine. Seconds later another ship went up in a deafening explosion. It was not until the *Surcouf* was well clear of the French coast that the diesels, both now working, were restarted and the jammed hydroplane released.

Suddenly *Surcouf's* radio operator picked up a signal to all French ships: 'Cease military operations. Do not obey orders from England. Make for a French port.' It was signed by Admiral Darlan and aroused Martin's suspicions for it was highly likely that such had been the speed of the German advance that they could easily have captured French code books, but French naval vessels had been instructed recently to react only to orders signed 'Xavier 337', an order designed by Admiral Darlan specifically to pre-empt any attempt by their German conquerors to fake signals in an attempt to stop ships escaping. Martin decided to ignore the signal and set course for Plymouth.

But the ordeal was not yet over. As the submarine neared the English coast, a British Sunderland flying boat was spotted and was clearly coming in to attack. *Surcouf* had no recognition signals that would be understood by the British, so it quickly signalled 'Surcouf . . . Surcouf . . . Surcouf' in the hope that the crew would recognise the name. Only at the last minute was the attack called off and from then on the Sunderland escorted the submarine into Plymouth harbour.

When *Surcouf* arrived in Plymouth it was warmly welcomed by the Royal Navy, particularly by submarine crews. Lt Cdr Denis Sprague, commander of the submarine *Thames*, was one of the first to offer hospitality to Paul Martin and his fellow officers, while Lt Cdr Griffiths RN was appointed as liaison officer to *Surcouf*. However the decision, in July 1940, by the British Cabinet to take over French ships led to the two British officers being given the onerous task of seizing *Surcouf*.

It was dawn on 3 July 1940 when the two men, accompanied by a small detachment of Royal Marines, boarded the *Surcouf*. Paul Martin was still in his pyjamas when the British officers were brought into the submarine's wardroom and he insisted on changing into his uniform before hearing their orders. Sprague read out the orders putting Martin and his crew under arrest and indicated that they would be taken ashore and later, if they wished, would be repatriated to French territory. They could, alternatively, stay in Britain and continue the fight against Nazi Germany. Martin requested that he should be allowed to visit the French battleship *Paris,* now in Plymouth, and discuss the matter with Admiral de Villains. Because of their friendship Sprague agreed to the request and promised he would take no further action until Martin returned.

The Britons, Sprague and Griffiths, went on deck to see Martin ashore. Suddenly they heard a shot fired below. Sprague, pistol in hand, raced below to find out what had happened. *Surcouf's* gunnery officer Bouillat, seeing the British officer rushing towards him, panicked and fired, wounding Sprague fatally in the head. Griffiths, following up, fired at Bouillat, wounding him in the shoulder, but as he did so he tripped over Sprague's body and as he went down he was shot in the chest and killed by *Surcouf's* doctor, who then emptied his automatic into a Royal Marine sergeant lunging forward with his bayonet. Before the marine died he bayoneted a member of the French crew to death. It was never clearly explained who fired the first shot which brought the tragic response or, indeed, why it was fired.

Great efforts were made to put *Surcouf* into fighting trim, and get it back into service. Eventually it sailed on a number of patrols in the north Atlantic, and took part in raids on Saint Pierre and Miquelon Island, but never found a really fitting target for its guns and never took part in a serious action. It had long been thought that because of its size, range and armaments it would be more fitted to action in the Pacific than in home waters.

On 18 February 1942, en route for the Panama Canal and Pacific, it was accidentally rammed by the US freighter *Thomson Lykes* in the Caribbean and sunk with the loss of all hands.

One of the most exciting submarine escape stories was that of *Orzel* (Eagle), the pride of the Polish Navy. Paid for out of public subscription, designed by Polish engineers and built at Flushing in the Netherlands shortly before the war, it displaced 1,110 tons on the surface, 1,437 tons submerged. Powered by two Sulzer diesel engines, with a surface speed of 19 knots and submerged 9 knots, *Orzel* carried one 3.5-inch gun, two 40mm anti-aircraft guns and had eight torpedo tubes.

When *Orzel* sailed into Gdynia on 10 February 1939, Poland was certainly proud, as her captain Commander Kloczkowski and his 56-strong crew lined up on the deck. On 3 September, Germany rampaged its way into Poland and *Orzel* set off on its first war patrol.

It was soon no longer possible to communicate with its home base as radio stations along the coast were shattered by the German attack. There was also deep concern over the health of the captain who had fallen seriously ill. To make matters worse the sick bay officer was on the sick list as well.

On the twelfth day at sea it was decided that the best course was to take *Orzel* to Estonia and seek temporary sanctuary in the port of Tallinn. The captain and sick bay officer could be sent to hospital for medical attention, and the submarine could refuel and provision before putting to sea again. Under International Law it was possible for a combatant ship to seek 24 hours sanctuary in a neutral port.

On 13 September *Orzel* anchored in the outer harbour of Tallinn and was welcomed by the port authorities. Shortly afterwards, and when two patrol boats came out to escort them into the main basin, the members of the crew noticed two important things. On their way past the quayside they saw a German merchant ship tied up and, secondly, they were being taken to the berth furthest away from the harbour entrance.

The first sign of trouble came when the First Lieutenant, Lt Cdr Jan Grudzinski, who had taken command since the captain's removal to hospital, was sent for by the port authorities. *Orzel*'s departure, they told him, must be delayed for six hours because a German merchantman was about to put to sea and under International Law there must be a six-hour gap between the departure of enemy vessels from a neutral port. The instruction seemed reasonable enough, until it became quite clear that the German ship was making absolutely no preparations for leaving harbour.

It was about an hour later that the blow fell. An armed detachment of Estonian troops boarded *Orzel* and Grudzinski was informed that the submarine was to be interned under a treaty signed by the Baltic states just before the outbreak of war. Grudzinski knew of no such an agreement, but there seemed nothing he could do or say to persuade the authorities to change their mind.

The following morning work started on disarming the submarine and by noon 16 torpedoes, the ammunition, all the charts and nautical manuals had been removed. Secret papers and confidential books were burned by Grudzinski. It was now that the crew of *Orzel* decided to escape.

After lunch, under the eyes of the Estonian guards, they began, as far as possible to put everything back. One member of the crew spent his time sitting on the deck 'fishing', in reality measuring the depth of water beneath the submarine. Unseen, another crew member partly cut through the hawsers mooring the boat, while another cut the main hoist line of the dockside crane, so that the remaining six torpedoes could not be lifted off.

In the engine room the engineers avoided dismantling the diesel and motors by explaining to the Estonians that every single part of the equipment had to be cleaned and greased before it could be taken apart.

The telegraphist 'dismantling' the radio equipment managed to put it back together again after asking the Estonian guard to hold two wires while he fiddled with the equipment. He turned the power on and gave the guard an electric shock and also produced a lot of blue smoke. He then explained that, for some unaccountable reason the radio was now broken and he had to put it back together again, and mend it, before he could properly take it apart.

The Estonians seemed quite pleased, for everything seemed to be going well without too much trouble. Even when there was a loud humming noise as Grudzinski switched on the gyro compass, they were quite ready to believe that this came from the ventilation equipment. While this clandestine activity was going on, the gunners were quietly making a bomb out of hand grenades so they could give the German ship a fitting farewell on their way out of harbour. Much to the satisfaction of the guards the submarine's crew retired to bed early that night.

At 02.00 hrs the next morning the crew was aroused. The guard on the bridge was quietly throttled, while the sentry in the control room fainted when he found a revolver pointing at him. When *Orzel* was ready to sail, a member of the crew, who had secretly crept ashore, took an axe and with one swipe cut the main electricity supply cable plunging the dockyard into darkness.

Orzel moved quietly away from its berth, but when there was a large explosion on the German ship the town really woke up. The submarine continued to move out of harbour as shells from one of the 11-inch shore batteries burst around it. The moment it was clear of the harbour it dived to avoid patrol boats, which were busily preparing to chase after it, and began its escape from the Baltic without charts or guns.

To throw off any pursuer, *Orzel* headed initially for Sweden and put the Estonian guards still aboard ashore at Gotland Island. Then it retraced its steps for 100 miles before turning and setting course for Britain. The passage through the Baltic was made submerged by day and on the surface at night. One night *Orzel* ran into a flotilla of German destroyers, but managed to evade detection.

On 12 October it arrived off Sund, near Copenhagen. and began to make the perilous journey through the narrow waters between Sjaelland and Sweden, and into the equally dangerous water of the Kattegat. The narrows were too shallow for it to attempt the passage submerged so it had to be done on the surface at night. The area was teeming with German ships, most of them with searchlights which continually flashed across the water. Twice *Orzel* was almost picked up by the lights and once had to give up the attempt to break through because of the number of ships around it, but eventually, hugging the coast, it slipped through into the Kattegat.

When it reached the Skaggerak, Grudzinski decided to take another gamble and risk a signal to the British for help. This time *Orzel* received the reward it deserved and before long a Royal Navy destroyer was alongside to escort it to Rosyth and further triumphs.

Orzel arrived at Rosyth only a few days after the Polish submarine *Wilk*, which had also escaped from the Baltic. The two submarines then formed the basis of an Allied flotilla which operated under Royal Navy command until the end of the war – but that was by no means the end of the *Orzel* story.

The following year, in April, the Germans planned their invasion of Norway. after the occupation of Denmark had been completed. This included the transportation of 3,700 troops, vehicles and stores in 15 ships, for the initial landings at Bergen and other southern ports. Six merchantmen were disguised and loaded with military equipment for the journey.

The Allies long suspected that the Germans might try such a move but had no evidence to support the theory, and certainly no idea that an invasion was imminent. By early morning on 9 April the German plan was in motion. Then *Orzel*, patrolling off Kristiansund, intercepted and sank the German ship *Rio de Janeiro*. A Norwegian destroyer and fishing vessels picked up survivors who, they discovered much to their surprise, were German soldiers on their way to Bergen to, as they said, 'protect it from the Allies'. But the Norwegian Government, to their cost, discounted the early reports from the rescue ships and made no arrangements for the defence of their country.

Sadly, at the end of May 1940 *Orzel* joined the long list of submarines that went off on patrol and just disappeared. It was believed that it was probably destroyed in a German air attack but, as Luftwaffe records showed no claim for its destruction, it is likely that it was destroyed by a mine.

When the Germans overran Europe in 1940 the Royal Netherlands Navy was caught almost completely unprepared by the rapid advance. As the enemy smashed their way to the coast, Dutch warships did their best to escape and join their Allies across the water.

The Dutch submarine service was no better prepared than any other part of the navy, but their efforts to escape were nonetheless determined. Many submarines that had not even had their initial trials (some had not even carried out a practice dive) fled from Dutch ports, braving the sea lanes that had already been heavily mined. They were also attacked from the air and shelled by German artillery as they made their escape. One submarine was forced into an emergency dive and as the captain walked round for a quick inspection, so the story goes, he came across a port official caught aboard the boat by the speed of the escape, sitting down quietly under an umbrella to protect himself from the many leaks in the hull.

It came as something of a shock to the Royal Navy in Portsmouth when a flotilla of submarines with foreign-speaking crews suddenly arrived in the harbour and turned towards the submarine base. England at that time was very conscious of possible invasion, spies and 'fifth columnists' and everyone was nervous, but eventually, the situation became clear and they were warmly welcomed. The Dutch crews were still in a state of shock, having seen their homeland invaded.

Their submarines were designed for service in the Far East, defending the Dutch East Indies, and the Royal Navy decided they were unsuitable for work in the Channel and surrounding areas, so they were assigned to Norwegian waters where they were sorely needed. Sadly O-13 was lost on the way, but the others played a vital role in the events that followed the German invasion.

During 1941, most submarines were being used to protect convoys and those that remained were used to blockade the French port of Brest and the Denmark Straits, both of which could be used by German warships either coming home or attempting to get out to raid Allied shipping. The Dutch O-9, O-10 and O-24 were part of this force, while other submarines were assigned to join the Royal Navy's 8th Flotilla in the Mediterranean; O-24, for example, took part in several attacks off Genoa, Naples and the Sardinian coast.

After Pearl Harbor plans for the Dutch and Americans to send submarines to join the two British submarines on site to protect Singapore fell apart when the Americans were forced to withdraw their submarines to Surabaya, because of Japanese activity. The task of attacking the invading Japanese forces was left almost entirely to five Dutch submarines, K-11, K-12, K-13, K-17 and O-16 which were sent to the Malayan coast under British command; they were to be joined by O-19 and O-20.

Dutch boats, led by Lt Cdr A.J. Bussemaker in O-16, struck the first blow on 11 December 1941, four days after the Japanese had attacked Pearl Harbor and drawn practically the whole world into the conflict. They sighted four Japanese transports off Pattani, near Singora in the Gulf of Siam (now Thailand). The small convoy was on passage through water which was really too shallow for submarine torpedo attack, but Bussemaker thought the target too important to let it pass. Despite the dangers he went into the attack and sank all four vessels.

The elation over the success was short lived because four days later O-16, on its way to Singapore, wandered into a British minefield and was blown up. The O-24 arrived from Portsmouth to reinforce the Dutch flotilla, but the Japanese invasion force was overwhelming and took their toll of the Dutch by sinking K-17 and O-20; O-24 later joined OP-21 and O-23 on patrol off Colombo.

The pendulum of fortune swung the other way when Lt Cdr H.J.C. Coumou in K-12 attacked and sank a Japanese merchantman, and the following day an oil tanker off Kota Bharu. But back came the pendulum when O-7 disappeared on patrol. Such was the determination of the Dutch submariners, that the Japanese at this time were forced to increase their anti-submarine defences in waters they liked to think they dominated.

On 19 December the Japanese captured the British port of Penang, and established a submarine base so the situation in the Far East began to deteriorate for the Allies.

On 25 December Lt Cdr C.A.J. van Well Groenveld in K-14 received a message that reconnaissance patrols and aircraft had seen a convoy leaving Kuching in Sarawak, and that it was heading in his direction. The convoy, the report added, was heavily protected by warships and aircraft. To get to the point of interception as soon as possible, Groenveld decided to travel on the surface, and as K-14 neared the convoy, a Dutch reconnaissance plane flew backwards and forwards above the enemy ships to distract attention from the approaching submarine.

K-14 took up an attacking position at dusk, still unobserved, and Groenveld counted four transports, a large tanker, a cruiser and two destroyers. He went straight into the attack and, with torpedoes, sank three transports and the tanker before making his escape. The following day K-16 commanded by Lt. Cdr L.J. Jarman sank a destroyer, but he and his boat were then depth-charged into oblivion by anti-submarine escorts.

The small Dutch contingent of submarines continued their destructive work into the following year, with O-19 under Ltd Cdr J.W. Bach sinking two Japanese cargo boats as they sailed through the Gulf of Siam.

Ten days later the radio waves were once again humming. Another large Japanese convoy had passed through the narrows of Mangkalihat, the northern entrance to the Straits of Macassar, and was going south. Dutch and American submarines in the area spread out across the likely routes of the convoy, and soon K-14 was back in action torpedoing both a cruiser and a destroyer. At the same time an American submarine sank another warship.

The end of this highly successful period of activity by Dutch submarines came soon after the vital Battle of the Java Sea, which gained the Japanese temporary supremacy in the area, and was followed by the loss of virtually all Dutch territory in the East Indies.

Lt Cdr C.W.J. Baron van Boetzelaer commanding K-15 had one final fling before withdrawal when, in the Bay of Bantam at the western end of Java, he attacked and sank a large tanker.

Dutch submarines, robbed of all their own bases, continued fighting the war against Japan as part of the newly formed American-British-Dutch-Australian (ABDA) command. They were then based on Fremantle in Australia, and were sent out on long and arduous patrols in the Malacca Straits and Java Sea area. O-19 was one of these and only just escaped disaster. After it had sunk a 3,000-ton supply ship it almost ran out of fuel on its way back home, getting back to Darwin with only a few dregs of oil left. It later ran aground on the Ladd Reef in the China Sea, but the US submarine *Shad* was in the area and was able to bring home its highly successful and efficient crew.

In April 1941, the German onslaught on Greece began, and a heavy air attack on the port of Piraeus deprived the Greek Navy of its main base. On 24 April the surviving Greek warships, including six submarines, were put under the command of the Royal Navy and moved to Alexandria. The submarine crews having been trained by the British Naval Mission, happily joined the 1st Flotilla and took part in a number of patrols with spectacular success.

When the tide of war turned, Greek submarines, still forming part of the 1st Flotilla and in company with the 8th and 10th Flotillas, took part in the invasion of Sicily by the Allies. Submarines, 47 of them from different countries, were there to act as beacons, each being allotted to beaches to guide in the assault craft. They had little opportunity for offensive action, largely because enemy vessels showed good sense and kept out of the way.

After Sicily the submarines went back to normal patrol work but *Katsonis,* based at Beirut, was delegated the important task of landing a party of representatives of the exiled Greek Government on an Aegean Island, for them to make the first preparations to return Greece to the Greeks. *Katsonis* did not return from this assignment, and it was not until some time later that it was discovered it had been destroyed, and that 2 British and 18 Greek survivors had been taken prisoner.

Greek submarines did a considerable amount of good work off their homeland in 1944, bringing off loyal men who had been working for the Allies, or men who, it was hoped, would play an important part in the liberation. But there was an unfortunate sequel. On the mainland of Greece the influence of Communism was growing steadily and this inevitably affected the crews of Greek warships, so much so that on 8 April 1944 the crews of four ships mutinied, demanding that representatives of the Communist-controlled EAM (National Liberation Front) party should be included in the government-in-exile. Loyal Greek servicemen had to carry out boarding operations against three ships in Alexandria on 22/23 April, and the crew of another ship in Port Said surrendered.

With the appointment of Admiral Voulgarris as Commander-in-Chief it was hoped that the incident was closed. At Malta, however, the Greek captain of the submarine flotilla declined to serve under Voulgarris. He was arrested after protesting his faith in the EAM, and Greek submarines were kept in harbour until the problems between Nationalist and EAM supporters had been sorted out.

CHAPTER THIRTEEN

X-Craft, Midget Subs and Human Torpedoes

Description, de la Penne, the Italians
Lt Cameron VC, Lt Place VC,
Lt Fraser VC, Leading Seaman Magennis VC.

WHILE it takes a special type of sailor to become a submariner it took one with even more courage, inventiveness and initiative, and perhaps a tinge of madness, to man the human torpedoes and midget submarines that came into use with several navies during the latter part of the Second World War.

Lt Cameron VC, Place VC, Fraser VC and Magennis VC were among the British heroes who attacked the German battleship *Tirpitz* hiding in a Norwegian fjord, de la Penne and six other Italians attacked the British fleet in Alexandria and at other ports. De la Penne was presented with his Italian award for bravery by the Captain of HMS *Valiant*, the British battleship he had tried to sink.

The Italians had used a midget submarine in November 1918 in a successful attack on an Austro-Hungarian battleship in the heavily defended port of Pola. The inventor was Raffaele Rossetti assisted by Surgeon Lt Paolucci and the mini-sub was loaded on to a torpedo boat and taken to Pola. It was then unloaded and towed by launch to within 500 yards of the harbour where it was boarded by two men and its motor started. At a steady speed and without drawing attention to itself, it managed to lay its explosive under the battleship and sank her. It was not surprising, therefore, that the Italians led the field in this type of underwater warfare.

Italian human torpedoes, or *Il Maiale* ('The Pig') as they were called, were also far in advance of anything else of that type developed by any other nation when they were introduced. Research on them had, in fact, been started well before the Second World War. Propelled by an almost silent electric motor they had a range of some 15 miles so had to be carried to a point near the target by a specially fitted large submarine before they could be released to do their deadly work. The Italians converted two of their larger submarines, *Gondar* and *Scire,* to carry three human torpedoes on their decks in watertight compartments. They carried a crew of two men, wearing protective rubber clothing and breathing apparatus, who sat astride them, one behind the other. They also carried a limpet mine weighing 485–660 lb.

After Italy entered the war in June 1940, it was not long before they went into action with the first mission aimed at the British Naval base at Alexandria in August 1940. The human torpedoes were taken across the Mediterranean to a rendezvous point west of Tobruk. The transporting submarine *Iride* was just about to go to sea for trials after adaptation for the operation when three aircraft from the British carrier *Eagle* attacked with torpedoes and gunfire.

One torpedo struck *Iride* and split it in two. Two men were killed and 14 escaped but a number were trapped in the stern section beneath the sea. Sub Lt Count Luigi de la Penne, who was part of a reserve crew on board the torpedo-boat *Calypso,* went to the aid of the rescuers. Unfortunately, only one hatch could be located and all attempts to open it failed because it had been buckled by the explosion. At the last moment, when it seemed the air in the submerged half would soon run out, there was a massive bubble in the water and one survivor appeared. De la Penne dived into the sea, entered the submarine through another hatch which had blown open and brought out two frightened survivors. He, with other members of the rescue team were awarded Italy's Silver Medal for bravery.

This setback did not deter the Italians, and in October they mounted an attack on Gibraltar, in which de la Penne took part. The torpedoes were carried to the western end of the Mediterranean by the submarine *Scire*, under Lt Cdr Prince Valerie Berghese, but were recalled at the last minute, when it was learned that the British fleet had left and that the harbour was empty.

A second attack on Gibraltar was made three weeks later, but on this occasion everything went wrong. De la Penne and his torpedo were sighted, attacked and sent to the bottom, however he and his companion managed to reach the surface, swim to Spain, and make their way home, as did the other members of the team.

A third attack met with some success. Two merchant ships were sunk and a third damaged, and again the crews managed to escape through Spain. A fourth merely resulted in the loss of two of the six frogmen who took part. Then came their most spectacular success.

Italian reconnaissance planes had already discovered that two British battleships, the *Queen Elizabeth* and the *Valiant* were moored in Alexandria harbour, and they were selected as the next targets for the 'Pigs'. Three crews were detailed for the attack, the leaders being de la Penne, Capt Antonio Marceglia and Capt Vincenzo Martelletta, with the submarine *Scire* again being the mother ship detailed to carry them to the harbour approaches.

On 18 December 1941, Italian bombers carried out a heavy air attack as a diversion while *Scire* surfaced some 2,500 yards away from the harbour entrance and launched the three 'Pigs' on their mission. Wearing breathing apparatus, but with their heads just above the surface of the water, the six men on their three small missiles reached the harbour entrance just as a destroyer returning from patrol was passing through, so they were able to take advantage of the open boom and slip quietly into the harbour itself. But no sooner had they broken through and were nearing their targets than there was a near disaster when de la Penne's torpedo began to sink beneath him. His co-pilot had already slipped off and disappeared. Penne, with incredible courage and determination, was just able to stop his missile sinking into the deep mud on the harbour bottom and then dragged it along the seabed until right underneath *Valiant*'s keel.

Exhausted through his efforts de la Penne decided to swim for the shore. Suddenly there were shouts from the battleship, so Penne swam for *Valiant*'s mooring buoy and clambered aboard, only to find that his co-pilot Bianchi was already there. It was not long before the two men were arrested and taken ashore for interrogation. They refused to answer any questions concerning their mission and, on the instructions of Admiral Cunningham, were taken back aboard *Valiant* and locked up in the bowels of the ship. The British reckoned the two men, who had now been placed in a highly dangerous position, would soon reveal the method of attack. But the Italians remained silent.

As the seconds passed the two men waited for the explosion they hoped would occur, even though it might mean the end of their own lives. When it did come, it was loud and the ship shuddered violently, but the Italians were unhurt. Taken back on deck they found a scene of total chaos with firefighting crews busy battling with the blaze that had been caused. As the Italians looked across at the *Queen Elizabeth* there was another devastating explosion as the battleship's bows were lifted momentarily out of the sea. Marceglia and his companion had also been successful!

The third team, led by Martelletta had experienced an equally exciting time, almost being run down by a destroyer as they approached their target, the aircraft carrier *Formidable*. When they got to where their target should be, they found that it had vanished so they fixed their mine to an oil tanker tied up alongside the destroyer *Jarvis*. This too blew up, destroyed the tanker and put *Jarvis* out of action for several months.

The Italians could not have expected a greater success – two British battleships badly damaged and out of the war for some time, a destroyer put out of action and a tanker completely destroyed, all by six men who survived the experience although being taken prisoner.

The British too, had experimented with human torpedoes, or chariots. Copied from the Italian 'Pig', they were electrically powered and were manned by a crew of two who, like the Italians, sat astride their weapon and attempted to fix a limpet mine or other explosive to the hull of the target ship.

In September 1942 the chariots made their first offensive move against the great German battleship *Tirpitz* which was anchored in a fjord near Trondheim in Norway. They were carried to Norwegian waters by the fishing trawler *Arthur* manned by a crew of Norwegian resistance fighters.

With two chariots secured underneath his ship the Norwegian leader, Leif Larsen, managed to bluff his way past German patrol boats, even though his craft was carefully examined by German officers (who failed to look far enough under the boat), and to get within two miles of their target. Unfortunately at this point the weather deteriorated rapidly, and with the trawler being buffeted around by high winds and strong seas, the chariots broke adrift and the operation had to be abandoned.

Chariots were tried again, with greater effect, when a number of them were moved to Malta for an attack on the Italian ports of Palermo and Maddalena. The submarine P-311, carrying two chariots, was attacked and sunk on the way to the targets but two other submarines, *Trooper* and *Thunderbolt*, managed to reach Palermo with their chariots and launch them into the harbour. The new light cruiser *Ulpio Traiamo* of 3,360 tons was sunk and a large liner severely damaged. Sadly none of the chariot crews managed to return to their mother ship.

The British reaction to the Italians' activities in Alexandria, and their own experiences with the chariots was to vastly step up the development of midget submarines or 'X-craft'. Work that had been going on to complete X-3 (the first two were experimental and had been abandoned) was increased on the personal orders of Winston Churchill. Scientists and technicians, diving instructors and senior submariners all concentrated their efforts on bringing the project to fruition.

The 'X-craft' was a complete submarine in miniature, except that it did not have torpedo tubes. It had a maximum surface speed of 6 knots on diesel engines and could dive for 36 hours on batteries. The crew of four worked in four hours on, four off watches with one man, the captain, being responsible for navigation and steering, another for the motors and hydroplanes, and a third responsible for all the machinery. The fourth member of the crew was the diver, who would go out and cut through anti-submarine nets if necessary, or when the target was reached, fix limpet mines or other explosives to the bottom of the target ship. Their range, like that of the human torpedoes, was strictly limited and they had to be towed to a point near the target by a conventional submarine – a most hazardous operation. They were also used to survey the D-Day beaches, act as beacons and, in the Far East, cut lines of communications between Japanese-held islands.

They could be exceptionally dangerous to handle. X-22, for example, was being towed by the submarine *Syrtis* during which a combination of heavy seas and gale force winds caused the Officer of the Watch of *Syrtis* to be washed overboard. The submarine turned sharply to pick him up but in doing so struck X-22 and sent it to the bottom with its crew.

The crew lived in a space roughly 30 feet long and only 5 feet at its highest point. There were none of the 'comforts' of the conventional submarine for the 'X-craft' was fitted purely as a weapon of war. It is hardly necessary to point out that the crews were all volunteers and, without exception, extremely fit young men.

The first target, and in fact almost the whole purpose of the X-craft project, was the destruction of the *Tirpitz*, still lurking in Norwegian waters. Considered the most dangerous warship in the world, the German battleship had spent almost all its life in those waters, and the British had made a number of attempts to destroy her by chariots and aerial bombing. Nothing had so far been achieved.

The attack on the *Tirpitz* by X-craft began on 11 September 1943 when X-6 under Lt Donald Cameron was towed away by the submarine *Truculent*. Five more followed, each on the end of a nylon towing rope, and the little flotilla began its long haul across the North Sea. The towing submarine was able to surface each night, and sometimes during the day; the X-craft, manned for crossing by special crews, were only able to surface for 15 minutes four times a day in order to avoid the danger of detection.

Tirpitz was the main target for the attacking X-craft flotilla, X-5, X-6 and X-7; meanwhile other midgets, X-8, X-9 and X-10 also had vital targets. X-8 was to attack and disable the battleship *Lutzow,* and X-9 and X-10 the battleship *Scharnhorst,* all lying in roughly the same area.

Tragedy occurred on the journey across when X-9 broke away from its tow line and foundered with the loss of all hands. At the same time X-8 broke its tow line and although the crew managed to blow ballast tanks and surface they found their towing submarine, *Sea Nymph*, had sailed on not knowing that the tow was broken, and there was no sign of her. After considerable anxiety X-8 was discovered by the submarine *Studders* which was towing X-7, but then lost again before being eventually reunited with its parent boat and continuing the crossing. It had, however, sustained some serious damage and eventually had to be scuttled.

On 20 September the four remaining X-craft left their parent submarines and made the dangerous crossing of a German minefield to the mouth of the Altenfjord. After spending the night recharging batteries, X-6 went into the attack, slipping up Altenfjord and into Kaafjord where the *Tirpitz* was hiding. At a depth of 60 feet Cameron took his boat through the anti-submarine nets in the wake of a small German coaster and then through the anti-torpedo nets following a small picket boat. They were well and truly in enemy territory.

As X-6 approached the *Tirpitz* through shallow water it ran aground but managed to clear herself without being spotted. Then their luck really changed. When only 80 yards away from its target X-6 hit an underwater obstruction and Cameron had to surface, only to be greeted by rifle and machine-gun fire from the battleship's deck. He quickly submerged again and by sheer guesswork managed to manoeuvre the boat beneath the *Tirpitz*. Despite a hail of hand grenades being hurled at him from above, Cameron managed to release his explosive charge under the battleship's keel, set its detonation for one hour ahead, scuttled his boat and bailed out.

The four crew members were picked out of the water by the *Tirpitz*'s boats, taken on board the battleship and put under guard. They were not interrogated immediately, but the Germans sent divers beneath their ship. The *Tirpitz* was called to action stations and preparations were begun to move her away from any possible danger. As the giant ship began to move, and with the four British submariners nervously glancing at their watches, there were suddenly two mighty explosions which lifted the huge ship five or six feet before she began to list to port. The explosions also threw up the X-7 which was immediately fired upon by the battleship's gunners.

X-7 had had a tough time getting to the attack point, having fouled the anti-submarine nets; her gyro compass had then gone wrong and she had been caught in the nets yet again. Nevertheless it had eventually forced its way to where the *Tirpitz* was anchored, not knowing that X-6 was already here, and had laid charges under the starboard side of the battleship. Once X-7 was forced to the surface and the boat became uncontrollable, the captain, Lt Place, decided it was time to get out.

While the officers and crew of the *Tirpitz* were busy trying to assess the damage to their ship caused by the explosions, X-5 was sighted outside the anti-torpedo nets. The battleship's light guns opened fire hitting it several times, it sank out of sight and was never seen again.

X-10 missed all this excitement. While the others were creating havoc around the German ship, Lt Kenneth Hudspath and his crew were lying in 150 feet of water in Altenfjord, trying to repair the many defects that had developed. The compass was not running true, the depth-gauge was not functioning and the periscope hoist motor had burned out. They heard the explosions created under the *Tirpitz* but, as they could make little headway with their own task of attacking the *Scharnhorst* they decided to abandon it.

On 22 September, Hudspath brought X-10 back down Altenfjord and out to the point where he was scheduled to rendezvous with the mother ship. After waiting almost 48 hours, the submarine *Stubborn* hove into sight and took Hudspath and his crew aboard; X-10 was scuttled.

The battleship *Tirpitz* was virtually knocked out of the war by the attack. Six men from the three X-craft that had made the hazardous journey to the *Tirpitz* were taken prisoner; six others died. Lt D. Cameron of X-6 and Lt B.C. Place of X-7 were awarded the Victoria Cross.

X-craft made another attack in Norway when on 14 April 1944, X-24 got into the port of Bergen and sank its target, the Laksvaag floating dock, although it was in some ways disappointing for the floating dock was empty at the time.

In the first week of July 1945 X-craft were sent to the Far East and placed under the command of the C-in-C, US 7th Fleet, who gave them two major assignments – to cut the telephone cable between Singapore and Hong Kong, and to attack simultaneously Japanese heavy cruisers in the Johore Straits, Singapore.

On 27 July the submarines *Spark*, *Stygian* and *Spearhead* left Brunei in Borneo each with a midget submarine in tow. At the same time another midget was being towed from Subic in the Philippines by the submarine *Selene*. Two of the X-craft were to attack the Japanese cruisers, and two were to cut the cable as required.

XE-4 had absolutely no trouble with its task, Lt M.H. Shean carrying out the operation perfectly, not only cutting the Hong Kong–Saigon and the Saigon–Singapore cable efficiently, but also bringing back a foot of each cable to prove it.

XE-5 made several attempts to cut the Hong Kong–Singapore cable, and spent over three days inside the heavily defended waters off Hong Kong, but all attempts to cut the cable failed.

The attack on the cruisers was made by XE-3 commanded by Lt Fraser, and XE-1 under Lt Snart. X-3 found its target, the cruiser *Takao* and managed to place limpet mines, which was not as easy as it sounds. XE-3 found that there was just enough water to allow it under the cruiser and then spent 40 minutes pushing along the seabed before getting into position only to find it was jammed under the enemy ship. When Leading Seaman J.J. Magennis, the boat's diver, was sent out to investigate, he found that the hatch, through which he was supposed to get out, would not open fully but squeezed himself free after a short struggle. Then he found he could only place the limpets on the cruiser's bottom with great difficulty, before struggling back into the mini-sub.

Fraser managed to place the main charge and withdraw successfully but then Magennis had to get out again and clear the hydroplanes of some limpet carriers that had become entangled. Again, he managed to get back safely. Both Fraser and Magennis were awarded the Victoria Cross for this attack.

XE-1, which should have attacked a second cruiser, found itself in some difficulty after having to spend time avoiding a patrol craft, putting it well behind schedule, which would have meant that it would still be on its way to the target when *Takao* was scheduled to be blown up. The attack on the original target was therefore abandoned and mines were laid under *Takao* as well. Needless to say *Takao* was destroyed.

The Japanese, who had a tradition of suicide missions in all services during the war, developed their human torpedoes with the same outlook. Known as the Kaiten series they were quite literally manned torpedoes about 70 feet long. Armed with a devastating warhead of some 3,418 lb, they were powered by a unique engine burning petrol and stored gaseous oxygen. The operator sat astride the torpedo under a transparent dome, the missile being catapulted from a cradle on a surface vessel. Once under way it was the operator's task to set course for the enemy vessel, running underwater most of the time, but surfacing occasionally to allow him to fix his position.

The plan was to carry them on larger ships and then launch them in the path of oncoming enemy ships but, in fact, they were only used to penetrate enemy harbours. A great deal of research and development went into the production of these deadly Kaitens, and several large submarines were modified to carry them. Although the operator had no chance of returning from his mission, there was no shortage of volunteers to man them. As was typical of Japanese submarine warfare at this time, a great deal of effort was wasted since the Kaitens were hardly used.

The Japanese were late with their development of their midget submarine, even though the subject was first considered as far back as 1934. But by 1941 they were able to equip their fleet with five models for the attack on Pearl Harbor. As described elsewhere they completely failed in their task of entering the harbour to attack American warships and none of them survived the operation.

They were sent on another mission, this time to Sydney Harbour, in May 1942. Two midgets were launched from their parent submarines, I-16 and I-20 and managed to penetrate the harbour itself, but were spotted and destroyed by patrol boats.

On 29 May they had more success with an attack on Diego Suarez, Madagascar. Early in the day a Japanese plane had been sighted over the harbour, and as a precaution the British battleship *Ramilies* anchored there got under way and started steaming round the bay as a defensive measure to avoid attack from the air. Two Japanese submarines lying outside the harbour launched their midgets, which then penetrated the bay and torpedoed the battleship, putting her out of action for several months.

The Japanese persevered with the development of midget submarines, building over 60 of them. Some were sophisticated weapons with a crew of five, rechargeable batteries and a range of over 1,000 miles. Before they had the opportunity to use them to full advantage, however, the war was over and yet another Japanese underwater project failed to live up to its expectations.

The Germans entered the midget submarine business too late for them to be put to any good purpose. A commando unit, known as 'K' force, was built up to man the new weapons but when one of the new recruits, on seeing his first midget, asked for an instruction manual, he was told it was not available as it had been captured by the British.

German midgets made several abortive attacks on Allied shipping but did not record any worthwhile successes. The Germans also turned towards developing human torpedoes which were deployed against Allied shipping during the Normandy invasion and, although they sunk several ships, they did not play a vital part in the defence of the European mainland.

The most successful design was the Type 127 midget submarine, the *Seehund*, and nearly 140 were commissioned, the plan being to eventually construct a thousand. They had a crew of 2 and carried 2 torpedoes slung underneath, and a range of 185 miles. Some had an additional fuel tank which increased their range to 300 miles at 7 knots. In the first four months of 1945 they were sent out on 142 assignments, lost 35 and sank only 8 enemy ships with another 3 damaged.

CHAPTER FOURTEEN

The Nuclear Age

The advent of the nuclear submarine.
Prospects for the future.

WHEN the Second World War ended the universal hope was for a long period of peace and stability, but it was not to be. Within months it became clear that there was a growing antagonism between the Western democracies and Eastern block Communist countries.

In the immediate post-war period conventional submarines were replaced by diesel electric boats varying in size from around 3,000 tons down to 450 tons. Fitted with long-range torpedoes, radar homing anti-ship missiles and the latest sonar technology they had a top speed of 20 knots submerged.

Then came a dramatic and far-reaching development which revolutionised not only submarine warfare but warfare in general. The Americans introduced *Nautilus*, the world's first nuclear-powered submarine. The submarine, which used to be almost a secondary weapon supporting the mighty battleships and aircraft carriers, and in many cases was used as a defensive rather than offensive weapon, became what is now the major weapon that most leading maritime nations possess.

A Second World War submarine could stay submerged for only a matter of hours, depending on the state of its batteries and was capable of about 10 knots submerged, 15 knots on the surface. Its main weapon was a torpedo which it could send a maximum distance of 8,000 yards. It was able to dive to around 350-400 feet and its presence and position could be detected by ASDIC. It could stay at sea for only about two months, slightly longer when the Snorkel (Snort) breathing mast, was developed.

Compared to this a nuclear submarine can stay submerged for months, the limit only being determined by the amount of food supplies on board and, of course, by other humanitarian considerations. It can travel at 20 knots submerged and nearly 30 knots on the surface. It can fire a ballistic missile between 2,500 and 4,000 miles and dive to at least 1,000 feet. It cannot be reliably detected, can launch attacks without giving away its position and is immune from ballistic missiles or other methods of mass destruction. In fact, if ever there was a world-wide nuclear war it is highly likely that only nuclear submarines would survive.

The main reason for this transformation in underwater warfare is the power plant of a nuclear submarine which is based on a nuclear reactor. This produces a vast amount of heat which boils water into steam – the holy grail of *Resurgam*, the development of which was abandoned in the eighteenth century because at that time only coal could be used to produce steam. This drives two main engines for propulsion and two turbine generators for electrical power. Refuelling is necessary every ten years although the latest submarines will not need refuelling during their expected 25-year life. Heavy shielding protects the crew so that members receive less radiation on submerged patrol than they would from natural resources on land.

Developments with air purification and conditioning, sophisticated navigation systems which depend on gyros and electronic equipment rather than sun, moon and stars, improved underwater sensors, and nuclear propulsion have all contributed to the transformation. The nuclear submarine of today with unlimited endurance does not even have to surface to fire its main weapon – no longer a torpedo but a ballistic missile or similar offensive weapon – which can be done while the submarine is many fathoms deep.

Since 1945, the world has stepped back from the brink of total war mainly because of the nuclear deterrent. These were originally expected to be delivered by aircraft but now submarines have taken over the role of missile launchers. Aircraft carriers and aircraft by contrast can be spotted and attacked and so are extremely vulnerable.

In 1945 British Prime Minister Winston Churchill spoke of the 'Iron Curtain' that had fallen across Europe and of the spectre of an atomic war. US President Kennedy, talking about the atom bomb, spoke of a 'Sword of Damocles' held over the heads of all nations. It was not long before it became clear that the nuclear submarine, armed with nuclear missiles, was that 'sword'. The weapons with which it was equipped, apart from modern electric torpedoes, were developed from the Polaris missile to the Tomahawk and up to the Trident which has a range of over 5,000 miles.

Within a year of the United States commissioning *Nautilus* the Soviet Union introduced its first operational nuclear submarine and in 1960 Britain launched *Dreadnought*. The 'cat and mouse' game which the United States and Britain had played with the Soviet Union reached new dimensions with boats that were silent and could not be detected, had improved periscope photography both above and below the surface, and faster communications.

Probably the only torpedo that has been fired in anger by a nuclear submarine was in May 1982 following the invasion of the Falkland Islands by Argentine forces. A British military force was sent to regain possession and a 200-mile total exclusion zone was placed around the Island. When two Argentine naval forces approached the exclusion zone and one, led by the cruiser *Belgrano*, got close enough to lob shells at the British forces on land, it was decided to take aggressive action. The British nuclear submarine *Conqueror,* one of three in the area, was ordered to attack and fired three torpedoes. The second one hit and sank the *Belgrano* with the loss of 368 lives. The Argentine fleet went home.

The Cold War between East and West ended in 1989 after 40 years with the collapse of the Soviet Union and a more placatory attitude by the new Russia. Once again it was greeted with relief that a more peaceful world would result. But again it was a misplaced hope. The invasion of Kuwait by Iraq in August 1990, although quickly resolved by American, British and European forces, seemed to herald an era of international terrorism.

Nuclear submarines were given a role in this conflict, notably in response to the terrorist attack on the World Trade Centre in New York on 11 September 2001. The immediate aim of an anti-terrorist alliance of nations was to wipe out the Al Queda terrorist organisation believed to bear responsibility for the attack, and based in Afghanistan.

Three British nuclear submarines, *Superb*, *Trafalgar* and *Triumph* were sent to the Persian Gulf and opened the Allied attack on the terrorist camps with a 1,300-mile ballistic missile bombardment.

The development of the first Polaris-firing US Navy nuclear submarine was startlingly fast due to the inspiration of Admiral H.G. Rickover, who was earlier the driving force behind the development of nuclear submarine propulsion. The keel was laid in June 1952, the boat was christened in January 1954, made its first test voyage in January 1955 and joined the US fleet in April 1955. In May it went on its shakedown cruise, covering 1,300 miles in 84 hours, roughly ten times faster than any other submarine could have achieved, reaching an incredible 16 knots submerged, and later 20 knots.

In August 1958, it completed a trans-polar voyage from Pearl Harbor in Hawaii, to Portland Harbour in England, under the geographic North Pole, an amazing voyage which impressed the world's navies.

Submarines have certainly come a long way since Cornelius Drebbel started developing a diving ball with propulsion way back in the 1600s and even further back to the type of submersible chamber Aristotle describes as being used in 352 BC, or the Chinese variation on the theme that could move on the bottom of the sea in around 200 BC.

The modern submarine does, however, retain some of the features of the older boats that did such tremendous work during the Second World War. For example, it still requires ballast tanks in order to dive and surface and high-pressure air to enable it to perform these manoeuvres. It still has hydroplanes to control diving and surfacing, and periscopes for search and attack. Torpedo tubes have changed little in appearance, neither has the torpedo, except that it can be wire-guided towards the target until it makes contact itself and homes in on the target. The control room, however, which used to be a steamy place of pipes, handles, levers and nuts and bolts, is now a controlled-atmosphere room of dials and electric switches, of navigation control systems, weapons launching systems, communication systems and high-technology sonar. Now there is a missile control centre which is connected by computer to the navigation centre.

The modern submarine has three decks and is wide enough to allow a main passage down the centre with accommodation on either side. The missile compartment, which holds around 16 missiles, needs the height of all three decks in order to hold its deadly weaponry. The missiles, on average, are nearly 10 metres long and have a diameter of 1.5 metres and a weight of roughly 16 tons. Together they have the explosive power equal to all the bombs dropped by both sides, including the two atom bombs, in the Second World War.

Instead of noisy, smelly diesel engines, which used to impinge themselves on every aspect of life on a submarine, there is now the clinically clean, quiet, nuclear reactor which gives the submarine its propulsion.

Although the living space is still cramped, compared to a surface warship, the crew has a recreation space and library, something quite unheard of in bygone days. Instead of the crew grabbing their food and eating wherever they could find a space to sit down, there is now a dining hall. Catering is of the highest quality with variable and interesting menus. They also have a lounge, showers, wash room, a constant supply of fresh water and bunk space. Music and a substantial library of films help to provide amusement for the leisure hours.

Even the character of the crew has changed. Instead of a polyglot assembly of seamen, stokers, engineers, torpedo men and signalmen under the control of a captain, first lieutenant, navigator and engineer there are now highly trained navigators, torpedo and sonar officers, supply officers, technical officers, weapons electrical officers, marine engineers, a Polaris (or other missile) systems officer and, of course, a surgeon. Even the ratings now have their specific titles and duties covering marine engineering, electrical equipment, ordnance, radio, underwater control, radar, weapons control, seamen and, naturally, a galley staff.

The missile now carried by nuclear submarines is a far deadlier weapon than the old torpedo. The Polaris, for example, is a two-stage ballistic missile with a nuclear warhead and its own inertial guidance system, which has a maximum range of 2,500 miles. Although it can be launched from a submerged submarine, it has such deadly accuracy that it can be landed, even at that great distance, within only yards of its target.

To attain this high degree of accuracy it has to be fed with all the relevant information regarding the position of the target, the precise position of the submarine, its speed and direction and its behaviour regarding trim and attitude. All this information is provided by a computer linked to the missile's inertial guidance system which takes over when the missile is launched. When this system decides that the nuclear warheads will reach their target they separate from the missile second-stage motor and go on to wreak destruction.

The latest in a long line of nuclear submarines developed by the United States is the Trident class, by far the biggest submarine in history. It is faster and has a longer range than any other submarine and the range of its missiles, some 4,000 miles, means that it can cover its potential target from millions of square miles of ocean.

The British Polaris submarine was originally developed when the British Government bought three Polaris 'A' missiles, without warheads, from the United States in 1962. In 1967, four special British submarines were designed to carry the missile, the warhead for which was also developed by the British. They were the 7,500-ton surfaced, 8,400-ton submerged *Resolution*, *Repulse*, *Renown* and *Revenge*, which carry 16 missiles. They were followed by the Swiftsure and Trafalgar classes, both of which carry Tigerfish and sub-Harpoon missiles.

The French too have continued with development of nuclear-powered submarines and their latest class is the Sons-marin Nucleaire Lance-Engins (SNLE) built to deliver the French-built nuclear deterrent. It also carries conventional torpedoes, seen mainly as a defensive weapon, but the main armament is 16 Mer-Sol Balistique Strategique (MSBS) missiles. The submarine's main task is believed to be to take up a specific position and wait there until ordered to fire. The propulsion of these submarines is believed to be a pressurised water reactor fuelled by highly enriched uranium.

The heart of the SNLE is the data-processing centre, where all numerical information on board is handled by four digital computers. They control targetry, trajectory and launch. The submarines currently in use are *Le Redoubtable*, *Le Terrible*, *Le Foudroyant*, *L'Indomptable*, *Le Tonnant* and *L'Inflexibale*.

By far the greatest nuclear fleet was that built by the Soviet Union but, naturally, following the many changes that have taken place in recent years, such as the break-up of the Soviet Union, the current situation is unclear. The latest nuclear submarines are based on the 18,000-ton, 150 feet long, Oscar-class cruise missile boats. They have a complement of 130, are capable of 30 knots and carry 24 missiles The missiles are believed to be capable of carrying a nuclear warhead right across North America, and are considered more powerful in terms of payload and range than any equivalent Western missile except the Trident. Happily, with the end of the Cold War, such details are of less importance than they once were.

The development of the nuclear submarine has not all been plain sailing and there have been over 30 accidents since *Nautilus* was launched. The American, British, Russian, French and Israeli navies have all suffered, with most of the accidents being collisions or fires. There have been seven nuclear submarines lost, five of them Russian and two American. According to the Norwegian environmental Bellona Foundation, six nuclear submarines still litter the floor of the ocean bed, the most recent loss being the 18,000 ton Oscar-II cruiser missile submarine *Kursk* in August 2000. Commissioned in 1995 it was one of the newest and biggest in the Russian fleet. It was on a major naval exercise off the north-west coast of Russia when it sank in 350 feet of water in the Barents Sea, 85 miles from the Russian naval base of Severomorsk, with a crew of 116 aboard.

Bad weather made immediate rescue attempts impossible and it was not known whether any of the crew remained alive. Desperate rescue attempts were made, with some help from the Royal Navy, but they failed and the long procedure of bringing the submarine to the surface began.

Reported not to have any nuclear warheads on board, three possible reasons for the loss were given by the Russian authorities: that water had entered the submarine after a torpedo was triggered; that there had been a serious collision; and that there had been an explosion in the front of the boat where the torpedoes were housed.

Oscar-class submarines are capable of 30 knots – they were designed to chase US aircraft carriers – and are totally silent. In full operational mode they carry 24 cruise missiles and 36 torpedoes with a range of over 300 miles and can carry nuclear warheads.

In April 1963, the USS *Thresher* sank 8,530 feet while off the New England coast, with the loss of 129 officers and men. In May 1968 the USS *Scorpion* went down east of the Azores in the Atlantic with 99 men, and now lies at 9,860 feet.

The Soviet Union lost a nuclear submarine in April 1970 when 52 people died, now lying 15,354 feet down in the Bay of Biscay. In October 1986, another caught fire and sank 16,404 feet, east of Bermuda, but only four sailors were lost. In April 1989, *Komsomolets* caught fire and sank off Norway killing 42 of the 69 sailors on board; it now sits at a depth of 4,500 feet.

Submarine accidents since the Second World War have not been confined to nuclear submarines – Britain has lost two since 1945. In January 1950 the 1,450-ton *Truculent* was in the Thames Estuary when it collided with the Swedish merchantman *Divina* and sank within minutes, with a crew of 61 and a number of dockyard builders aboard. Everyone managed to get into the engine room and prepared to escape but there was not enough escape equipment for everyone, so the civilians were given preference. Sixty-four men managed to escape into the icy waters of the Thames but rescue operations could not start until dawn and by then it was possible to rescue only ten men.

The last British submarine to be lost was *Affray* in April 1951, with the loss of 75 lives. A search for the missing submarine started immediately but it was 59 days before the wreck was discovered in 50 feet of water 45 miles south of Portland Harbour and some 100 miles from Portsmouth. Navy divers found that the snort mast had been broken off; recovered from the seabed it was found to be of faulty manufacture. It was thought that the broken snort together with a possible battery explosion contributed to *Affray*'s fate.

The French lost *Minerve* when it ran aground in bad weather off Portland Bill in southern England in September 1945; the Japanese lost HA-204 when it was stranded in the Pacific and wrecked in October 1945; and the Spanish lost C-4 when it was rammed by the destroyer *Lepanto* off the Balearic Islands in June 1966.

Nuclear submarines constantly patrol the world's oceans, as advancement in terms of producing ever faster and stealthier craft continues unabated by specialist research and development teams, as does weaponry development.

Most experts agree that the nuclear submarine will continue to be the dominating weapon of sea power, and that sea power will play an increasingly dominating role in any future conflict.

Bibliography

Official Histories

Admiralty Naval Staff History, Second World War. Operations in Home, Northern and Atlantic Waters, 1947

Admiralty Naval Staff History, Second World War. Operations in the Mediterranean, 1947

Submarine Operations in World War II by Theodore Roscoe, United States Naval Institute, 1949

Books

Blair, Clay, *Hitler's U-boat War, The Hunters 1939–42* (Cassell & Co, 1998)

Blair, Clay, *Hitler's U-boat War, The Hunted 1942–45* (Cassell & Co, 1998)

Brennecke, Jochen, *The Hunters and the Hunted* (The Elmfield Press, 1958)

Boyd, Carl & Yoshita, Akihito, *The Japanese Submarine Force WWII* (Airlife Publishing, 1996)

Hezlet, Arthur, *The Submarine & Sea Power* (Peter Davis, London, 1967)

Lipscombe, F.W., *The British Submarine* (Conway Maritime Press Ltd, 1954)

Mulligan, Timothy P., *Neither Sharks Nor Wolves* (Chatham Publishing, 1999)

Padfield, Peter, *War Beneath the Sea* (Pimlico Publishers, 1995)

Ring, Jim, *We Come Unseen* (John Murray (Publishers) Ltd, 2001)

Roskill, S.W., *The War at Sea* (Her Majesty's Stationery Office, 1961)

Sharpe, Peter, *U-boat Fact File* (Midland Publishing Ltd, 1998)

Tall, Jeff, *The History of the Submarine* (Ticktoch Publishers Ltd, 1998)

Index